THE ART OF WRITING

André Maurois

THE ART OF WRITING

Translated by Gerard Hopkins

THE BODLEY HEAD
LONDON

BIBLIOGRAPHICAL NOTE

The essays on Voltaire, Rousseau, Stendhal, Balzac, Flaubert, Proust, Goethe, Leopardi and Tolstoy were originally published in a collection entitled *Lecture Mon Doux Plaisir* (Paris, 1957).

The essay on Gogol was originally published in a collection entitled *Robert et Elizabeth Browning, Portraits* (Paris, 1955).

The essay on Turgenev was originally published in *Tourgueniev* (Paris, 1931).

The essays on The Writer's Craft and on Tchekov are here published for the first time in book form.

The publishers gratefully acknowledge permission granted by Messrs Gerald Duckworth to quote from *Six Famous Plays* (Tchekov), translated by Julius West and Marian Fell.

The essays from *Lecture Mon Doux Plaisir*
© Librairie Arthème-Fayard, 1957
English translation © The Bodley Head, 1960
Printed and bound in Great Britain for
THE BODLEY HEAD LTD
10 Earlham Street, London W.C.2
by Staples Printers Ltd., Rochester
Set in Monotype Plantin
First published 1960

OCLC

CONTENTS

CHAPTER I

THE WRITER'S CRAFT

1. The Writer's Life

THE STARTING-POINT of a writer's life is the sense of a vocation. The child or the adolescent feels impelled to give expression in the written word to the emotions or the ideas which people and things have aroused in him. At a very early age Marcel Proust was conscious of a desire to lay hands on an imprisoned beauty which, so he believed, was hidden under the appearance of certain objects. He had a confused notion that it was incumbent upon him to free some captive truth from confinement. At that time in his life he was as yet incapable of reaching down to truths which he felt to be lurking under the bushes, the orchards and the sunlight of La Beauce. In *Louis Lambert* Balzac gives us a portrait of himself as a youth chock-full of works clamouring to be born. Victor Hugo, Byron, Musset, Valéry all wrote poems when they were young. It occasionally happens that the vocation of letters is a late-flowering growth (as in the case of Rousseau), but when that is so, numerous attempts in secret have preceded the ultimate fulfilment.

How comes it that this vocation is present in some people and not in others? One may say in answer to that question, though without laying it down as a rule, that the need to express oneself in writing springs from a mal-adjustment to life, or from an inner conflict which the adolescent (or the grown man) cannot resolve in action. Those to whom action comes as easily as breathing rarely feel the need to break loose from the real, to rise above, and describe it. That is why so many of the finest writers have been the victims of ill health (Poe, Proust, Flaubert, Tchekov), men whose lives have known frustration from an early age or found their natural development impeded by some obstacle. Dickens, Balzac, Hugo, Kipling and Stendhal all had an unhappy childhood which was too soon dislocated by family conflicts. With others the conflict was social or religious (Voltaire, Anatole France and Tolstoy), while in some an over-sensitive nature has been driven back on itself as the result of some invincible timidity (Merimée). I do not mean that it is enough to be maladjusted to become a great writer, but writing is, for some, a method of resolving a conflict, provided they have the necessary talent.

It may be objected that many writers have been happy in their lives and endowed with a healthy temperamental balance. That, no doubt, is true, but I do not know a single instance in which that balance has not had to be achieved by a struggle from which a considerable body of work has resulted. Although after 1875, when he was an astonishingly vigorous old man with a firmly established reputation, Victor Hugo had certainly no right to complain of the way in which life had treated him, yet it should never be forgotten that a difficult youth, thwarted love affairs, and sorrows brought upon him by death and political strife had made of him a sorely troubled and tormented individual—and a poet. Chateaubriand, at the time of the Restoration, as an ambassador and a Minister, had not the same motives as once he had had for voicing melodious sorrows. Nevertheless, because he was conscious of his genius, and knew on what food it flourished, he deliberately kept the old conflicts alive, or sought new ones. Paul Valéry, as I remember him, was a man of a strong and sunny temperament, but his lined and wrinkled face was eloquent of much former pain and struggle. The only writers I have known who were perfectly contented with themselves and with the world in which they lived, were, I am sorry to say, bad writers. This is not to say that in order to write well a man must be a pessimist, but only that "optimism in an artist is something that has to be won by hard fighting" (Alain).

First, then, the vocation and the early attempts at authorship. Next, the problem of publication. Why is it so necessary for a writer to have a public? If his purpose is to express himself, ought it not to be enough for him that he should succeed in doing so? Is a cloud of witnesses really essential? The answer to this question is almost always in the affirmative. I say "almost" always because there have been writers of memoirs, Saint-Simon, for instance, and Pepys who cared nothing for public applause. They wrote for themselves or for a posterity which they could never know. But such cases are rare. Nearly every writer wants to have readers, even though they should amount to only a small number of the elect. That is but natural. He has written with the deliberate purpose of revealing the truth about himself and about the world as he sees it. The revelation can have no point unless it reaches those for whom it is intended. To find readers who shall understand him, who may perhaps love, or at least admire him, is reassuring to an author, and if his own conflict resembles that of many of his fellow men, it may, through his efforts, become less obsessive and troublesome to them, in which case he will have the additional pleasure of having been helpful.

The aim of a writer worthy of his chosen profession is never merely to achieve Power and Glory. It does sometimes happen that these rewards come the way of those who deserve them, but many great men have been cheated of them in their lifetime. Mallarmé was the idol of a few discriminating admirers: to the wider public he was unknown. Stendhal said, with considerable perspicacity: "I shall have readers in 1860"; he has still more in 1960, but he had few before his death. Tolstoy, on the other hand, Balzac and Dickens, enjoyed an enormous popularity. Success proves nothing either for or against a writer. It is desirable, because it gives him an assured independence, on condition that it does not come to him through scandal, the employment of such artificial means as excessive publicity, or vulgarity. The public interest in certain literary prizes does ill-service, in the last analysis, to those who receive them. A sudden and exaggerated notoriety leaves them precisely where they were before. They may, indeed, show themselves worthy of their fame, and capable of responding to the hopes reposed in them. If, on the other hand, they drop back into obscurity, then failure is the more painful by reason of the generous promises of success so unexpectedly extended to them.

The writer who has achieved a certain degree of celebrity will find that many additional "jobs" almost inevitably come his way in the shape of newspaper articles, lectures, talking on the radio and appearing on television. What should his attitude be? To say no to all of them, especially if he be young, would prove either an abnormal pride, or incapacity. I know that some types of mind do not take kindly to public life, but many writers are fully competent to play a part in it, and, in so far as they may usefully influence a wider public by doing so, why should they not? Valéry, certainly, treated none of the offers that came to him with contempt; in fact, he was always delighted to have the chance of writing on a theme supplied to him. Some of his best work (for example, his *Preface to Montesquieu* — an astonishing manual of pure politics) was produced on commission. Hugo's best poems are those inspired by some national or international event—which is only another form of commission. But the extra labours involved in activities of this kind must never be allowed to take up so much of the writer's time that he has not enough left to give to his main occupation, which is to write what he feels he must write. In France, especially, where literary men find themselves far more involved in public affairs than elsewhere, either because they occupy some post under Government, or, on the contrary, are active supporters of the Opposition, he must be very careful to retain a necessary freedom.

Is a writer justified in making material success the main object and aim of his work? In other words, is earning a livelihood ever a sufficient reason for turning author? It cannot be denied that the need to provide for himself and his family has proved a useful stimulant to many a man of letters. A few authors, though only a few, have accumulated enormous fortunes: Hugo, Bernard Shaw, some modern American novelists, and several French dramatists. It is easier to do so today than it once was because the possible reading public is vast and international in extent, and because literacy is far more widely spread. Balzac and Dumas, in spite of their great success, were often short of cash. Consequently, they published a great deal. That, in itself, is no crime. We should always remember that a great writer, even though circumstances keep his nose to the grindstone, may still produce masterpieces. Balzac was in urgent need of the money he was to receive for *La Cousine Bette* and *Le Cousin Pons*, but those books are no less admirable for having been written under financial pressure. The English have a word for books written to "keep the pot boiling". They call them "pot-boilers". But why should not the fire which keeps the pot simmering also keep the mind in a state of effervescence?

But Power, Glory and Money are only secondary objects for the writer. No man can be a great writer without having a great philosophy, though it may often remain unexpressed. That is true even of those whose lives were far from edifying. George Sand's own life was, like that of most of us, warped, mediocre and frustrated. Yet, in *Consuelo* she could create a unique model of femininity in which every woman can find something to imitate, and every man something to understand and to love. A great writer has a high respect for *values*. His essential function is to raise life to the dignity of thought, and this he does by giving it a shape. If he refuses to perform this function, he can be a clever juggler and play tricks with words such as his fellow-writers may admire, but his books will be of little interest to anybody else. If, on the contrary, he fulfils it, he will be happy in his writing. Borne aloft by the world as reflected in himself, and producing a sounding echo of his times, he helps to shape it by showing to men an image of themselves which is at once true and disciplined.

2. The Writer's Craft

"There is as much craft in the making of a book as there is in the making of a clock," said La Bruyère. About this one might argue up and down for a long time. Undoubtedly, the making of a book involves the learning of a craft, and one that is mastered by the exercise of writing. Few succeed at the first attempt. Those whose earliest published efforts seem to show real skill are not, as a rule, strictly speaking, beginners. They will be found to have worked long and arduously in the privacy of their study, either writing themselves or absorbing the secrets of the masters. But though authorship is a craft it differs from that of the clockmaker in that the latter assembles pieces ready to his hand in a strictly determined order, whereas the writer, in the very process of putting pen to paper, has to invent not only the constructional plan of his book but the materials which go into it. Of what a nature, therefore, should his training be?

A book is made up of words. The first concern of the writer-to-be is to acquire a vocabulary and to master the rules of grammar. He must have so infallible a knowledge of his native tongue and its syntactical usages that he will never run the risk of employing a word to convey a meaning other than that normally attached to it, or of constructing an unintelligible or defective sentence. I am quite prepared to have it pointed out to me that very great writers have sometimes given a new meaning to an old word, or played tricks with syntax. That is so, but such liberties, though they may win approval when they stand out against the background of a perfect norm, will seem ridiculous when taken by a beginner, for in his case they will merely give the impression of ignorance. The musical composer of genius is entitled to introduce discords into his score and to spring surprises on the ear. All the same, he must have begun by learning harmony. The good painter may distort, not because he does not know how to draw, but because, knowing perfectly well how to draw, he has a right to indulge in daring experiments.

The first essential, therefore, on which the young writer must concentrate is the acquisition of an accurate vocabulary. Should it be more than usually extensive? No general rule can, I think, be laid down. Some of the great classic writers could say everything they had to say with a very small vocabulary. No better example of this could be found than Racine. Others, on the contrary, no less great in their way, accumulated a rich treasure of solid technical terms. Chateaubriand made a practice of collecting, and restoring to their place in the language, a great number of archaisms. Balzac was fully acquainted with the turns of speech in common use among bankers, journalists, police officers, lawyers and the members of many other professions. Valéry, in his prose writings, owed much to the language of science, for the rigour of which he had a marked liking. The beginner's choice depends upon the nature of his subject. Technical phrases, admirably suited to the treating of technical matters, will seem pretentious when applied to narrative.

The clear and simple words of common usage are always better than those of erudition. The jargon of the philosophers not seldom conceals an absence of thought.

The best training for the young writer is to be found in a reading of the masters. A close study of them will show him how a masterpiece is made. Familiarity with the methods of the great will provide him with great examples. At first he will read for pleasure, like any young enthusiast with a taste for books. Then, having become familiar with this or that work, he will return to it again and again with the purpose of "taking it to pieces" and seeing just how its effects are obtained. In what way is a Balzac novel, a Tchekov story or a Shakespeare play built up? Obviously there can be no such thing as a recipe for genius. Nevertheless, the art of description, of construction and the use of dialogue can be learned. If we want to give life to our characters in the manner of Tolstoy, we shall find that he managed it by stressing gestures, tricks of behaviour and linguistic mannerisms. Proust's way of moving from general ideas to individual actions deserves careful study. He had learned much from George Eliot, Dickens and Ruskin. How? By constantly reading them, by translating and annotating Ruskin, by amusing himself with the composition of "pastiches".

But is there not danger in following a master too slavishly? What we ask of a young writer is not that he should be a second Balzac, a new Dickens, but himself. The danger is, I think, imaginary. In the first place, should the young writer suddenly and miraculously produce the very novel, dealing with our contemporary society, which Balzac himself would have written had he been alive today, that would be a great and happy event. In fact, if he is truly gifted, nothing of the sort is likely to happen. He will have learned from his masters certain tricks of the trade, but he will use them differently. Even if he deliberately sets out to imitate them, a moment will come when, his own genius having taken charge, he will forget all about the imitation, take a good look at his subject, and handle it in his own way. Mauriac once attempted to produce a faithful imitation of Bossuet. The result was good Bossuet, but, all of a sudden, it also became first-rate Mauriac. Nobody expects us to write as though no one had ever written before we came upon the scene. In literature everyone is somebody's spiritual child. Musset owed a great deal to Byron, who, in his turn, owed a great deal to Voltaire, who had incurred a debt to Swift. What matters is that the beginner, by studying other men's styles, should ultimately develop a style of his own.

But what, precisely, is style? It is the hallmark of an individual, which shows clearly in his use of language and in his view of life. Every man has a temperament which is personal to himself. But most men are incapable of impressing their temperaments on what they write. For most, the act of writing is something outside their usual competence. Consequently, they lack that flexibility which would allow them to give free rein to their instincts and their passions. As soon as they get a pen between their fingers, they find that nothing comes but a flood of commonplace clichés. They are used to reading bad prose, and cannot break free from it. Saint-Simon, who was a master of language and wholly indifferent to popular applause since he was writing only for himself, could give full play to his furies and his memories. The supremely right adjective came to him simultaneously with the thought he wished to express, or, rather, a cascade of adjectives which gradually encircled it. Passionately intent on what he was feeling and wanted to record, he did not much worry about the form in which it should be presented. He took the first word that occurred to him, no matter how trivial, with the result that he hit on those astonishing "finds", those powerful images which both surprise and flay. So torrential is the movement of his prose, that the incidents flood the page. Circumstances come into his mind even while he is in the act of writing, but the very disorder in which they jostle gives life to his words. The touchy duke shows through the writing. That is what style means.

There are as many variants of style as there are men of originality who know how to write. Chateaubriand was no less passionate than Saint-Simon, but he could exercise greater self-control, and he wrote to be read. His style shows traces of the great classic age. It was only towards the end of his life that he freely abandoned himself to his genius. Freely?—yes, but with this reservation, that he was fully conscious of the self-portrait he was painting. Saint-Simon let himself go: Chateaubriand watched himself letting himself go. If, now and again, he fell into an easy negligence he was perfectly well aware of what he was doing, and was careful to enshrine it in one of those long, sonorous, violoncello passages of which he was a master. He knew, none better, what images could best set his pages singing, and played tunes on many of his favourite themes—old age saddened by regret for past loves: the approach of death: the vanity of fame: the moon which brought to his mind the trees of Combourg. Even God, even the Cross, were but so many adjuncts to the sublimity of his personal drama, and all these things, which make his style, are the man himself.

I knew Rudyard Kipling well. When listening to his talk one was immediately reminded of his way of writing, of his mannerisms, of that air he had of insinuating more than he said: "What I am going to tell you would appear to be impossible: but that is how men are, and I know men"—all the while maintaining a zone of mystery, for he had to perfection the art of leaving motives in shadow, at the same time saying just enough to enable one to make a pretty shrewd guess at what they had been. Lying in the grass, with his head supported on his hand, and those astonishingly alert eyes under wild and bushy brows, he *lived* Kipling. I remember him talking to me one day, round about 1930, about Germany, which was already becoming dangerously transformed, and suddenly saying: "A people always ends by resembling its shadow . . ."—a typically Kiplingesque oracle, the veiled warning coupled with a refusal to elucidate its meaning, a distant echo of those Indian sages and those Old Testament prophets who were his masters. That was how he thought and how he wrote.

Some may think that this definition of style as the hallmark of a temperament stamped on the material in hand is over-romanticized, and attaches too much importance to the individual. The great classic writers, it will be said, sought rather to proclaim universal truths than to leave their imprint on them. But this view will not stand up to examination. Nothing is less like the

style of Racine than the style of Corneille. We have only
to read one single line of Pascal to recognize its author.
Any schoolboy in a junior form could distinguish a
passage of dialogue in Molière from a scene by Beau-
marchais or Marivaux. Bossuet and Voltaire are both
classical writers, but they have nothing in common
except the precision of their language. There does, no
doubt, exist a sort of classical perfection which has no
recognizable face of its own, and is, so to speak, anonymous, but it is to be found only in uninspired writers
who are not, strictly speaking, writers at all.

Alain laid it down that in anything worth calling style
two conditions must be fulfilled: grace and ease in the
movement of the prose, and, in the work itself, its visible
trace. Grace and ease can be acquired as a result of that
double training to which I have already referred: reading
and working. A certain degree of modesty must also be
linked with them. He who takes too much obvious
trouble to write well falls below the highest level. Flaubert in his letters, where he is being himself without
effort, is better than the Flaubert of the novels, in which
every sentence has been so frequently worked over that
the style loses all natural movement and becomes rugged
or clumsy. Let me, once again, quote Alain: "Style, like
good manners, should never be self-conscious, but must
express a free improvization in a way that laborious
application can never achieve." The resistance of the
material will do the rest, as can be seen in hand-wrought
iron-work or sculptured stone. That is why, as we realize
in classical tragedy, style is the outcome of constraint.

It is useless to advise a writer who is seeking to express
himself to be a Kipling, a Chateaubriand, a Flaubert or,
indeed, anyone but himself. But it is not easy to be oneself.

Many writers have died without ever finding their true selves, or, at least, without succeeding in imparting their selves to their style. This is sometimes due to lack of culture and of skill in the handling of words, though sometimes, on the contrary, to an excess of culture. They have admired so many styles that they have failed to form one of their own. What advice, then, should be given to the beginner? That he should remain a rough diamond? No, for the rough diamond has no lustre. The source of light is doubtless in it, but it remains invisible. My own advice would be to seek out those masters who best suit the young learner, those for whom he feels a natural sympathy and, having found them, to be assiduous in his study of their work. Mauriac has never given up reading Chateaubriand and the Pascal of the *Lettres Provinciales*. Others may seek their nourishment in Voltaire or Anatole France, and others still in Hemingway or Stendhal.

Nulla dies sine linea. The aspiring author, whether genius or not, should never let a day pass without writing at least a few lines. The habit of writing is a good one, always on condition that one sets down on paper what one *really* wants to say, and does not fall a victim to the allurements of the easy cliché. Journalism can easily become a danger if it is not conducted with passionate sincerity. There is an art of saying nothing which is the very reverse of style. Journalism undertaken in the manner of Paul-Louis Courier or Diderot is, on the contrary, a wonderful training-school of good and succinct writing. Goethe's advice—start with short pieces —is, I think, excellent. The very fact of carrying through a piece of work *to the end* is of great encouragement to the beginner. To embark upon a "saga-novel" at twenty would be doubly foolish. At that age few men have the necessary technical skill or a sufficient first-hand experience of life on which to draw. Writing should never be allowed to become a substitute for living. Style cannot breathe in a void. It should not be forgotten that Dickens was at one time a reporter, Balzac a lawyer's clerk and Tchekov a country doctor. Art is different from life but cannot exist without it.

"The business of getting going," says Alain, "should be reduced to a minimum," by which he meant that one should never spend months and years in planning how to start on a book. I have known writers, or, rather, men who wanted to be writers, whose whole life has been wasted in deciding to take the first step. "I still lack certain important elements," they say, "before I can begin my novel," or "I am burning to get on with this biography but there are still several essential documents on which I haven't, so far, been able to lay my hand." So, time goes by, and nothing is done. Once the choice of a subject has been made, one must jump into a book as one jumps into water. If one goes on testing the temperature with one's toe one will never learn how to swim. Once the plunge is taken, the swimmer will soon learn to adapt himself to cold and currents. The initial decision is what matters, for, without it, no work will come to anything. Once begun, the book will "serve as its own model", or, more precisely, the author, sitting down at his desk in the morning and reading over what he has written the previous day, will feel instinctively how he must go on, and, not infrequently, will surprise himself.

The first thing that a certain Scots professor used to say to his students when they handed in their essays was: "Did it never occur to you to tear up the first page?" Without reading it, he could guess that it was bad, because beginnings are the most difficult things to manage successfully. "It is there", said Tchekov, "that we do most of our lying." Before we are properly warmed up, we run the risk of being flat and pedantic. Speaking personally, I am never quite sure how I am going to begin, but, once afloat, instinct takes over the controls. That is why so many of the great masters make an abrupt opening. They fling the reader straight into a dialogue between characters about whom he knows nothing. It is for him to strike out and find his own way. The Scots professor was right. It is an admirable rule to "cut" the first page which is almost certain to be groping, slow and didactic, as well as wholly unnecessary for the intelligent reader.

As to the art of concluding, that depends on the nature of the subject. If the whole purpose of a book has been to argue a thesis, it should end, as Beethoven ended, with a passage of affirmation in which the musical material was resolved. In biography and history it is well to gather all the *motifs* in the final pages, after the manner, say, of Wagner. In the case of a novel, or any imaginative work, especially if the tone is poetic, my own preference is for ending with a touch of symbolism which shall leave the reader brooding. A fine novel, a well-written story, "proves" nothing. Certain characters have played their parts, life goes on, and the final passage may be allowed to remain with one foot in the air, as is the case with some of Chopin's conclusions. But there is no absolute rule in such matters, and there are epic novelists who like to end on a powerful crescendo, as Ravel does in *Bolero*, or Dvorak in the *New-World*

Symphony. Composition has features which are common to all the arts, and the author can learn as much about his business in the concert hall as in the library.

3. Periods and Forms

I have said that a writer is a man who, more than anyone else, feels a need to express himself. But the *form* of that expression will differ in different periods. Had Valéry been born in the sixteenth century he would have written ballads: in the thirteenth, mystery plays. Art and religion are, in their origins, allied. There is a close connexion between sacred books and epics. The Bible is an epic. Homer was a religious poet who gave to the Greeks their essential myths. The poet is a magician. He has his incantations and his spells. Whenever poetry takes on new life it turns back to its source, that is to say, to the magic of words.

The theatre too, as everybody knows, originated as a place in which a representation of the religious mysteries was given. That is clearly visible in the practice of Ancient Greece where the play was at once a ritual and a State ceremony. We see the same form of drama reappearing in the Middle Ages with the enacting of the Passion in the open spaces in front of cathedrals. Tragedy, the form most in favour with the French writers of the seventeenth century, bears traces of this double origin, with Greek drama preponderating. Racine owed much to Sophocles and Euripides. What matters most to us is that Racine utilized the tragic convention for the purpose of getting himself into focus and of depicting the passions of his day. Period determines form: the writer uses it.

[23]

In the same age the moralist was in high favour. Court and City alike, comprising, as they did, a leisured élite, delighted in analysing the varying shades of sentiment, and formulating their findings in Maxims and Characters. What a man of our own day would express in the novel, La Rochefoucauld stated in concise epigrams. The new freedom of thought which came with the eighteenth century changed the moralist into a philosopher. Tragedy became platitudinous and withered away. The great writers of the time were those who devoted themselves to the exposition of ideas, science and history. Simultaneously, the novel gradually became a popular means of expression (*La Nouvelle Héloise*, *Les Liaisons Dangereuses*, *Le Paysan Perverti*). In England, books like *Tom Jones* and *Clarissa Harlowe* were treading the same road.

The writers of the eighteenth century, however, still looked on the novel as a minor form of literature. Voltaire took more pride in his tragedies than in *Candide*. It was not until the dawn of the nineteenth century that the composition of novels became a sufficient activity in itself. With Balzac, Flaubert, Maupassant and the great Anglo-Saxon, Russian, Spanish and Italian story-tellers, fiction grew to be *the* form of expression *par excellence*, a means to the dissemination of ideas among the general public. Now, in the twentieth century, the predominance of the novel is unlikely to be challenged until such time as the emergence of some new form of expression shall make it obsolete.

Let us now study briefly the technique best suited to two specific departments of literature: fiction and biography.

4. The Novelist

The production of fiction, which has reached vast proportions in all countries, is what attracts and holds the attention of the public. The reputation of a great novelist easily out-distances that of the historian or the essayist, though not, perhaps, that of the dramatist. The Nobel Prize will go to ten novelists for every *one* philosopher. I know that the imminent death of the novel as an art-form is constantly being dinned into our ears. Some of these harbingers of woe tell us that its possibilities have been exhausted, that it depended for its popularity on the existence of a bourgeois society, that only such a society provided material for the portrayal of manners, that the individual, whose passions form the stock-in-trade of fiction, is losing his importance in an increasingly authoritarian and collective world. Others think that a craving for fictional narrative is still alive and kicking but finds its satisfaction in the dramas of the screen (whether cinema or television) and that novels written to be read are already under sentence of death.

Before passing on to consider the technique of novel-writing, I wish to say a few words about this sweeping assumption. No useful purpose could be served by discussing a form of literature which is destined to disappear almost immediately. I will, therefore, say at once that I refuse to believe that there is any danger of its sad demise. Why should the novel depend upon the existence of a bourgeois society—which, by the bye, still lives on even if its health gives cause for anxiety? Collective thought has not yet destroyed individual passions, even in collectivist civilizations. Novels are still being written in the U.S.S.R. and some of them are good. The demand in Russia for French fiction is very much in evidence. We are told that the Russian sales of *Le Rouge et le Noir* now amount to seven million copies, and that of a book which is a masterpiece of fiction. As to the dramas of the screen, they, I am convinced, can never take the place of novels in the eyes of ardent and searching readers. There is something scrambled and hustled about a portrayal of dramatic happenings which lasts, at the most, for two hours. The cinema is a far greater threat to the theatre. It may have a specific beauty of its own, but it does not permit that constant re-reading, that meditative brooding, those turnings-back to passages heavily charged with meaning, which form the especial pleasure of the novel-reader.

It is further declared that even if the novel does continue, it stands badly in need of renewal; that the old methods of fiction which, as used by a Balzac or a Proust, have many masterpieces to their credit, have now been squeezed dry: that the younger generation will refuse to a man, as Valéry refused not so long ago, to write such sentences as: "The marquise took a chair, sat down, and said . . .": that the analysis of feelings—false at the best —must give place to a concern with objects. I must confess that I have no more belief in this revolution than I have in the other. Obviously, the form of the novel changes whenever a novelist of genius appears. Proust is totally different from Balzac. But though that is true, he differs far less from George Eliot and Dickens. It may be possible, it may even be probable that the novel is finding fresh inspiration in the technique of the screen: that dialogue is supplanting the author's comments on the action of his story (Compton Burnett, Claude Mauriac): that the "interior monologue" (what the characters think, not what they say) has now a recognized place in the technique of fiction (Nathalie Sarraute): that concentration on external objects is the sole means of expressing the interior world—but these variants will not change the essential nature of the novel.

Almost all the great novels have as their *motif*, more or less disguised, the "passage from childhood to maturity", the clash between the thrill of expectation, and the disillusioning knowledge of the truth. Proust extracts the very essence of this movement when he shows us a young boy confronted by a world of things, attaching to *names* ideas which, later, he will have to root up one by one before he can make the names coincide with a perceived reality. Swann is in love with an Odette who exists only in his imagination. The transformation of this fictitious Odette into the formidable Odette of flesh and blood is, in itself, a subject for a novel. Natasha, in *War and Peace*, passes from mistake to mistake. One of our younger novelists, Michel Butor, sets before us a youthful Frenchman arriving in an English town. He cannot understand it; to him it seems monstrous. The subject of the novel is the hero's coming to grips with the real nature of the town. *Lost Illusions* is the undisclosed title of every novel. By this I do not mean that the mental development of the protagonist necessarily proceeds from illusion to cynicism. One can love a real woman after having loved her imagined counterpart. Similarly, one can adapt oneself to a society which, previously, one held in contempt. Another blanket title which would fit all the finest novels is *The 'Prentice Years*.

But if the main subject of fiction is always of the same

general nature, every gifted writer chooses the variant which will allow him to express his own personal view of it. There are autobiographical novels, though they are so only in part. The really great novel, on the contrary, tends to be the exact negative of its author's life. "The characters crowd onto the page", writes Mauriac, "there to accomplish all those things which the personal destiny of the author has kept at bay. All temptations overcome, all frustrations of love, combine to produce the embryo of a being who slowly takes on form and substance until, at last, he emerges into the light of day, uttering his newborn cry. The road never trodden by the father, the child will surely tread." That is true enough, but the choice of a subject is, all the same, linked with the secret desires of the writer, and this explains how it is that the greatest novelists never cease, under a variety of masks, from writing the same book. Fabrice and Julien Sorel are two aspects of the man Stendhal would have liked to be: Mme de Rênal and Clélia Conti, of the woman he would have liked to love. In Mauriac the conflict is always between Faith and Flesh. The truth is that, from the immense spectacle of the world, each novelist retains the one adventure which enables him to give expression to his own essential self, just as the painter sees in nature only pictures painted in *his* manner.

The subject once decided upon, what part, in treating it, is played by the observing eye, what by the inventive imagination? Most novelists base their work on a *milieu* with which they are thoroughly familiar. Balzac's world is vast because life had brought him into close contact with many different types of men. Fictional characters are not portraits, but they are transpositions of real

people. We are told that Rastignac was M. Thiers, and
Micawber, Dickens' father. We may, however, be sure
that many of the peculiarities of those characters were
borrowed from other models. The Duchesse de Guermantes was Mme Straus, but she was also Mme de
Chevigné. The really good novel is never a *roman a clef*.
Nevertheless, it needs the support of reality, and the
background of an actual society, otherwise it will not
stand firm. If a novel is to come to life it must make
contact with the facts of a society, its operative influences,
its external relations, its politics and its rituals. The
pastoral idyll is always a defective novel, because the
lovers live their lives in isolation, as though situated in
some enchanted bubble.

On the other hand, the external world in a novel must
be seen through the eyes of its hero. In that form of
novel which we call our life, we circle round many human
beings, we see them under a succession of different
lights, we are witnesses of the changes which take place
in them, and it is thus that they hold our attention.
Similarly, in a well-written, well-constructed work of
fiction, the world presented will be three-dimensional
only if it circles round the reader as well as round the
hero. There are many different ways of writing novels.
The story may be told directly by the author speaking
as eye-witness of the action, in which case his surprises
must be our surprises. The hero, on the other hand,
may be the narrator, speaking in the first person, and
this is the easiest method because in it the confidential
tone comes naturally. Finally, the novel may be written
"from the point of view of God". Of this type, *War and
Peace* is a good example. In it the world revolves round
several different persons, and the reader sees it now

through the eyes of Prince André, now through those of Pierre Bezoukhov, now through Natasha's.

To be more precise: in the great novels of the world the characters fall into two main types—objects and subjects. A novel presents us with the picture of an individual life in such a way that we get to know it as well as we know our own. This life belongs to the "subject" (or to more than one subject), and all the other characters who make their appearance in the course of the narrative are objects only. Old Grandet is an object to his daughter. But *she* is a subject, and that is why the book is called *Eugénie Grandet*. Balzac's famous descriptions, which some critics find too long, are the visions of a subject-character, and, as such, are made vividly alive. What is described is not Grandet's house *in itself*, but Grandet's house as seen by Eugénie and her cousin, Charles.

It may be objected that some novels are purely imaginary (fantasies, philosophic tales, prophetic imaginings, science-fiction). That is a mistaken view. The more different the world described is from day-to-day life and the experience of the reader, the greater the need for factual precision and an illusion of solidity. *Gulliver's Travels* can make even absurdity *seem* true. Voltaire's *Micromégas* brings Fontenelle to mind, and *Candide*, Leibnitz. The novelist who relies wholly on invention is not a realist, but he must provide his fantasy with a substratum of reality.

5. The Biographer

The biographer has two duties: he must be a portrait painter and an historian. As the former, he must provide a portrait which shall be "like", and, at the same time, a good piece of painting in itself. As the latter, he must assemble a number of genuine facts, arrange them intelligibly, and give to his work an artistic form. A biography should give us "the faithful picture of a human being on his way through life": and when I say faithful, I mean to say that the biographer must base his work on solid documentation, and organize his findings in such a way as to produce a good book.

How is he to get at, and arrange his facts? First, by reading all that has been written about his hero, his hero's friends and enemies, and the period in which all of them lived. Next, he must seek out material which has never before been made public. There is always something new to be found, since the great public libraries and numerous private collections are very far from having been exhausted. He should, too, visit the places associated with his hero's life, and, if he has been dead for only a short time, hunt up and question those who knew him. Finally, he must weigh the written against the spoken evidence with a critical eye, comparing one with the other. He must so thoroughly soak himself in the contents of his documents as to be able, if necessary, to write without further reference to them.

Having assembled his facts, he must arrange them chronologically, taking care to observe the following rules: (1) The reader must not be swamped under a flood of documentation. What is redundant should be suppressed, and, where possible, the contents of this or that document carefully summarized. Except where a letter is of capital importance, a few lines should suffice to convey its "gist". (2) Great attention should be paid to such small details as will make the characters live—the most important being habitual tricks, gestures and turns of speech. (3) A proved fact must never be suppressed because it falsifies the biographer's preconceived idea of his hero. He must, on the contrary, constantly be at pains to retouch his picture, as a portrait painter does, adding something here, modifying something there, coming closer and closer to the truth. (4) In certain cases (happily rare), the existence of relations or close friends of the subject may necessitate a few omissions. But, though it is permissible not to tell the *whole* truth about a man, what is told must be true.

The invention of facts not justified by documents or by living witnesses is strictly forbidden. To attribute to one's subjects thoughts which cannot be proved, to present the reader with imaginary dialogues, is to be guilty of an infringement of the laws of biography, which are those of history. Fictional biography is a bastard literary form. On the other hand, a well-written biography should to this extent resemble a novel, that the reader should be enabled to watch the hero's progressive discovery of the world. Not only is that in accordance with the standards of serious history, but it is very necessary. It should be obvious that, for instance, Disraeli as a young man did not see English society in the same way as did Disraeli the ageing Prime Minister. It is for the biographer to discover, in the writings of his hero, in the evidence of his hero's contemporaries, in the memoirs of the time, the traces of this progressive development.

Interpretation of the available facts should be undertaken with the utmost care and be solidly supported. It is often indispensable. Was Balzac really in love with Mme Hanska, or did she behave very badly to him? Did George Sand exercise a pernicious influence on Musset and Chopin, or did she, on the contrary, contribute to the maturing of their genius? Did Bonaparte, in the days of the Consulate, behave as a tyrant or as a wise friend to genuine liberty? The reader wants an answer to these questions. So far as he can, the author will provide the facts and leave the reader to draw his own conclusions. Should he feel bound to intervene where the truth is in doubt, he must indicate all the possible hypotheses. Lytton Strachey was a master at the biographical game, at saying whether the truth lay here, or, more probably, there. He excelled at enveloping in a luminous fog the obscure points which are to be found in every life, in art no less than in real life.

Should biography have a moral value? Yes, to the extent that all great art has a moral value. I do not mean that it should take the form of a deliberate lesson in vice and virtue. But biography may well have a beneficial effect upon the reader. "Here," he will think, "is a man, or a woman, who was very like me in more ways than one, exposed, just as I am, to the exigencies of passion and to the frustrations of existence. Nevertheless, he (or she) succeeded in making something great and lovely of life." A true portrait should be a reconciliation with the sitter. A great biography should, like the close of a great drama, leave behind it a feeling of serenity. We collect into a small bunch the flowers, the few flowers, which brought sweetness into a life, and present it as an offering

[33]

to an accomplished destiny. It is the dying refrain of a completed song, the final verse of a finished poem. Such a biographer as Strachey showed himself to be the equal of a great musician or a great poet. Therein lies the technique of biography, and, indeed, of all art.

CHAPTER II

VOLTAIRE
Novels and Tales

PHILOSOPHICAL FICTION is a difficult, because a hybrid,
literary form. Since the author uses it for the purpose of
espousing or attacking certain accepted ideas, it belongs
to the class of essays or pamphlets. But because it nar-
rates a sequence of imaginary events, it can also claim
the title of fiction. It cannot, however, have either the
seriousness of the essay or the credibility of the novel.
Not that it even pretends to be credible. On the contrary, it deliberately stresses the fact that it is an exercise
in intellectual ingenuity. Not Voltaire when he created
Candide, nor Anatole France when he wrote *L'Île des
Pingouins,* nor Wells when he invented *The Island of Dr
Moreau* believed for a moment that the reader would
mistake these fictions for reality. On the contrary, it was
their considered intention to present these stories with
a philosophical content as fantastic tales.

But why, it may be asked, should an author have
recourse to this whimsical and indirect method of
philosophizing? In order to enjoy greater freedom in
expressing ideas which, in an essay, might seem to be
subversive, shocking and unacceptable to the reader.
The more he can be made to feel that he has been transported into a world where nonsense reigns supreme, the
more reassured will he feel, and the readier to digest

many surprising truths. Swift was able to say a number of disturbing things about human nature and the England of his own day, merely by pretending to describe a nation of midgets, a kingdom of giants, or a country in which horses ruled over human beings. Montesquieu was able, through the mouth of an imaginary Persian, to mock at customs for which his birth and position compelled him to make a show of respect.

The philosophical tale, or novel, will, therefore, be peculiarly well suited to a period in which ideas are changing more quickly than institutions and manners. Writers, tormented by the need they feel to say what they think, but hampered by the severity of police regulations, censorship or an Inquisition, will be tempted to take refuge in the absurd, and to make themselves invulnerable by making their books incredible. Such was the position in the France of the eighteenth century. To all appearances the monarchy was still powerful. It was the protector of religious and philosophic orthodoxy. Its judges administered the Law with a heavy hand. But, in fact, the writers and the members of the privileged classes had been won over to the new ideas, and were eager to air them. It was not altogether impossible for them to do so openly, as is proved by the publication of the *Dictionnaire Philosophique*, the *Essai sur les Moeurs* and the *Encyclopédie*. But there still remained a number of themes on which it was difficult to touch. There was, however, a good chance that, if treated as elements in a fictitious narrative, they could be brought to the notice of a more timorous and, therefore, a wider public, the more so since this type of reading matter was very much in the fashion. Ever since the publication of *The Arabian Nights* in Galland's translation (1704–1717) and of the

Lettres Persanes (1721), the oriental mode had become the favoured and transparent mask of those who, in this way, could temper their audacities with prudence. Voltaire, more than anybody else, had recourse to it.

I

It is a matter for no little surprise that he should have adopted this lively and, in both senses of the word, free form at a comparatively advanced age. Apart from the *Aventures du Baron de Gangan* which never found its way into print, though its existence is proved by a series of letters exchanged between the author and the Crown-Prince of Prussia, Voltaire's first philosophic tale was *Le Monde Comme il Va*, written in 1747. It was at this time that, as the result of an unfortunate episode, he, together with Mme du Châtelet, took refuge with the Duchesse du Maine at Sceaux. It was under her roof that *Babouc*, *Memnon*, *Scarmentado* and *Zadig* were composed. Voltaire wrote a chapter every day, which he showed to the Duchess in the evening. "Sometimes, after supper, he would read a tale or a short novel which he had written during the day for the express purpose of entertaining her. . . ."

These philosophic fictions, always contrived so as to illustrate some moral truth, were written in a gay and charming style, and the Duchesse du Maine took so great a delight in them that others soon expressed a wish to share her pleasure, with the result that Voltaire was compelled to read them aloud to a wider circle. This he did with the skill of a trained actor. The tales enjoyed a great success with his listeners, who begged that he would have them printed. For a long time he refused to do so, saying that such trivial works, designed for the amusement of a small and intimate circle, did not deserve to be perpetuated. Writers are bad judges of their own productions. At the age of eighteen Voltaire had believed that he would go down in literary history as a great tragic dramatist: at thirty, that he was destined to be a famous historian: at forty, an epic poet. He could not have foreseen, when he wrote *Zadig* in 1748, that it would still be regarded as entertaining reading, together with his other short tales, in 1958, whereas *La Henriade*, *Zaïre*, *Mérope* and *Tancrède* would be condemned to an eternal sleep on library shelves.

In this matter Voltaire's contemporaries were no less wrong than he was. They attached but little importance to frivolous stories in which what struck them most forcibly were numerous allusions to the author's personal enemies. "It is easy to recognize Voltaire under the disguise of the sagacious Zadig. The calumnies and spite of courtiers . . . the disgrace of the hero are so many allegories to be interpreted easily enough. It is thus that he takes revenge upon his enemies . . ." The abbé Boyer, who was the Dauphin's tutor and a powerful ecclesiastic, took in very bad part the attacks on one whose identity was but thinly concealed behind the anagram *Reyob*. "It would please me mightily if all this to-do about *Zadig* could be ended," wrote Mme du Châtelet, and it was not long before Voltaire disowned a book "which some there are who accuse of containing audacious attacks upon our holy religion". In point of fact the audacities of *Zadig* were pretty mild, and were limited to showing that men, at different times and in different places, have had different beliefs, though the solid basis of all religions is the same. Such a thesis was the most obvious common sense, but common sense was, at that time, most certainly not in general circulation.

Those who dared not attack Voltaire's theology accused him of plagiarism. That has always been an easy method of belittling a great writer. Everything has been said before—not excepting the statement that everything has been said before—and nothing is easier than to establish a connexion between passages in two different authors. Molière imitated Plautus who, in his turn, had imitated Menander who, no doubt, had imitated some earlier model unknown to us. Fréron (some twenty years later) charged Voltaire with having borrowed the best chapters of *Zadig* from sources "which that prize copyist took great pains to conceal". For instance, the brilliant *L'Ermite* chapter was borrowed from a poem by Parnell, and that entitled *Le Chien et le Cheval* (an anticipation of Sherlock Holmes) was lifted from *Le Voyage et les Aventures des Trois Princes de Serendip*. "Monsieur de Voltaire", wrote the treacherous Fréron, "reads often with intention, and much to his advantage, more especially in such books as he thinks have now been long forgotten. . . . From these obscure mines he brings a great many precious jewels to the surface."

Is that so terrible a crime? Must an author refuse to touch seams which have not been completely worked out? What honest critic has ever maintained that a writer can create *ex nihilo*? Neither Parnell's *The Hermit* nor *Le Voyage de Serendip* were original productions. "All these brief tales", says Gaston Paris, "were told long ago in many languages before being recast in that flexible and lively French which, today, gives them a seeming novelty . . ." The unique and brilliant character of Voltaire's *tales* lies not in originality of invention, but in that combination of diverse and seemingly contradictory qualities which are their author's own and unequalled contribution.

He had been educated by the Jesuits, and from them had learned intellectual discipline and elegance of style. During a temporary period of exile in England he had read Swift and studied his technique. "He is the English Rabelais," he had said of the author of Gulliver, "but without Rabelais' bombast." Under the influence of Swift he had developed a liking for strange fancies (whence *Micromégas* and *Babouc*), for travellers' tales which were no more than an excuse for satiric writing, and a literary variant of what we, today, should call a "poker face" which enabled him to give expression to the most monstrous propositions as though they were obvious and natural truths. Onto this living tree had been grafted the Galland of the *Arabian Nights*. "The combination of the classic French mind, with its love of proved statements, its lucid deduction of conclusions from strict logical premises, and the completely illogical view of life common in the fatalistic East, might have been expected to produce a new dimension: and this it did."[1] The subject matter was provided by stories as old as the human race: the technique contained elements drawn from Swift, from Eastern story-telling and from Jesuit teaching: but it was the inimitable synthesis of all these influences that produced the tales which Voltaire continued to concoct over a long period of time.

It has already been pointed out that he began his experiments in this, for him, new literary form, in 1747,

[1] *Alain.*

that is to say, when he was fifty-three. He wrote his masterpiece in that kind, *Candide*, when he was sixty-five; *L'Ingénu*, which is another of his most successful products, when he was seventy-four, in the same year that saw the publication of *La Princesse de Babylone*; and he was over eighty when he brought out such minor works as *L'Histoire de Jenni*, *Le Crocheteur Borgne* and *Les Oreilles du Comte de Chesterfield*. Hence, Paul Morand's generalization to the effect that French writers are never younger, never more free from constraint, than when they have passed their sixtieth birthday. By that time they have broken free from the romantic agonies of youth and turned their backs on that pursuit of honours which, in a country where literature plays a social rôle, absorbs too much of their energies during the years of maturity. Chateaubriand was never more "modern" than in his *Vie de Rancé*, and in the concluding sections of the *Mémoires d'Outre-Tombe*. Voltaire wrote his best book at sixty-five, and Anatole France his, *Les Dieux ont Soif*, at sixty-eight. The old writer, like the old actor, is a master of his craft. Youthfulness of style is no more than a matter of technique.

2

It has become customary to bring together under the blanket title of "Romans et Contes de Voltaire" a number of works greatly differing in kind and in value. Among them are such masterpieces as *Zadig*, *Candide* and *L'Ingénu*: there are the relatively unimportant *Princesse de Babylone* and *Le Taureau blanc*; there are *Cosi-Sancta* and *Le Crocheteur Borgne* which are no more than

short stories of ten pages or so, and genuine novels of a
hundred; there are rough sketches of the general type of
Les Voyages de Scarmentado, which is really only a fore-
taste of *Candide*; *Les Lettres d'Amabel* which belongs to
the tradition of *Lettres Persanes*, and dialogues like
L'Homme aux Quarante Écus, in which there is no fictional element at all, but only a discussion about political
economy reminiscent of *Dialogues sur le Commerce des
Blés*, by the abbé Galiani, or Voltaire's own *Oreilles du
Comte de Chesterfield* in which theology is argued instead
of economics.

What have all these odds and ends of writing in common? First and foremost, the *tone* which, in Voltaire, is
always mocking, mercurial and, at least apparently,
superficial. There is not, in all these fictions, a single
character who is treated with genuine seriousness. All
are either embodiments of an idea or a doctrine (Pangloss
stands for optimism, Martin for pessimism), or fairy-tale
heroes from a lacquer screen or a piece of Chinese
embroidery. They can be tortured or burned to death
without the author or the reader feeling any real concern
for them. Even the beautiful Saint-Yves, when dying of
despair because she has sacrificed what she calls her
honour in order to save her lover, can weep without
bringing the slightest hint of moisture to the eyes of
anybody else. The stories, catastrophic though they may
be, are always dominated by the author's wit, and so
rapid is their *tempo* that the reader is given no time in
which to be deeply distressed. A *prestissimo* has no
place in a Funeral March or a Requiem Mass, and the
prestissimo or the *allegretto* are Voltaire's favourite
"movements".

Puppets, variously labelled, jig to this devil's tattoo.

Voltaire delighted in bringing on to his stage priests, to whom he gave the name of *magi*; judges, whom he called *mufti*; financiers, inquisitors, Jews, innocents and philosophers. Certain routine enemies reappear in all the tales, variously disguised. Of women he has no very high opinion. To judge from his treatment of them, their minds are exclusively occupied by the prospect of making love to handsome young men with good figures, though, being both venal and timid, they are prepared to hire their bodies to old inquisitors or soldiers if, by so doing, they can save their own lives or amass riches. They are inconstant, and will gladly cut off the nose of a husband fondly mourned in order to cure a new lover. For such conduct he does not blame them. "I have", says Scarmentado, "seen all that the world can offer of the beautiful, the good and the admirable, and am determined for the future to confine my attention to my household gods. I took me a wife in my own country: I was cuckolded, and concluded that my state was the pleasantest that life can give."

It is from the author's philosophy that these writings truly derive a unity. It has been described as "a chaos of lucid ideas", in short, incoherent. Faguet accused Voltaire of having considered everything, examined everything, and never gone deeply into anything. "Is he an optimist? Is he a pessimist? Does he believe in free-will or predestination? Does he believe in the immortality of the soul? Does he believe in God? Does he deny the validity of metaphysics? Is there something in him of the agnostic spirit, but only up to a certain point, in other words, is he really a metaphysician at heart? . . . I defy anybody to answer any of these questions with an unqualified yes or no."

All that is perfectly true. There is something of every-thing to be found in Voltaire, and also the opposite of everything. But the chaos is reduced to order as soon as one sees the apparent contradictions against the back-ground of his times. In his case, as in that of most men, a personal philosophy was in a continuing state of evolution throughout his life. *La Vision de Babouc* and *Zadig* were written when Fortune was smiling on him. He was enjoying the favour and protection of Mme de Pompadour, and, consequently, of a considerable section of the Court. All the kings of Europe were inviting him to visit them. Mme du Châtelet was attending to his sensual needs, giving him affection and assuring his independence. He had every reason, therefore, for finding life tolerable. That is why the conclusions reached in *Babouc* are, relatively speaking, lenient.

"Would you have me chastise Persepolis or destroy it?" the djinn Ituriel asks him. Babouc has an observant and impartial eye. He is present at a bloody battle, in which, on neither side, do the soldiers know why they are killing and getting killed, but that same battle is the occasion for innumerable acts of bravery and hu-manity. He enters Persepolis and finds there a dirty and ill-favoured people, temples where the dead are buried to an accompaniment of harsh, discordant voices, and women of the town on whose activities the magistrates turn an indulgent eye. But, as he continues his tour, he comes upon finer temples, a wise and polished people who are deeply attached to their king, an honest mer-chant. It is not long before he comes to like the city which is, at once, frivolous, scandalmongering, pleasant, beautiful and intelligent. When he reports his findings to Ituriel, the latter decides not even to try to correct its shortcomings, but "to let the world go its way, since, though everything is far from well, everything is not too bad".

Zadig sounds a somewhat deeper note. In it Voltaire shows, by a series of ingenious parables, that it would be a rash man indeed who would maintain that the world is bad because it contains a certain number of evils. The future is hidden from us, and we cannot be sure that from these seeming errors of the Creator salvation may not come. "There is no evil", says the Angel to Zadig, "of which some goodness is not born." "But", asks Zadig, "what if everything were good and nothing evil?" "Then", says the angel Jesrad, "this world would be a different place: the interconnexion of events would belong to a different order of wisdom, and this different order, which would be perfect, could exist only in the eternal dwelling-place of the Supreme Being . . ." — a form of reasoning which is far from being irrefutable, since, if God is good, why did He not confine the world within the bounds of that eternal dwelling-place? If He is all-powerful, why did He not, in creating the world, keep it free from suffering?

Voltaire was far too intelligent not to have asked himself these questions, and, in *Micromégas*, he gives them a disillusioned answer. Micromégas is an inhabitant of Sirius who travels from planet to planet in the company of a dweller in Saturn. One day, the giant discovers the Earth and the almost invisible animalculae who live upon it. He is amazed to find that these tiny creatures can talk, and is outraged by their presumption. One of these midgets, wearing a doctor's cap, tells him that he knows the whole secret of existence, which, he says, is to be found in the *Summa* of St Thomas. "He looked the two celestial beings up and down, and informed them that their persons, their worlds, their suns and their stars had been created for the sole purpose of serving Man." Hearing this, Micromégas gives vent to Homeric laughter.

This laughter is Voltaire's own. So, human beings complain that the world is ill-made, do they? But ill-made for whom? For Man, who, in the immense design of the Universe is no more than an unimportant mould! The probability is that everything in this world which we think is botched or erroneous has its reasons at a totally different level of existence. The mould endures, no doubt, a small amount of suffering, but somewhere there are giants who, huge in stature as in mind, live in a state of semi-divinity. This is Voltaire's answer to the problem of evil. It is not very satisfactory because the mould need never have been created, and, in the eyes of God, it may well be that mere size is of no importance.

But *Micromégas* is still comparatively optimistic. Ridiculous though these human insects may be when they presume to speak of philosophy, they astonish the celestial visitors when they apply the principles of their science, and measure with accuracy the exact size of Micromégas, and the distance of Sirius from the Earth. That these all but invisible mites should have penetrated so deeply into the mysteries of the Universe in which they are themselves, perhaps, no more than accidents, was already causing no little wonder in Voltaire's time, and would still more surprise a Micromégas who should make a similar voyage of discovery in our own day. Pascal had already said as much, and so had Bacon. Men may be no more than mites, but mites who dominate the Universe by obeying its laws. Their absurdities are counter-balanced by their intelligence.

In *Micromégas* we have the second Voltaire of the "tales". The third is a far sadder figure, for he has come to understand that Man is not only absurd but also extremely wicked. By that time he had had his own personal misfortunes. Mme du Châtelet had deceived him with his best friend, and, got with child by Saint-Lambert, had died in labour. The Kings, whether of France or Prussia, had treated him badly, and he found himself condemned to live in exile. True, it was a very comfortable exile. Neither Les Délices nor Ferney could be called unpleasing residences. But such happiness as he enjoyed there he owed to his own prudence, and not at all to his fellow men among whom he had met with such bitter persecution. But his worst sufferings resulted from public disasters. Too many wars, too much intolerance. Then, in 1755, to the cruelty of men was added the enmity of Nature. It was the year of the Lisbon earthquake which destroyed one of the finest cities in Europe. It had a profound effect upon him. No longer was it possible to maintain that everything is tolerable. The present, for him, was hideous.

> *One day, all will be well.* That is our hope.
> *All is well now*, that is an illusion.

One day all would be well, but only on condition that men set to work to transform society. In this poem we see the first sketch of a doctrine of progress and of the philosophy of *Candide*.

Candide was the outcome of Voltaire's own experiences and of the exasperation bred in him by the works of certain philosophers, such as Rousseau who had written:

[47]

"If the Eternal Being has not done better, the reason is that he could not," or Leibnitz who laid it down that all was for the best in the best of all possible worlds. This generalization Voltaire put into the mouth of Pangloss, the teacher of optimism, and, to show how false it was, sent wandering about the world a simple-minded disciple of that same Pangloss, the young Candide, who saw at first hand armies, the Inquisition, murders, thievings and rapes, the Jesuits of Paraguay and conditions in France, England and Turkey. As a result of what he found in all these places, he came to the conclusion that everywhere and always Man is a very vicious animal. All the same, the last words of the book are: *Il faut cultiver notre jardin*—we must cultivate our garden—in other words, the world is mad and cruel: the earth trembles and the skies shoot lightning: kings engage in wars, and the churches tear one another to pieces. Let us limit our activities and try to do such humble work as may come our way, as best we can. That "scientific and bourgeois" conclusion was Voltaire's last word, as it was to be Goethe's. Everything is bad, but everything can be bettered. It sounds the prelude to our modern world, to the wisdom of the engineer, which may be far from complete, but is useful all the same. Voltaire, as Bainville said of him, "cleared the world of many illusions". On the ground thus swept and tidied it is possible to build anew.

Certain writers of our own day have discovered that the world is absurd. But in *Candide* Voltaire said all that can be said on that subject, and he said it with wit and intelligence, which is a good deal better than merely growing irritable, and leaves to us that legacy of courage which we need for action.

3

Candide was the high-point of Voltaire's art. Of the tales that followed it, *L'Ingénu* is the best. It still has the swiftness of the true Voltaire *tempo* and all his charm, but the themes round which it is constructed are of less importance than those of *Candide*. *L'Histoire de Jenni* is a defence of Deism, "the sole brake on men who are so shrewd in the committing of secret crimes. . . . Yes, my friends, atheism and fanaticism are the two poles in a Universe of confusion and horror." *Les Oreilles du Comte de Chesterfield* is a story which sets out to prove that fatality governs all things in this world. So, why reason and why worry? "Swallow hot drinks when you freeze, and cool drinks in the dog-days. Steer a middle course between the too much and the too little in all things. Digest, sleep and take your pleasure, all else is mockery." That is the conclusion of *Candide*, minus the poetry.

For the dominant quality of Voltaire's prose in his days of happiness is poetry. "There is", said Alain, "a prayer in every great work, even in Voltaire's tales." The poetry in all great writing is born, to a very large extent, of the fact that the madness of the universe is expressed by the disorder of ideas, but dominated by rhythm. In this, Shakespeare was a master with his witches' chants and his fairies' songs, so incoherent and so perfect. Voltaire's best work has the same two characteristics. Unforeseeable cascades of factual absurdities splash every page, yet the rapidity of the movement, the return at regular intervals of Martin's lamentations, of Candide's simplicities, of the misfortunes of Pangloss and of the Old Woman's stories, bring assurance to the mind of that tragic repose which only great poetry can give.

And so it is that Voltaire, who wanted to be a great poet in verse, and worked so hard at his tragedies and his epic, ended, though he did not know it, by finding pure poetry in his prose tales which he wrote for fun, and without, for a moment, thinking that they were important. Which proves, as he would have said, once again, that bad is good, good bad, and that fatality rules the world.

CHAPTER III

JEAN-JACQUES ROUSSEAU
The Confessions

THERE ARE few writers of whom it can be said: "But for him the whole of French literature would have taken a different direction." Rousseau is one of that few. At a time when the life of society exercised the chief formative influence on all writers, as a result of which they passed, by stages, from the majestic nobility of the seventeenth century, to the wit, and then to the dissolute cynicism of the eighteenth, the citizen of Geneva who was neither French nor noble, nor so much as touched by aristocratic influences: who was sensitive rather than well-bred, and more responsive to the solitary pleasures of a country life than to those of the *salons*, threw wide open a window which gave on to the landscape of Switzerland and Savoy, and let in a current of fresh air.

To him Chateaubriand owed the music of *René*, the thoughts and even the phraseology of his heroes. Without Rousseau we should never have had the swallows of Combourg, the sound of the rain pattering on the leaves, the song of Mlle de Boistilleul, in the *Mémoires d'Outre-Tombe*, the idea of which must have come to Chateaubriand when reading, in *The Confessions*, that passage, so deeply marked by an "intimate and domestic sensibility", in which the author tells of the song of Aunt Suzon. "Why, I do not know," writes Rousseau, "but I find it impossible to sing that song through, without being forced by my tears to stop before the end."

René is Rousseau transposed. "The young noble, the traveller on a grand scale", enamoured of Indian women and of Sylphs, was a changed version of the youth who did his travelling on foot, of the engraver's apprentice, the lackey with a touch of rascality, the squire of women of mature charms. If Chateaubriand had not read the *Confessions*, he would have remained in ignorance of many of those sources of beauty which combine to give a peculiar charm to his *Mémoires*. Rousseau was the first French writer, as Sainte-Beuve points out, "to give a country freshness" to our literature. The days of "charm, enchantment and delight" which Chateaubriand spent with Natalie de Noailles, are evocative of the "lively, tender, sad and touching impression" which Mme de Warens made upon the youthful Rousseau. Jean-Jacques set the tone for René.

No less was the debt that Stendhal owed him. Not only would the strength of feelings and the courage to acknowledge them have been impossible without that precedent. The whole character of Julien Sorel is modelled by the Rousseau of the *Confessions*. Julien in the house of the Marquis de la Mole is Rousseau in the house of the Comte de Gouvon. The one is stung by Mathilde's show of disdain, the other wishes to attract the attention of Mlle de Breil. Rousseau, like Julien, breaks through the barrier of disdain by exhibiting his knowledge of Latin. "Those present looked at me, and at one another, without uttering a word. Never was there such a display of astonishment. But what flattered me still more was the expression of satisfaction so clearly visible on the face of Mlle de Breil. She, so disdainful, deigned to give me a second glance which was at least the equal in value to the first: then, turning her eyes upon her grandpapa, she seemed to be waiting, in a sort of impatience, for the praise he owed, and did, in fact, give me in full measure, in terms so unqualified, and with so satisfied an air, that the whole table was in a rivalry to echo him. All this lasted but for a moment, but how sweet to me in every way that moment was . . ." Might that not be straight from *Le Rouge et le Noir*?

Would Gide, a century later, have written *Si le Grain ne Meurt* with its frank avowal of the specific nature of his sensuality had not Rousseau provided the first famous example of such a confession? True, there is more of hypocrisy in Gide, more of smugness in Rousseau, but that is because Gide belonged to the upper middle class and Jean-Jacques to the lower. Still, the fact remains that the taste for, the cult of, sincerity did not, before Rousseau's day, come naturally to men. In the classic age of French literature propriety was more highly prized than truth. Molière and La Rochefoucauld dressed up their confidences. Voltaire indulged in none. Not until Rousseau came upon the scene do we find a writer who took pride in telling all.

*

There is in the Neuchâtel Library an early manuscript draft of the opening pages of the *Confessions*. It is better than the somewhat theatrical exordium of the final version with its references to the Last Trump and its appeal to the Supreme Being, and makes clear the "singularity of the author's intention".

"No one can write the story of a man's life except himself. The workings of his mind, his life as it was truly lived, is known only to him, but, in setting it down on paper, he disguises it. Under the pretext of telling his story, he embarks upon an *apologia*. He exhibits himself as he would wish other men to see him, and not at all as he is. At best, the most sincere are truthful only in what they say, but they lie in their reticences, and what they do not confess so changes what they make a pretence of avowing that, by reason of recounting only one part of the truth, they tell us nothing. I would rank Montaigne as the chief of these *falsely* sincere, who set themselves to deceive by writing truly. He reveals his blemishes, but only such as are agreeable. *No man admits to being odious*. Montaigne paints a portrait of himself, but in profile only. Who can be sure that a scar upon the hidden cheek, an eye missing on the side we do not see, might not have entirely changed his physiognomy?"

The project which he had in mind to undertake raises two problems. Was not Rousseau himself one of the falsely sincere? Is complete sincerity possible when painting a self-portrait?

Admittedly, Rousseau believed, quite honestly, that he was being sincere. That is what he meant to be, even to the point of, at times, revealing himself in the most unflattering light, as when he confesses his precocious delight in solitary self-indulgence, the pleasure he found in being beaten by Mlle Lambercier, his timidity where women were concerned, due to an excessive sensibility which made him partially impotent, the almost incestuous nature of his love affair with Mme de Warens, and, above all, the strange form assumed by his exhibitionism. But, at this point, it is very necessary for the reader to note

that this sincerity is employed only in connexion with
Rousseau's sexual behaviour, and is, therefore, in itself, a
form of exhibitionism. To write of what he had so enjoyed doing meant that thousands would be spectators of
his dissolute ways, and, to that extent, increase his pleasure. To adopt a cynical attitude towards these matters is
one way of forcing one's way into the intimacy of the
abetting reader, one's counterpart and brother.[1] An
author who adopts this line, is inclined to lie by over-,
rather than under-, statement.

It is true that Rousseau accuses himself also of theft,
or bearing false witness (poor Marion's ribbon) and
ingratitude in his dealings with Mme de Warens. But
the thefts were trivial, the false-witness due, as he is
careful to point out, more to weakness than to malice,
and the "desertion", of which he makes such a point,
took place at a time when he had already long left the
house of Mme de Warens, and was no worse than what
many men might have done. He confessed these sins
with a will, knowing that his readers would absolve him.
On the other hand, he skates rapidly over the abandonment of all his children, as though it were a matter of
little moment. One cannot help wondering whether he
did not, himself, belong to that class of the "falsely
sincere" who reveal their blemishes, but only such as
are agreeable.

To this Rousseau would, no doubt, reply: "Let any
man, if he dare, say that he has been more sincere than
I!" And there he would be within his rights. For total
sincerity implies that a man can observe himself as

[1] It is, perhaps, worth pointing out that M. Maurois is here
evoking a memory of Baudelaire's famous line: *"Hypocrite
lecteur, mon semblable, mon frère!"* (Translator).

dispassionately as he would an inanimate object. But no one can be certain that the observing intelligence has not flaws and distortions. The author who sets out to tell his story has only memory on which to rely, and, since he is both artist and casuist, that memory has already conducted a preliminary sifting. He attaches capital importance to a few episodes of which he has retained a lively recollection, while passing over, without so much as a thought, the thousands of hours when he was a perfectly ordinary individual. Georges Gusdorf has demonstrated this mechanism in his *Découverte de Soi*: "Confession never tells everything. Perhaps because the real is so complex that no description can recover a truly faithful image. . . . The reading of an old diary can be very revealing. What we think we are recording of day-to-day occurrences, the immediate interpretation of daily events is found to have no relation to that same reality as retained by the memory . . ."

The writer of a volume of confessions believes that he is evoking his past, whereas the truth is that he is recounting the past *as it has become* in his present. Fouché, recalling in old age his memories of the Revolution, began: "Robespierre said to me, one day, 'Duc d'Otrante' . . ." He had quite honestly forgotten that he had not always been a Duke. In the same way, subsequent events colour our memory of decisions taken much earlier. The constant need we feel to be "all of a piece" makes us look for reasons that will justify actions which, when they took place, were due to an accident, to a bad digestion, or to the tone in which someone we were talking to, spoke. "The more I want to have a true picture of something", said Valéry, "the more do I distort it, or, rather, the more do I change the object." We think we are remembering some episode of our childhood, but what we are really doing is remembering how that episode was told to us by somebody else.

There is something of pretence in every man. Not only do we play a part for an audience, but for ourselves as well. We feel the need for continuity, and this leads us to attribute to ourselves actions of which, instinctively, we should never have been conscious. All morality is based upon a second and more consistent nature. Every human being is a sum total of different characters. Perfect sincerity would consist in describing all of them, but they are contradictory, and that is something which an author finds it difficult to admit. Stendhal, both in his treatment of his heroes, and in his own *Journal*, shows a mixture of waywardness and logic, but even this alternation is more constant in a writer's work than in his life. What would art be, if it did not impose on nature a greater degree of order than it actually contains?

No confession can be other than a work of fiction. If the confessor is honest, then the *facts* will conform as closely to historic truth as memory and interpretation will permit. But the *feelings* will inevitably be the product of imagination. Rousseau's *Confessions* is one of the best of all picaresque novels. All the elements of good fiction were ready to the author's hand when he sat down to write it: the adolescent hero turned in upon himself: a great variety of conditions, characters and places: love affairs and travels: the slow discovery of society by a man who, up till the age of forty, had been almost a complete stranger to it. This was just the material from which to construct a sentimental *Gil Blas*, and Rousseau was equal to the task.

What strikes us as strange is that it was his honest

belief that his presentation of past emotions was more accurate than the record of events. "So far as facts are concerned, I may be guilty of omissions, transpositions and wrong dates, but I cannot be mistaken about what I felt, nor yet about what my feelings made me do, and that is what really matters. The aim of these confessions is to give a true picture of my inner self in all the situations of my life . . ." Such a statement presupposes that a man is able to know his inner self and to distinguish it from external appearances—which I do not believe. The truth about Rousseau is not to be found in his moments of self-examination, but in the relation of facts, for which he declared that he felt only contempt.

The man who sets out to tell the story of his life paints a true portrait of himself, though quite unconsciously, by showing that he is constantly relapsing, without wishing to do so, into the same sort of situation as before. Stendhal with Angela Pietragrua is the same man who knelt at the feet of Mélanie Louason. Rousseau finds himself making one of a *ménage à trois* with Saint-Lambert and Mme d'Houdetot, after having occupied a similar position with Mme de Warens and Claude Anet. Many of his attitudes were determined by physical ailments. Bladder trouble was the cause of his turning his back upon the world, and round that compulsory abstention he built a doctrine. He expresses astonishment that "with senses so inflammable, and a heart all steeped in love, I was never truly on fire for any specific woman". But, unconsciously, he provides us with an explanation: "That infirmity was the principal reason for my absenting myself from social circles, and finding it impossible to enjoy any genuine intimacy with women . . ." The mere thought of having planned a meeting with some woman who pleased him produced such an extraordinary state of nerves, that he arrived at the appointed rendezvous in a condition of complete exhaustion. To the imperfections of his body, Jean-Jacques owed his unhappiness: to his comparative impotence we owe the *Confessions* and *La Nouvelle Héloïse*. "A writer finds such compensation as he can for the injustices of Fate."

Self-knowledge is possible only if the intelligence can be made sufficiently objective to apply to those feelings which the writer thinks that he has discovered in himself, the same correctives which are forced upon him by the other elements of his situation: his origins, his childhood, his social class and the consequent prejudices which have been bred in him: his body, and the limitations it imposes on him, the circumstances which have fashioned its reactions and desires: the atmosphere of the period in which he has lived, with all its manias, infatuations and superstitions. One might imagine M. Teste stripping himself bare of everything except the essential characteristics of self. But what would be left? Is not true self-knowledge nothing more than knowledge of the world in which we live?

*

There are several things to be said about Rousseau's sensuality. For women he had had, from childhood onwards, that lively and authentic craving which contributes so much poetry to his narrative when he is under the influence of the tender passion. Nothing could be more pleasing than his description, in the fourth book of his *Confessions*, of the walk he took with Mlle de

Graffenried and Mlle Galley, and of the unmixed delight
it gave him.

"We ate our dinner in the farmhouse kitchen, the
two young women sitting on one of the benches which
stood on either side of the long table, with their guest
between them, on a three-legged stool. Oh! what a
meal was that! and how brimful of charming memories!
When, at such little cost one can enjoy so much pure
and genuine pleasure, why should one go in pursuit
of others? No supper in a discreet Parisian villa could
ever hope to be the equal of our feast, not merely in
gaiety and sweet happiness, but in the satisfaction of
the senses, too.

When dinner was ended, we played at thrift. Instead
of drinking the coffee left over from our breakfast, we
kept it, to be taken later with the cream and the cakes
which the ladies had brought with them, and, to give
ourselves an appetite, we went into the orchard and
wound up our dessert with cherries. I climbed into
the tree and threw the clusters down to them, and they
tossed back the stones to me between the branches.
On one occasion, Mlle Galley, spreading her apron
and throwing back her head, made so fine a target
that I, with careful aim, sent one little bunch between
her breasts. What laughter greeted my success! To
myself I said, O that my lips were cherries! how gladly
would I throw them down! . . ."

No less charming is his idyll with Mme Basile, nar-
rated in the second book:

"With her I experienced delights which are beyond
the power of words to express. Nothing that I have

ever felt when possessing of a woman can compare
with the two minutes during which I knelt at her feet
without daring so much as to touch her dress. There
is nothing in the ecstasies of the flesh to equal the joys
which an honest woman whom one loves can bestow.
All with her is a favour. The tiny movement of a
beckoning finger, a hand pressed lightly to one's lips
—such were all that I ever received from Mme Basile,
but, slight though they were, the memory of them can
thrill me even now . . ."

Sainte-Beuve rightly admired the delicious description
of his first meeting with Mme de Warens, and the
novelty, in French literature of such passages, revealing,
as they do, a world of sunlight and freshness undreamed
of by the ladies of Versailles, though it lay at their very
doors. "They are filled [these pages] with a mingled sweetness of sensibility and nature, with only just enough of
sensual swooning as is permitted, and, indeed, is needed,
to free us from the false metaphysic of the heart, and a
conventional respect for what is spiritual." But he de-
plores the fact that a man who could write so deliciously
of pure delights should have shown such lapses of taste as
he does in recording the episodes of the horrible More,
of the abbé of Lyon, and of Mlle Lambercier. And
why, he asks, should he have called Mme de Warens
"Mamma" at the very moment when she became his
mistress?
Sainte-Beuve, who was class-conscious to an extent
beyond anything we now know, explains these flaws, as
well as certain "low and repellent turns of phrase which
a gentleman would not have used, or, probably, known",
by the fact that Rousseau had been a lackey and grown

familiar with the language of his kind. When a man has led a rough-and-tumble existence he can speak openly of many objectionable things without making us feel sick. But we have changed all that, and the vocabulary of cynicism is no longer the property of any one class. Rousseau's "frankness", which so deeply shocked the nineteenth-century critic, seems, in these days, almost bashful.

Is it a matter for regret that Rousseau and his imitators should have dared to confess what all men know, and all women ought to know? It is sheer hypocrisy to praise freedom of speech so long as it avoids essential matters, and to wax indignant when it describes men as they really are. There is something pleasing in open references to sexual matters, because it awakens the reader's sensuality by association, and gives him a fellow-feeling with the author which is distinctly reassuring. To find in another man, and a great one to boot, the desires and, sometimes, the perversions to which he has yielded, or, by which, at least, he has been tempted, strengthens his self-confidence. His repressions become "unrepressed". So far, so good. But there are dangers involved. For a whole epoch to live in a climate of sensuality is never conducive to health, and periods more than normally marked by cynicism in sexual matters have almost always been periods of decadence. The Rome of Heliogabalus made men regret the Rome of Cato. On the other hand, an excess of chastity can be the cause of many painful frustrations. To sit too heavily on a safety-valve may lead to unpleasant consequences, and in Rousseau there was, most certainly, a touch of sex mania.

Like most manias, however, it was for the most part restricted to the imagination. Actually, there were very few women in Rousseau's life: Mme de Warens, Mme de Larnage, la Padoana, the "little girl" offered him by Klupffel, and Thérèse Levasseur, make up, I think, the full total. Those whose love affairs are frequent are not those who talk about them most often. Rousseau talked a great deal about his amorous prowess, and, as a result, got badly on the nerves of his friends to whom he preached those very virtues which he would have dearly liked not to practice. If we are to understand the cruel hostility shown to Rousseau by a whole social world and two religious confessions, we must be mindful of the philosophy which, round about 1750, had suddenly made him the fashion. He had taken the smart circles of Paris by assault in the guise of a sober citizen, the friend of virtue, who scorned sophisticated pleasures, and was the declared enemy of "civilization". But this opponent of the theatre produced an opera at Court: this proud republican accepted fifty louis from Mme de Pompadour: this apostle of conjugal love lived in sin with a woman whom he had seduced when she was still a girl: this author of a truly remarkable treatise on education had deposited all his children on the steps of the Foundling Hospital. He certainly went out of his way to put serviceable weapons into the hands of his enemies.

*

There was no lack of enemies in his life, and the whole of the second part of the *Confessions* is an effort to clear himself of their calumnies. The first six books, which were written in England, at Wootton, carry the story of Rousseau's life up to 1741 and paint a sunny picture of his years of apprenticeship. The last six were composed, after a two years' break, in Dauphiné and at Tyre, between 1768 and 1770. The narrative stops at 1766 when, persecuted by France, Geneva and Berne, he decided to seek an English refuge. This second part deals with his first contact with the life of Paris, his liaison with Thérèse Levasseur, his début in the literary world, his emotional friendship with Mme d'Houdetot and its unfortunate consequences. This panel of the dyptich still contains passages of great beauty: the joy he felt when Mme d'Epinay invited him to l'Hermitage there to renew his contact with the world of Nature which called to him and was his friend, and to see again green fields, flowers, trees and running streams: the birth of *Julie* under the influence of this intoxicating happiness, and his experiences of love with that Sylph born of his brain: his walks with Mme d'Houdetot, their first romantic meetings, their rendezvous at night in a bosky grove—all this is sheer delight and as fascinating as the earlier pictures of Les Charmettes.

But, little by little, rancour begins to cast a shadow on the pages. The smell of candles and corruption mingles with the scented summer sweetness. Rousseau believed himself to be the victim of a secret persecution. "This is where the clouds begin to gather in which, for the last eight years, I have been enveloped; the terrifying obscurity which, do what I may, I cannot pierce . . ." Was this mere persecution mania? Was there, in fact, no solid reason for so much self-pity? For a long time the commentators thought so because Rousseau's adversaries, most of them men of letters and wielding great power, had found credit with posterity. But one has only to read Henri Guillemin's book, *Un Homme, deux Ombres*, to realize that enemies there most certainly were, bent on ruining him for different but convergent reasons.

Humble, unhappy, unknown and original, he had, in
his forties, been well received. Fashionable women took
pride in having discovered a new talent. Then success
had come to him, and the success of others is what men
are least ready to forgive. Grimm and Diderot who, so
he thought, were his most faithful friends, were growing
sick of hearing him praised. Grimm was animated by
malice, and, though Diderot was little addicted to that
vice, he could not forgive Rousseau for being a Christian.
The fact that intimacy with the Encyclopaedists had
strengthened rather than shaken the faith of the Citizen
of Geneva, threatened danger for the whole sect and for
the successful propagation of their doctrine. But at least
he could have had the Christians on his side had he
attached himself firmly to one of the two great per-
suasions. First a Protestant, then a Catholic, and, lastly,
a Protestant again, he laid claim to a purely personal
form of the Faith, that of the *vicaire savoyard*, stripped
of all the "rubbish of petty formulae". This independent
attitude, praiseworthy but dangerous, leagued against
him Jesuits and parsons alike.

There remained the women, at that time so powerful,
who for a long period had rewarded with their protection
the tenderness with which he spoke of their sex. But
them, too, he succeeded in alienating. They asked of him
that he should charm away their boredom: they sought
his company. But he much preferred his solitary walks
and day-dreams to the boudoirs of the fashionable. His
infirmity unsuited him to undertake the heavy duties of
courtier or favourite. Mme d'Epinay wished him well,
but he mortally offended her by falling in love with her
sister-in-law, Mme d'Houdetot, and parading his passion.
He carried simple-mindedness so far as to confess it to

C

Diderot whom he believed to be his friend, though he was so no longer. No one can be more cruel than a former friend, for, to justify himself in his own eyes for what he knows is a bad action, he sets himself with a will to blacken the man he has betrayed. Diderot abused the confidence reposed in him. With consummate art Grimm dripped poison on to everything. Mme d'Houdetot, whose affections were engaged elsewhere, grew tired of a lover who was, at one and the same time, platonic and indiscreet—two unpardonable faults. Suddenly, Rousseau found himself beset on all sides by the denizens of that little world which once had seemed so enchanting to him. He had to leave l'Hermitage. This produced a sensation. Reading the story, one is reminded of Balzac's unhappy *Curé de Tours* who, also, was a victim of long-smouldering and concentrated hatreds.

The rest should have been silence. The packets of letters, the uneasy analysis of sentiments indulged in by the Holbach coterie, the pettiness of the folk of Berne or of the Val-Travers, cannot but have a certain interest for the literary historian. For the impassioned reader, however, the charm of the *Confessions* vanishes completely in the twelfth book. All the same, he cannot withdraw from Jean-Jacques either his admiration or his respect. The work ends, as it began, with a profession of sincerity:

"I have told the truth. If anyone knows things contrary to what I have set down, then I say that what he knows, even though it were to be proved a thousand times, is false and deceptive. If he refuses to join with me in probing and casting light upon these matters while I am still living, then is he no friend to justice or

to truth. Loudly and fearlessly I declare that if anybody, even though he has not read my writings, after
examining for himself my nature and my character,
my morals, my leanings, my pleasures and my habits,
can still believe me to be dishonest, he deserves to be
strangled."

There is every reason to think that Rousseau told the
truth, his truth, in so far as human weakness makes such
telling possible.

CHAPTER IV

STENDHAL

Le Rouge et le Noir

(The text here printed was delivered as a lecture. I feel it necessary to point this out in order to explain its didactic and conversational tone.)

SHOULD A NOVELIST take his subjects from real life? I intend, by studying *Le Rouge et le Noir*, to show how a true story, followed very closely, can, in its passage through a creative mind, become a genuinely original piece of fiction.

★

In 1827 a case which had caused no little sensation in the neighbourhood was brought before the Criminal Court of Grenoble. A young man, Antoine Berthet by name, was accused of murder, and pleaded guilty. The circumstances were as follows.

Berthet was the son of a village blacksmith. He had been brought up by the curé of Brangues who had found him a position, when he was nineteen, as tutor in the family of a certain M. Michoud, a local industrialist. Mme Michoud was a woman of about thirty-six. What exactly happened we do not know, except that Berthet most certainly made love to her. Whether she became his mistress was never clearly established in the course of the trial, but it is an undoubted fact that M. Michoud got rid of him. Some months later the old curé persuaded

him to enter a seminary. His stay there was short, and
he was expelled for reasons which never came to light.
We next find him, again as a tutor, in the house of a
M. de Cordon, a nobleman, and once more, after a stay
there of only two years, he was discharged on the ground
that he had made passionate advances to the daughter
of the family. He tried to find other employment, but
without success, and imagined, rightly or wrongly, that
his failure was due to the fact that Mme Michoud, from
motives of revenge or jealousy, was making it impossible
for him to earn a living. It was then that he took a
strange decision. One Sunday he went to the church of
the village where Mme Michoud lived, and, during High
Mass, at the moment of the elevation, when Mme
Michoud had her head bowed, shot her in the back with
a pistol. She fell to the ground, and Berthet attempted
to commit suicide. He, too, fell, bleeding profusely. He
was carried from the church and his life was saved. Mme
Michoud did not die, nor did he. He was arrested and
sent for trial.

The scene in Court must have been a strange one. The
accused was dressed in black—half a seminarist—his
head enveloped in bandages because his wound was not
yet entirely healed: he was a young man whom the
Public Prosecutor had accused of being a monster, and
to every question put to him, he answered with:

"Kill me, sentence me to death: that is all I ask."

His Counsel confirmed this attitude. Berthet himself
wrote to the Public Prosecutor:

"Monsieur: my wish is that I may be condemned
tomorrow, and be led out to execution on the day
following. Death is the sweetest pardon that I could

be granted. It does not frighten me, that I swear. I have already found life so hateful, that you, by your prolonged proceedings, can make it no more odious. Let me not longer be compelled to breathe the air of corruption. Permit me to make but a few appearances in Court, where, I promise you, I shall not open my lips."

Such, then, was the story which was filling the French newspapers, and especially those of the Department of Isère (and don't forget that Stendhal was a native of Isère) in the year 1827. . . . Stendhal read it. Let us now enquire why it so struck him. I have described what actually happened. I wish now to explain the nature of the mind that treasured up this record of facts, and transposed it. Who, precisely, was Stendhal?

He was born in 1783, that is to say, a few years before the outbreak of the Revolution, at Grenoble. His real name was Henri Beyle. His father, Chérubin Beyle, was a complete blunderer where women were concerned, thoroughly unlikeable, and interested only in money-making. His great confidante and abettor was Aunt Séraphie, for whom Stendhal felt an intense hatred all through his life. She is portrayed (in *Henri Brulard*) as a hypocrite who was for ever preaching the blessings of a happy family life, and, for ever by her actions making family life impossible. She accused young Beyle of being a monster. One day, when he was still a child—seven or eight years of age—he happened to be on the balcony playing, as children do play, at planting seeds in a flower-pot with the aid of a little knife. It slipped from his hand and fell into the street, close to an old woman, whom Aunt Séraphie swore he had deliberately tried to kill. It is not difficult to imagine the effect of such an accusation on the mind of a child. The idea of injustice became firmly lodged in him. In order to avenge himself on an old aunt, he would be prepared to annihilate a whole society. Stendhal detested his father's side of the family.

On the other hand, he adored his mother's. She had been a Gagnon, and his Gagnon grandfather was a true man of the eighteenth century who professed a philosophy which, later on, Stendhal was to call *fontenellisme*, that is to say, an easy acceptance of life. There was also an uncle, Romain Gagnon, a Don Juan for whom the young Beyle had a profound admiration, and Aunt Elizabeth who was in every way the exact opposite of Aunt Séraphie. In the Stendhal mythology the one stood for hypocrisy, the other for *espagnolism*, a Spanish attitude in all things. The word, for Stendhal, connoted an exaggerated sense of honour, bravura and audacity. Aunt Elizabeth loved *Le Cid*, as she loved everything that showed greatness of character. We shall come across her again, under many disguises, when we consider the novels.

Most of us are shaped by our childhood. By the time he is eight, a man has become either an optimist or a pessimist. He changes very little after that unless events bring him a maturity of great happiness after a childhood of great misery, or *vice versa*, and even so, there will always remain something of melancholy and timidity in the make-up of those whose beginnings were inauspicious. Stendhal's character was fully formed in childhood. Its direction was determined by his father's tyrannical methods, to which was added the further tyranny of a priest, the abbé Raillane. He divided the human race into two groups. On the one side were those whom he called the "skunks". Into this category fell his father, the abbé Raillane, and all who were hypocrites, bigots and royalists (because his father was a royalist) or "classics" (because his father loved the classics): on the other, were the noble and warm-hearted, Aunt Elizabeth and himself. The "noble" had all the qualities conspicuously lacking in the "skunks". They were romantic, they were lovers, though, at the same time, cynics, too. They were free of all prejudice: they were worshippers at the altar of reason, like the people of the eighteenth century, but, since they were also romantics, they were mad about poetry.

It immediately becomes apparent what a very complicated person he was. His outlook was aristocratic though, in theory, he was a republican. During the Terror, the Beyle family was horrified by what was happening in Paris. The young Stendhal, on the other hand, was secretly delighted, for he saw the cruelties of that time as a just vengeance on the "skunks". The idea that energy and violence were fundamental necessities had become deeply rooted in him during childhood as a result of the fierce struggle in which he had, himself, been involved. He had but one wish—to get away from Grenoble and play a part in the new society where it would be possible to live "à l'espagnole" and to become one of the "noble".

He set off for the capital while still very young, and was much daunted by what he found there. A certain M. Daru, a cousin and a man of importance in the world of the Consulate, and later of the Empire, procured his entry into the "salons". For the first time in his life he made contact with well-bred and interesting women who could talk of literature and music. He was tremendously thrilled. He had a longing to be loved and to love, but, at the same time, scarcely ventured to open his lips. No one has ever loved women as he did, nor been so deeply disturbed by them. His introduction into the smart world of Paris left him with a life-long memory of the contrast between violent emotions and the timidity of those who feel them. Out of these memories he was to construct part of *Le Rouge et le Noir*.

The Paris with which he became acquainted was a place full of life and movement. It was the Paris which was beginning to accept the early splendours of Bona-parte. All the young men, as was but natural, adored Bonaparte. To this adoration Stendhal remained faithful. At a later date, describing the youthful climate of those days, he wrote as follows:

"In our eyes, the inhabitants of the rest of Europe were despicable nit-wits. The dominant influence in the lives of all of us was a deeply-rooted emotion of which, now, not a trace remains. Those who are under fifty can get an idea of it only from books. What moved us most in 1794 can be summed up in one single feeling: a longing to be of service to our country. Everything else—clothes, food, advancement, were nothing to us but trivial and ephemeral details. Since there was no longer any society in the old sense, social success did not exist. In the streets our eyes filled with tears when we read upon the walls a citation to the honour of the young drummer-boy, Bara, who, at the age of thirteen, had chosen death rather than cease to beat his drum. For us, who had had no experience of great gatherings of men, there were tremendous national festivals, moving military ceremonies which added fuel to the burning emotion which ruled in all our hearts. It was our sole religion, and when Napoleon appeared and put an end to the continual defeats to which the spineless government of the Directoire had exposed us, we saw in him only the military value of dictatorship. He gave us victories, and we judged all his actions in the light of the faith which, since our earliest childhood, had set our hearts beating. We saw nothing worthy of respect but the serving of our country. . . . Even within the walls of the Tuileries, there were among those who sincerely loved Napoleon—men like Ducros, Lavalette, Lannes and a few others—some who, when they were alone together, agreed that the Emperor's actions could be measured only by the yard-stick of the national interest. Strange to relate, Napoleon himself could be included in the number, for Napoleon's attitude to France was that of a lover, with all a lover's weaknesses."

Stendhal followed the Emperor into Italy, and there, in Milan, liberated from Austrian rule by the coming of the French armies, he believed that he had found what he had looked for, unavailingly, in Paris: a land where the passions of love were ardent and artless. All his life long he treasured the intoxicating memory of his first arrival in Italy. Perhaps he attributed to Milan, and to the Italians, passions and virtues which were those of his own youth.

For fifteen years he followed the armies of Bonaparte in Germany, in France, in Russia. Then, suddenly, came collapse. Beyle, still a young man (he was only thirty-two) found himself a half-pay officer on the retired list, a man who could find no employment under the Restoration government. Then began a difficult and gloomy chapter of his life.

The period of the Restoration was romantic, to be sure, but dark and dismal. The Bourbons who had just come back, lived in fear of bonapartists and republicans alike. They felt the ground unsure beneath their feet, and spread far and wide the network of their police. All through his life, Stendhal was obsessed by the idea that he could not openly speak of what he most valued—his memories of the Revolution and the Empire. Even in his manuscripts, in the series of journals which he kept for himself alone, he behaved with a prudence which was little less than puerile. For instance, instead of writing "le roi" he wrote "le king", "le plus fripon (rascally) des kings"—as though the police could not read English! When he wished to speak of religion, he spelt it "gionreli". One gets the feeling, sometimes, that he was not so much intent on taking serious precautions, as playing at being frightened, like a child.

Paris was no longer for him a place in which he wanted to live. He returned to his beloved Italy and, for a long time, existed in poor circumstances at Milan, writing books like *Armance* and *De l'Amour* which had no success, and continuing to think about Napoleon who was still so very dear to his heart. I find a high degree of nobility in this man, who knew to the full the risks he ran in speaking of the Emperor, and had the courage to include in one of his books this admirable dedication to Napoleon:

"In spite of your faults, which have harmed you more than they have harmed our country, an impartial posterity will bemoan the Battle of Waterloo. It will realize that action creates and demands power, that without Romulus the Numas could not have existed. For fourteen years you suppressed in France the strife of parties, and were the first to succeed in compelling Chouans and Jacobins to be Frenchmen, and only Frenchmen. That appellation, Sire, you raised to so great a height that, sooner or later, Chouans and Jacobins will embrace at the foot of your massed trophies. That boon, the greatest that any nation can be granted, will one day ensure immortal liberty to France."

During that long residence in Milan, Stendhal's character became finally established. Of what nature was it, and what kind of a man was it who wrote *Le Rouge et le Noir*?

The most prominent element in his character was that to which, a while back, I gave the name of *espagnolisme*, a quality of noble-mindedness, the need he felt to be neither colourless nor base.

There was no vanity in him. Never has a human being spoken so frankly and with such serenity of the unpleasant, the shameful and the disagreeable things that happened to him. His Journal is one of the most honest and outspoken records that any man has ever produced of his own life. Nor was he tainted with the vanity of authorship. He looked upon his books as amusing playthings. As soon as each was published, and he had read what the critics had to say about it, he revised and corrected what he had written. There exists a copy of *La Chartreuse de Parme* which (after reading Balzac's "notice") he had interleaved with sheets of blank paper, so as to rewrite it, not for his readers, but for himself. I have seen Stendhal's manuscripts now preserved in the Public Library at Grenoble. The marginal notes are artless and brutal. Sometimes he writes, as nearly as I can remember: "This is absurd, but better leave it as it is: it will amuse the reader." As a lover he was never vain. Almost all the women whom he loved did not love him, and he makes no bones about admitting it. He sets down precisely how long he spent in courting them, how often his efforts to win them were fruitless, and how, on the contrary, the few women who *did* love him scarcely attracted him at all.

He was not ambitious. The only favour he ever received from the Monarchy of July was his appointment to the second-rate post of French Consul at Civita-vecchia: but he wanted nothing better. "Dear reader, do not spend your life in hating and being afraid." And again: "Life is too short to be spent in licking the boots of a few wretched nobodies." In brief, he succeeded, by virtue of his intelligence and his *espagnolisme* in subduing the passions which torment mediocre men.

What were his ideas? He was a Frenchman of the eighteenth century, with a respect for reason and logic. "To be a good philosopher, one must be clear-headed, like Voltaire, and without illusions." But with his "logic" he mingled the poetry of Napoleon, and also a system, which, according to him, he learned from the Italians— the "art of living". Frenchmen, he maintained, are often desirous of the happiness which vanity can give, but never find such pleasure in their passions as did, for example, the men of the Italian Renaissance. He felt a very special love for those who can abandon themselves to their passions. The most deeply rooted of these is, of course, love, and on the subject of love he wrote a whole treatise. In this he distinguished four different types. The only one worth serious attention is *amour-passion*. The passionate lover is he who thinks only of the object of his love. Nothing else exists for him, and vanity has no place in what he feels. On a lower level he places *amour-goût*, a taste for loving in general. In this, the lover still often thinks of the loved one, but, at the same time, can take an interest in other pleasures, such, for instance, as the acquiring of money or the satisfaction of vanity. Physical passion comes only third. Last of all comes *amour-vanité*, for which he feels profound contempt.

One of the most famous themes of *De l'Amour* is that of "crystallization". This I will briefly summarize. What Stendhal is trying to say is that love is a subjective emotion which depends more on the lover than on the beloved. We do not see the woman we love as she is, but endow her with many qualities which she does not possess. In the Salzburg salt-mines it is possible to leave a dead branch, a black and ugly piece of wood, and to find next day, when one returns, that it has become covered with salt crystals and is now a glittering object which it is a delight to behold. The woman we love, says Stendhal, resembles this piece of dead wood. In herself she is nothing. But love, and, more especially, absence and doubt, adorn her with a whole array of glittering crystals, so that we come to see in her what, in fact, she is not. This idea was, later, taken up again by Proust. Alain says:

"The best way in which women can exert their power is in being late for an appointment, or in not keeping it at all."

This formula would have delighted Stendhal, for it contains one of the conditions of crystallization.

Hence the subjectivity of love. It is nothing but a form of madness, since, when afflicted by it, we see others as they are not. But, thinks Stendhal, it is a delicious madness, and the only thing that makes life worth living.

He was to try to give expression to these ideas through the medium of certain "characters". You must, I feel sure, have come across those puppet-men who were once such a common sight in our villages, where they used to turn up with a box containing the king, the queen, the devil and the countryman. . . . Stendhal is rather like that. He confronts each of his "subjects" equipped with his little box of puppets. Of what nature are those puppets?

First of all there is *the man Stendhal would have liked to be*: a young man, usually handsome and worthy of being loved, but timid, because he, too, is capable of loving, and, consequently, deeply troubled by the object of his love.

"The more vividly we imagine the greatness and the beauty of what we love," says Stendhal, "the more timid we are."

But this hero, when he loves, can, by courage and determination, overcome all obstacles. It pleased Stendhal to show his hero in a variety of situations. In *Le Rouge et le Noir* he made him the little seminarist of the Berthet story, that is to say, a man of the people. In *Lucien Leuwen* he was imagining what he, Stendhal, might have been had his father been a banker. In *La Chartreuse de Parme* he painted a portrait of what Henri Beyle would have been like if he had been born a young Italian prince. Thus, all his novels are games which he

[79]

plays for his own enjoyment, in which an idealized Stendhal is the protagonist.

The second puppet is *the woman Stendhal would have liked to love*.

The woman he would have liked to love was a woman who has never existed, of perfect beauty and perfect purity, who, nevertheless, becomes his mistress. "Only noble spirits", he said, "deserve to be loved." This character is Mme Rênal in *Le Rouge et le Noir*, Clélia Conti, in *La Chartreuse de Parme*.

The third puppet is *the woman he thought he would have been, had he been a woman*. In *Le Rouge et le Noir* she is Mathilde, that is to say, a woman who, like himself, had the ardour and vigour of the Renaissance: a strong woman, whereas the women whom Stendhal actually loved were always somewhat weak, and allowed themselves to be dominated. In the novel entitled *Lamiel*, he thought it amusing to transform himself into a woman. You will remember, of course, that when Flaubert was asked who Mme Bovary was, he replied:

"*Madame Bovary, c'est moi.*"

Stendhal could have said:

"Lamiel is myself."

Or, more accurately:

"Lamiel is Julien Sorel."

The fourth puppet is what might be called the *deus ex machina*. Stendhal always liked to introduce into his novels a powerful and beneficent character, the *magician* who, with a wave of his wand, might have turned Stendhal into a man rich, honoured and in a position to gratify all his desires. Such a person, in *Le Rouge et le Noir*, is M. de la Mole, the great nobleman who takes Julien as his secretary, and gives him an opportunity to make a rapid career, which is what he wants. In *Lucien Leuwen* it is the great banker, Leuwen, and, in *La Chartreuse*, Count Mosca.

And always, as a counterfoil to this good and powerful character, the mocker who hides his goodness under a mask of irony, there is the master-rogue, the rogue-in-a-big-way, the *chief of all rogues*, who plays the part of the antagonist and prevents the hero from getting what he wants.

The pattern, therefore, of Stendhal's novels is always relatively simple. This does not alter the fact that they are masterpieces, but merely shows that the basic framework changes but little. The story is always that of a young man's apprenticeship to life, of the clash between the fairy world of childhood and the world as it is. Stendhal takes a generous-minded youth, and confronts him with the two women of different types between whom he is torn. He gives him a powerful protector as friend, and a rogue as enemy. Such is the permanent form of all Stendhal's fiction.

★

This, then, is the man, with the philosophy of life which I have just outlined, who, in 1827, read about Antoine Berthet in the newspapers. He was deeply interested—for two main reasons: first, because the trial was the story of an apprenticeship: second, because the type of young man concerned was one that particularly appealed to him. He loved energy, and thought that it, more than anything else, must be the outstanding characteristic of men who, like Berthet, were very young, very poor, educated, unhappy and ambitious. Bonaparte had had the requisite elements of education, poverty and ambition. It is men like that who become the great figures of history. That was why the drama of Antoine Berthet continued to fascinate Stendhal. In 1827 he was turning the subject over in his mind. The book came much later. He did not start on it until 1829. There can be little doubt that he could not have had it published under the Restoration: but the revolution of 1830 set his mind at rest on the score of censorship, and the novel appeared in 1831.

How did he handle the story of the seminarist? Antoine Berthet became himself. Mme Michoud, the first of Berthet's conquests, he transformed into Mme de Rênal, who is a far finer character than the original of the portrait had been. Mlle de la Mole was Mlle de Cordon—with differences; the abbé Raillane "sat for" that "rogue of rogues", the horrible abbé Castanède. What Stendhal did, in short, was to take the real story as he had learned it from the newspapers, and to introduce into it his own stock company of puppets. At the end of the book he had, if he was to remain faithful to his sources, to make Julien Sorel murder (or attempt to murder) Mme de Rênal, and here we have a curious example of a struggle between fiction and reality. Seen in the light of the characters as depicted by Stendhal, the attack with the pistol comes as a surprise. Julien was too noble and too intelligent to have had recourse to it, and Mme de Rênal too touching a figure for anyone to have thought of killing. But Stendhal wanted to stick closely to the facts of the case. He kept the attempted murder, therefore, and, in the event, made it fine and convincing.

*

At this point a number of comments are necessary.

More than one critic has found this dénouement hard to swallow, and has blamed Stendhal for the speed with which he contrives an incident which needed a great deal of preparation and explaining. Even Merimée finds Julien's action atrocious. I, on the other hand, agree with Alain that there is great beauty in it. The action at this point in the story had to be rapid and the interior monologue reduced to nothing, because in Julien the taking of a decision and acting upon it are always closely linked. What we are shown is Julien issuing a military order to Julien. Just as, one day, he had said to himself "at two in the morning I am going to enter Mme de Rênal's bedroom", so now, as soon as he had learned of the wrong she had done him, he says: "I am going to kill her" and, from that moment, thinks no more about the matter. But he loved her, didn't he? Certainly he loved her. The point is that his ideal is not so much true love as true pride, pride true to itself. He kills without hatred as he has loved without love—deliberately. The whole of his morality can be summed up in his having taken an oath to himself, and kept it. To die means little to him: in the first place, because death accepted with courage is part and parcel of his conception of honour: in the second, because he has never been happy and does not cling to life.

But here an astonishing change comes over the scene which does much to cast a revealing light on this difficult subject. Mme de Rênal does not die of her wound. She quickly recovers, and, not only does she bear him no grudge for what he has done, but does not blame him for avenging an action which she herself regrets and condemns. She therefore goes to see him in prison and tries to persuade him to appeal against the death sentence, which, so far, he has refused to do. She loves him still in spite of the pistol shot.

"As soon as I see you," she says, "duty ceases to mean anything to me. Love for you has emptied me of every other feeling, though love is too weak a word to express my meaning. I feel for you what I ought to feel only for God—a mixture of respect, love and obedience. I do not really know what the emotion is that you inspire in me."

Julien, too, when he once again sees this woman who is so perfectly simple and natural, who never indulges in inflated sentiments, realizes that he has never loved anybody else.

To be under sentence of death means nothing to him, if only she can come to see him every day. At last he understands that the only true happiness is to be found in those moments of tenderness when idle talk and kisses go hand in hand. Here, it seems to me, we find the true significance of the novel. Because Julien in his prison has, literally, no future, he is at last cured of his ambition. He has only the present to live in, and now he can enjoy it to the full. Mme de Rênal can almost share his tranquil gaiety.

"Formerly," Julien says to her, "when I might have been so happy on the walks we took together through the woods at Vergy, a fever of ambition was, all the time, forcing my thoughts to wander in imaginary places. Instead of pressing to my heart the delicious arm which was so close to my lips, I let my dreams of the future come between us, and was, all the time, busy in my mind with the struggles in which I should have to engage if ever I was to build the colossal fortune which it was my dearest hope to possess. . . .

But for your coming to see me in this prison, I should have died without knowing the real meaning of happiness. . . ."

There lies the difference between love and ambition. Love lives in the present and in memories from which it garners a harvest of pleasure, simple-minded perhaps, but genuine. Ambition, on the other hand, lives only on the joy it seeks to find in the future. And, so it is, that disappointment always lies in wait for it, because the future does not belong to man. The accidental hides in ambush for the ambitious, and may, in a second, destroy the patient labours of thirty years. The greatest geniuses have striven hard to guard themselves against ill-fortune, to foresee everything, to forestall the threatening future, to see it naked and unadorned. But none have succeeded. The lover, however, plucks the flowers which unfold under his feet. He is certain of a present happiness, and, furthermore, lays up for himself a lovely treasure of remembrance. In love, and I mean, of course, true love, that perfect harmony which is the gift of sincerity, is to be found the only wealth of which we can be sure. Hypocrisy could have saved Julien. He would not have lacked powerful protectors if, as the result of some conversion, political or religious, he had brought grist to their mill.

"What should I have left", he asks, "if I despised myself? I have been ambitious, and for that I feel no sense of guilt, for I was acting in accordance with the standards of the times. Now I live from day to day, but if I took the easy path I should be wretched indeed at playing the coward's part."

Hypocrisy can pay immediate or future dividends in

the shape of fortune and success, but it is not compatible with happiness. That was a thought so dear to Stendhal that he gives expression to it in all his novels. Those of us who are writers, artists, know that we are obsessed by certain situations (bred of memories or desires) and that, in spite of ourselves, they will turn up, in various forms in most of our books or pictures. Greuze could never paint a portrait without the model's face becoming that of Mlle Balbuti whom he had loved. Even Bonaparte, as depicted by his brush, took on a feminine, a Balbuti, look. Stendhal is curiously unchanging in his details. His hero invariably sets out to achieve the conquest of the woman by whom he thinks that he has been humiliated. What Julien was for Mathilde, Lucien Leuwen was for Mme de Chasteller. In both cases a fall from a horse constitutes one of the earliest episodes. One cannot help thinking that Stendhal must have been an inexpert rider. Often, too, it is in a prison, a cell high up in a tower, that the hero finds at last a curious happiness: Fabrice del Dongo in the prison of Parma, Julien Sorel in that of Besançon. Why? Because, as I have pointed out, prison, by suppressing all possibility of action, leaves the spirit free to dream. That, at least, was what Stendhal imagined, though it should be pointed out that he had never been a prisoner, and also that the prisons he described were governed by a less strict, more peaceful, and less odious discipline than any prison in real life.

Every invalid who has spent some time in a nursing-home or isolation hospital is familiar with this surprising sense of bliss. To be ordered a "rest-cure" is to find oneself freed from all material responsibilities, released from social obligations, let loose from professional routine. The victim of anxiety, once no action is expected of him, finds peace of mind in his new state, because others make decisions for him. The man tormented by ambition, relieved of the necessity of striving to exercise an influence on events, because something over which he has no control has intervened to stop him from doing so, enjoys his new freedom with all the zest of a soldier on leave. His nerves, stretched beyond bearing, respond happily to the slackening of tension. Julien and Fabrice in captivity are delighting, the one in a holiday from ambition, the other in a reprieve from adventure. They have, both of them, escaped from the difficulties produced by their own characters. For them, prison is tantamount to escape.

Julien's, thanks to his gaolers being bribed, is more than usually delightful. Not only does Mme de Rênal come to see him twice a day, but he is visited also by the pregnant Mathilde, who displays heroic courage throughout the drama. But neither that, nor her condition, moves him at all. The time she gives to him is, he feels, filched from Mme de Rênal. When the day of execution comes he faces it bravely.

"Never had that head been so poetic as at the moment when it was about to fall. The sweetest moments he had known in days gone by when walking in the woods of Vergy (with Mme de Rênal) crowded back vividly into his mind . . ." And then comes that astonishing brief passage which is the only direct reference to the guillotine:

"All was conducted simply, in a dignified manner, and without any histrionics on his part."

There is something of the dandy in his behaviour at the end, but also of beauty.

★

What, then, is the moral of the story? There is more

than one. The first is that the presence of passions in a man is no cause for regret. One might as well regret that he is a man. What would Julien have been without ambition and without love?—a peasant lad with a touch of priggishness and no future but that of a dull domestic servant. Only passions can raise a man above the level of the animal. To do that, they must be sublimated, but, before that can happen, they must exist. Fabrice, without love, might have been a commonplace rake. Count Mosca, without his passion, would be no better than his Prince of Parma. Only passion freed Lucien Leuwen from his petty susceptibilities. Stendhal loved temperaments cast in the Italian mould, and preferred the violent to the luke-warm.

The second lesson taught to us by Stendhal, and the nobler, is that beyond passion there is feeling. Passion is a disease, a necessary disease, no doubt, which, if it can be cured, has the effect of purging the spirit of certain humours, though, in its operation it may bring sharp and crazy sufferings. Feeling, on the other hand, is a wholesome and a stable condition to which a man attains when he has reached beyond a certain degree of passion. On the further side of ambition as passion—the desire to dominate others—is ambition as feeling, which is the determination to dominate oneself. It was to that high level, perhaps, that Stendhal's hero, and Sorel's, Napoleon, reached at St Helena. Indeed, it might be argued that the Emperor was never greater than when, on an island, with nothing left to hope for, he re-read Corneille. and found intoxication in the spectacle of abstract grandeur.

Similarly, beyond love as passion, from which both Stendhal and his heroes suffered, is love as feeling, free from all threat, because it is an experience within the personality and proof against all the events and accidents of life. About the *pleasures* of love, Stendhal reasons like a cynic, as might have done any character in Crébillon or Laclos. He admits that men seek them—and even advises that they should, for the sake of peace of mind and body. But he knows, and his heroes know, that, delightful though such pleasures are, they are unimportant in themselves and do not last. He knows, too, that love-as-ambition, the love which has as its purpose the satisfaction of pride or empty vanity (Julien's love for Mathilde) is always weak and vulnerable, paltry and mistrustful. It is for ever haunted by the fear of losing face. Its concern is not so much the beloved object, as the opinion that others may hold of it. In fighting its battle it does not hesitate to have recourse to all the trivialities of crystallization.

True love does not fear its object. Knowingly and deliberately it enters the lists unarmed. Mme de Rênal, at the end of the novel, cannot, and does not, wish to make Julien suffer, any more than my own Isabelle, in *Climats*, wishes to make Philippe suffer. These men know that these women will never give them cause for jealousy. They love them with a love which is beyond the crazy alternations of passion, because confidence, when it is complete, becomes sublime. When feeling reaches a certain degree of loftiness it completely masters our imperfect human nature. "Love, in these noble spirits, is guaranteed by a sort of grandeur which excludes all doubt." Of such a kind was Corneille, and, often, Stendhal. The love they value is not Romantic, for Romantic Love is garrulous and unrestrained. Rather, as Alain says, it is Ideal, something above and outside the laws of society. To reach the level of Ideal Love, it is not necessary to live on the heights or in a prison. The true possessors of an ideal love build their own prison, a well-defended place, upon the secret summits of their hearts.

Such is the lesson of *Le Rouge*. I would have you understand it and reach, beyond the passions, to where the real feelings of our nature live, ambition purified, and tender love. For in them is the secret of happiness. So long as a man is at the mercy of opinion and the contingent, he is infinitely vulnerable and necessarily unhappy. The ideal in fiction, as Hegel has so clearly shown, is the conflict between the poetry of the heart, incarnate in a hero, and the prosaic realities of the world. In the age of chivalry, champions waged war alike on pagans and on windmills: in that of Stendhal, on governments and the race of "skunks". Today, as yesterday, "each one of us finds himself in an absurd world, a world under an evil spell, against which he needs must fight. Our young men, in particular, are the Knights of a New Age, who must reach the light by forcing for themselves a way through the material and the matter-of-fact." The hero can achieve peace by reaching a point at which he depends only upon his own judgment, or upon another noble spirit of whom he can be as certain as he is of himself. Then, and then only, will he find salvation. Of such a nature are the truths which we find in Stendhal, and scarcely anywhere else. That is why he has so many readers at the present time, as he hoped to have, and foresaw that he would have.

"Dear reader," he said, "do not spend your life in hating and being frightened."

Let us show respect for this advice by transposing the negative into the positive:

"Dear reader, spend your life in loving and in willing."

CHAPTER V

BALZAC

1. Le Père Goriot

BALZAC WAS NOT only one of the outstanding novelists
of the nineteenth century. It is, today, almost universally
admitted that in France he was the greatest of them all.
There is more of style, no doubt, in Stendhal and more
dazzling passages of poetry: but, on the other hand,
Stendhal projected, through the medium of his characters, only a picture of his private world, whereas Balzac
created a world which is not only that of his own day,
but of all days and periods. Flaubert engendered a few
eternal types — Madame Bovary, Homais, Frédéric
Moreau, Bouvard and Pecuchet—but Balzac, "in com-
petition with the Registrar of Births", entered upon the
records of mankind, two thousand men and women who,
for his admirers, are more bursting with life than any
whom life itself can show.

His essential originality lies in the fact that he wrote,
not isolated novels but the history of a society peopled
by doctors, lawyers, judges, statesmen, merchants,
money-lenders, women of the world and courtesans who
reappear in volume after volume, and give to this world
of his its convincing air of solidity. At the time when he
was producing his first stories he had not, as yet, con-
ceived this monumental project. One would look in vain
for so much as a trace of it in the original versions of *Les*

Chouans, La Femme de Trente Ans, La Peau de Chagrin, Eugénie Grandet or in any of his writings published prior to 1834. The critics took the view that they were no more than a series of isolated fictions from the pen of a frivolous "entertainer". This verdict touched Balzac on the raw, the more so since he felt the desire, the need to construct a homogeneous whole. "It is not enough to be a man," he said, "one has got to be a system."

It is probable that this system, this idea of introducing the same characters again and again into different books, was suggested to him by his reading of Fenimore Cooper, the American novelist whom he greatly admired, and from whom he had already learned how to describe the Chouans as the Indians are described in *The Last of the Mohicans*. The famous trapper, *Leatherstocking*, is the central point of all Cooper's plots. It is he who ties and unties the intrigues, and occupies a position similar to that of Vautrin in the *Comédie Humaine*. Balzac had been struck by this feature of the *Leatherstocking* series. In Walter Scott—the second of the Anglo-Saxon writers who influenced him—he had always regretted the absence of any connecting link in the long sequence of the novels, and he hit upon the idea of giving unity to his work by stressing that of the world in which the stories were to be set. His sister, Laure Surville, describes how, one day in 1833, he came to see her in a state of tremendous excitement. "Congratulate me," he said, "for I am well on the way to becoming no more and no less than a genius." There and then he unfolded to her the vast plan which he had in mind: "French society is going to be the historian: I shall occupy the post merely of scribe."

Le Père Goriot, which dates from 1834, was the first

of the novels written by Balzac after he had taken his gigantic decision. He later fitted the earlier books into the pattern by changing the names of some of the secondary characters, and, for example, introducing the Baron de Guénic (who appears also in *Béatrix*) into *Les Chouans*, and the duchesse de Chaulieu and Baron Nucingen, who are two of the "regulars" of the *Comédie Humaine*, into *Eugénie Grandet*. But in *Le Père Goriot* the new method was applied from the very first. Almost all the characters of *L'Histoire des Treize* appear in it, and the disquieting de Marsay, who was one of the *Treize* and plays a leading rôle in *La Fille aux Yeux d'Or*, became, in *Goriot*, the very type and symbol of triumphant corruption, the young man endowed with good looks, youth, wit and cynicism, who attacks society from within, by pretending to comply with its conventions. De Marsay is the Byronic pirate transformed into a dandy, a part which had often tempted Balzac himself.

But Henri de Marsay, a symbol rather than a character, makes only a brief appearance in the book. It is not he who makes of *Le Père Goriot* the turn-table, the key novel, of the *Comédie*. Apart from Goriot himself, of whom I shall have something to say later, there are two men who give to the book its quality of greatness. They appear again in twenty further volumes, and both are incarnations of certain aspects of the author: Jacques Collin, known as Vautrin, and Eugène de Rastignac.

Vautrin is the rebel who has chosen to fight society by placing himself outside its pale, and pursues his self-appointed task by all and every means. He has decided that the two passions which determine men's actions are the love of money and the pursuit of pleasure, the latter being dependent on the former. Everything else, he maintains, is hypocrisy. In other words, Vautrin denounces the social contract. This escaped convict does not consider himself to be worse than other men: he is only less of a coward. "He is", writes Bardèche, "the great wild beast of this savannah, the Leatherstocking of the Parisian steppe, where he hunts his prey with all the cunning and stealth of the wild men of the prairie."

Balzac put much of himself into Vautrin. Like all the young men of his time, he was still haunted by echoes of the Napoleonic adventure. He worshipped strength, and believed that he was capable of setting worlds in motion and controlling them. In this belief he was justified, as the *Comédie Humaine* showed clearly. But, though he chose to be the creator of fictions, he had once dreamed of winning victories in the world of actuality, of conducting giant speculations, and making one in a formidable freemasonry of ambitious men. In the universe of his imagination he had been Ferragus, the leader of the *Dévorants*, and, sometimes, Henri de Marsay or Maxime de Trailles. Not that he was a monster, far from it. After all, a man's dreams, a novelist's characters, have nothing to do with direct action. On the contrary, they serve to purge the passions. Balzac never behaved like Vautrin, but he had a fellow-feeling for him. To some extent, he was envious of the power with which he had endowed him; to an even greater, because he valued cynicism above hypocrisy, but chiefly because Vautrin was capable of loyalty. The man might be a criminal, but he was not a traitor. Balzac, like everybody else, felt nothing but contempt for La Michonneau, who denounced him.

Rastignac, in *Le Père Goriot*, is a character in the

process of becoming. He personifies the passage from the illusions of youth to the harsh experiences of mature manhood. Still quite young, and newly arrived from the provinces, he has not yet outgrown the stage of good intentions. In the persons of his mother and his sister he has had constantly before his eyes examples of family affection and of all the virtues. He knows, therefore, that, whatever Vautrin may say, the world is not wholly bad. But, flung without money, like Balzac, at twenty into the Paris of the Restoration, where both love and glory were for sale, where young men rose in the world through women, and women through dotards, he succumbs. His only working capital is youth and good looks, and from Vautrin he learns how to turn them to account. There are few finer scenes in the whole range of Balzac's work than that in which Vautrin, casting aside the mask, reveals to Rastignac, for whom he feels a not wholly innocent affection (though less explicit than that which later leads him to put his terrible powers at the service of Rubempré) what, in his view, is the Royal Road to success.

"Do you know how one makes one's way here? I will tell you. There are two ways, and two ways only: either by having genius and exploiting it, or by the shrewd use of corruption. . . . To be honest is point-less . . . I challenge you to take two steps in Paris without encountering some devilish intrigue . . . That is what real life means. It is no better than a kitchen, and has much the same stench. You can't make an omelet without breaking eggs and dirtying your hands in the process. But never forget to wash them after-wards. That's what really matters, and it's about the only form of morality which means anything to the age in which we live. If I speak of the world like this, it has given me ample right to. I know it. Don't think that I am sitting in judgment. Not a bit of it. Things have always been like this. The moralists will never change anything. Man is born imperfect."

It must be clearly understood that Balzac was throwing himself heart and soul into this attitude of aggressive misanthropy. When he wrote that tirade, he *was* Vautrin, though that does not mean that he did not also have, like Rastignac, an affectionate and tender side to him. George Sand, who knew goodness when she saw it, makes that clear. "To say of this man of genius that he was fundamentally good is the highest compliment that I can pay him." But, like Rastignac, and like most people, Balzac was a man at odds with himself. No less than Rastignac he knew the value of faithful friendship. He respected the supreme quality of goodness when he found it in women like Laure de Berny and Zulma Carraud. One has only to read *Le Lys dans la Vallée* or *Le Médecin de Campagne* to realize how fresh and youthful his instincts were. But, again like Rastignac, he had known poverty shot through with desires and rages, and was determined, at all costs, not to repeat the experience.

The Rastignac of *Le Père Goriot* is still full of scruples. As he listens to Vautrin he feels a faint thrill of horror. The idea of taking money from Mme de Nucingen humiliates him. He does not want to become a Maxime de Trailles. He values the esteem of Horace Bianchon, and tends old Goriot with almost filial attention. He, and the servant, Christophe, are the only two mourners at the funeral. Nevertheless, in the long run, he capitu-

lates, or, rather, he comes to terms with the world. When
next we meet him, he is a baron, an Under-Secretary
of State, and, more or less deliberately, hand in glove
with his mistress's husband. In 1845 he becomes a
Minister, a Count and Peer of France, with a settled
income of three hundred thousand francs. "There is no
such thing as absolute virtue," he maintains, "but only
the changing face of circumstances." (*Les Comédiens sans
le Savoir, Le Député d'Arcis*.) It has been frequently said
that Thiers served as a model for Rastignac, and it is
by no means impossible that Balzac did borrow some of
his characteristics from that statesman. But it was in himself that he found the man's essential nature. Rastignac
in the house of Delphine de Nucingen, Rastignac taking
a childlike pleasure in his first well-cut clothes and the
small satisfactions of his vanity, is Balzac being entertained by the Marquise de Castries, or, later, by Madame
Hanska.

The greatest novels are those that tell of a young man's
"apprenticeship to life" (*Wilhelm Meister, Le Rouge et le
Noir, David Copperfield, A la Recherche du Temps Perdu*),
the essence of which is to be found in the conflict between
the hopes of youth and the relentless facts of life. *Le Père
Goriot*, seen as part of Rastignac's story, is just such a
novel of apprenticeship which reveals to the young
reader the spectacle of a world "red in tooth and claw,
but full of delights". *Les Illusions Perdues* is the really
telling title which covers the whole of the series. Mme
de Beauséant introduces the newcomer to life into the
world of fashion—that of the Faubourg Saint-Germain:
Mme de Restaud, into that intermediate zone where
some of Proust's heroines are to be found: Mme de
Nucingen, into the circles of finance and Big Business.

All this, *mutatis mutandis*, is as true of our modern world as it was of the nineteenth century. I have known more than one Rastignac, and could guess, without much difficulty, at the identity of their Delphines.

As to Goriot, he is one of the most famous examples of a man dominated by those passions which we rightly associate with Balzac the novelist because their implacable development, leading the victim to utter destruction, is one on which he loved to dwell. Whether that passion be Grandet's avarice, Hulot's depravity, the manias and the greed of Cousin Pons, the love of Henriette de Mortsauf, or Goriot's paternal devotion, it is of the sort that Balzac took delight in exhibiting as growing like a monstrous cancer which ends by strangling every other feeling. At the beginning of the book we see Goriot as a man who may still be saved. He has already squandered part of his fortune on his daughters; he is already reduced to living in the Pension Vauquer, but he still has a little something left. The plan of the novel—and the plan in Balzac is always much the same—is to lead him on from surrender to surrender, from sacrifice to sacrifice, until he is finally faced with unavoidable disaster.

Goriot treads the same road as Grandet or Balthazar Claës. His passion for his daughters, which is not without a certain beauty, turns, at last, into a sort of madness because it is monstrous, as are all excessive emotions. They destroy all sense of morality and social decency. "Goriot", says Balzac, "did not argue or reason: he loved." He loved Rastignac because his daughter loved him. Goriot grovelling on the ground to kiss the hem of his daughter's dress, is Grandet coveting the enamelled crucifix which the priest is holding to his lips, and making a shocking attempt to snatch it from him. The poetry of Balzac demands those symbols of absolute horror, and the true Balzac addict accepts them.

The old man, in his delirium, is completely oblivious of society. Balzac establishes it solidly round him through the medium of his secondary characters. The novel needs a firm and resistant world on which to lean for support.

It is in *Le Père Goriot* that Balzac's world begins to assume a density almost equal to that of the world of reality. In it we get to know Horace Bianchon, still a medical student, who will later reappear in many scenes of the *Comédie Humaine* as a famous doctor: and in it, too, lurks dimly the figure of Gobseck, the money-lender with the thin, pale lips. Later (in *Gobseck*) we are presented with the dénouement of the drama played out in the usurer's sinister house by Anastasie de Restaud, Goriot's elder daughter, and the formidable Maxime de Trailles—who is a replica of Rastignac, without his genius. *La Femme Abandonnée* shows us the sad end of Claire de Beauséant, a fine creature whose only fault was to believe too utterly in love. As for the widow Vauquer, *née* de Conflans, Poiret and the old spinster Michonneau —these walking-on parts are unforgettable. Even the cook and Christophe, the odd-job man, have only to appear upon the stage for a moment to establish themselves in the reader's memory. All these characters are, like Proust's, three-dimensional and, by changing in the course of the novel, give us a sense of the passage of time.

But for this imagined world to be accepted by the reader, the characters are not enough. The settings are a necessary part of the illusion, and must be more than mere stage decorations. This accounts for those long and admirable introductory pages which are almost always descriptive. Readers who know nothing of the novelist's craft find them too long, but it is true to say that they alone can create the atmosphere in which the drama is to be played. The rue Neuve-Saint-Geneviève is, as it were, the bronze frame within which a tragic group is to be exhibited. No effort must be spared to prepare the mind for the ensuing action by means of "gloomy colours and solemn thoughts". The picture of the Pension Vauquer is functional and carefully controlled. "The place exuded a smell for which there is no word in the language, and can best be described as 'lodging-house' smell. It was redolent of stuffiness, mildew and rancid butter. It clung damply to the visitor's nose and penetrated his clothes. The general atmosphere was that of a room in which a meal has just been eaten: it stank of the backstairs, the kitchen and the poor-house." There are layers of grease on everything: the top of the sideboard is sticky, and the furniture in general is in a condition of rickety and worm-eaten decay. Here is poverty without poetry, poverty in its most literal sense, concentrated and out-at-elbows. This piece of scene-painting provides a sharp and necessary contrast between the drab, gloomy and sordid dwelling where Goriot and Rastignac vegetate, and the grand, flower-filled houses, the gilded drawing-rooms and pink-draped boudoirs in which Mme de Nucingen and Mme de Restaud bloom and flourish.

The end of the book is justly famous. The final scene shows us Rastignac alone in the cemetery of Père Lachaise where the grave-diggers have just shovelled a few spadefuls of earth on to old Goriot's coffin. He gazes down on Paris "lying in a huddle along both banks of the Seine, with here and there a few lights beginning to show. His eyes fastened almost greedily on that quarter of the city, between the column in the Place Vendôme and the dome of the Invalides, where lived the world of wealth and fashion into which he so longed to gain an entry. The concentrated look he gave to all this humming bee-hive seemed already to be sucking out the honey, and to his lips there rose these words of bombast: 'Now it's between the two of us!' (*A nous deux maintenant.*)

The first challenge flung by Rastignac in the teeth of society was his acceptance of Mme de Nucingen's invitation to dinner."

The wheel has come full circle: the process of corruption has begun, the last tear has been shed. Rastignac, Balzac and the reader are ready to set out on the conquest of Paris. Not a word of blame is uttered. We must take the world as we find it. There is, in Balzac, as Alain said, a quality of reverence. He does not judge, he transcends. His task was not to make the world, but to paint its portrait.

A naturalist studying the relation of species finds that, in any given climatic conditions, there is a tendency for a certain balance to be established between the animal and vegetable worlds. This balance has nothing whatever to do with morality or immorality: it just *is*. Similarly, all human societies function by means of an indeterminate number of employers and employed, of doctors and farmers, parasites and dandies, money-lenders and convicted criminals, lawyers, women-of-the-world, householders and servants. No matter how much the social pattern may change, the species remain unchanged. Goriot's daughters are not monsters, but just daughters and wives.

"They have things to do, they are sleeping, maybe: they will not come. Only when one is about to die," says Goriot, "does one know what children are really like. Ah! my dear friend, never marry, never have children! You give them life, they give you death. . . . If I had still been rich, if I had kept my fortune, they would be slobbering round me now . . . A father should always be rich, and should ride his children on a tight rein like vicious horses. . . . The world is not a pretty place."

No, the world is not a pretty place. The young Rastignac, who had been present at the dreadful death of the abandoned father, murdered by his daughters, was appalled by the horrors he had witnessed. "What's the matter with you?" asks Bianchon, "you're as white as a sheet!" And Rastignac replies: "The sound of cries and lamentations is in my ears. There is a God: oh yes, there is a God, and He has prepared for us a better world, or else this earth of ours is nonsense"—which proves that the "absurdity" of life is no new idea. Balzac held it, but thrust it aside. He loved the world, he loved even its monsters, and that is why Alain declared that he was closer than Stendhal to true charity: "for he had an almost priestly power of detachment, and conducted his confessions at high speed". It is true that Balzac grants absolution very easily. There can be no doubt, in the light of Vautrin's speech for the defence, that, in the eyes of his creator, he is absolved. The fact, too, that Rastignac goes to dine with Mme de Nucingen on the evening of the funeral, is another form of absolution, or, at least, of acceptance.

The nature of a masterpiece has often been the subject of discussion. It was Paul Valéry, I think, who said that its distinguishing mark is this—that it would be utterly impossible to change anything in it. The genuine masterpiece is well constructed. It progresses with a continuous movement. Even in its contrasts it retains a surprising unity of tone. It neither slackens nor wanders. It has a clearly defined form. *Madame Bovary* is an example of the masterpiece in perfection. It is rounded and complete: it has no loose ends. *Le Père Goriot, La Cousine Bette* and even *Eugénie Grandet* exhibit the same characteristics. A reader of taste can find a great deal of pleasure in books of a different type, and mental sustenance in less perfectly constructed novels, such, for instance, as *La Femme de Trente Ans, Splendeurs et Misères des Courtisanes,* or *Lucien Leuwen.* But no novel has a greater degree of "finish" than the one I have just been discussing.

Because, in addition, it opens the most remarkable cycle of fiction to be found in the whole history of literature; because it contains in bulk the chief characters of the *Comédie Humaine*; because from this "central road junction", as François Mauriac has said, "lead the great avenues which Balzac cut through his human forest", and because a hundred dramas are there adumbrated, each one of which was to become, in its turn, the theme of a masterpiece—my choice of *Le Père Goriot* for extended treatment is not only justified but necessary.

2. *César Birotteau*

I

Balzac to Mme Hanska: "I am just now engaged upon a work of capital importance, *César Birotteau*, brother to the man whom you have already met, and, like him, a victim, but the victim, this time, of Parisian civilization, and not, like his brother, of a single man. The book is another, *Médecin de Campagne*, but set in Paris. It is the story of a stupid Socrates, drinking in obscurity his cup of hemlock, drop by drop, of an angel trodden into the mud, of an honest man misused. It is a canvas on the great scale, greater and more vast than anything I have so far attempted. I hope that, if you forget me, my name may be blown in your direction by the wind of fame, like a reproach."

"A work of capital importance." This novel was close to his heart because it was linked with his own life. Not that César Birotteau is a self-portrait by Balzac: the creature lacks the genius of the creator. But the torments inflicted on César were much like Honoré's own. Balzac, too, had pored, night and day, over profit and loss accounts. True, he had not actually known bankruptcy, but he had been near enough to realize its terrors and to feel a passionate hatred of its processes. He had had dealings with money-lenders, dubious bankers, and the type of close-fisted tradesman who turns up with his bill on the morning after a dinner-party. Few of his novels are based upon experiences so close to his own. Like Birotteau, he had furnished apartments too luxurious for his purse, in the rue Cassini and the rue des Batailles. Like Birotteau, he had been a businessman with a romantic temperament, always led on by his imagination to cross the borderline of the possible. The schemes upon which Balzac embarked had never included the manufacture of *l'Huile Comagène*. They had been far madder, and, just as Birotteau-Quixote was held in check by his practical-minded wife, Constance, so had Balzac constantly at his side a female Sancho in the person of the sensible and charming Zulma Carraud. Birotteau bought building plots near the Madeleine: Balzac allowed himself to become involved in a real-estate speculation at Ville-d'Avray, and had been caught up in the affair of the Sardinian Mines. But the essential difference between Birotteau and Balzac was that Birotteau could never rise above his mistakes, whereas Balzac mastered his, by using them as the raw material for his novel.

Of the other Birotteau (the curé of Tours) he said: "The poor fellow was lacking in that particular form of candour which enables both great men and scoundrels to stand back and look at themselves and their own actions dispassionately." Balzac himself most certainly had it. André Billy, in a very penetrating piece of analysis, has pointed out that he introduced elements of his own character not only into Birotteau, but also into the repellent du Tillet whose tastes in luxurious furnishings he most certainly shared. To du Tillet Mme Roguin gave money as Mme de Berny did to Balzac. To be able to attribute his own likings to a thief and traitor of so base a quality is the sign of a curiously split personality. "In his heart of hearts he admired du Tillet, much as he admired Grandet." We are here faced with a phenomenon analogous to that of Proust imputing to Bloch characteristics which he recognized, and detested, in himself.

A great novelist can describe all states of mind, though certain zones are more familiar to him than others and certain sensitive points in himself more vulnerable. When he presses upon these, when he shows himself in a bad light, he is more likely to stir his readers' feelings. In writing *César Birotteau* Balzac revived the memory of his own constantly recurring pains and torments and, by so doing, acquired a very special form of strength which had the advantage of novelty. One of the faults of the French novel in the nineteenth century was that, hitherto, it had sought to rouse the emotions by confining itself almost exclusively to sexual relationships. Balzac realized that so absolute a predominance given to love is false to human nature. Pride, ambition, avarice and cupidity are, all of them, passions which can carry the main weight of a novel no less convincingly than love. "Is not life a machine set in motion by money?" asks Gobseck. Great fiction depicts a struggle between an ideal imagined by the hero in conflict with the harsh realities of existence. The businessman, the priest and the miser secrete, no less than the lover, the stuff of fiction. "A bankruptcy can furnish matter for fourteen volumes worthy to stand comparison with *Clarissa Harlowe*." The fact that in *César Birotteau* love occupies only a subordinate place, and then in a static rather than a romantic form, does not prevent the book from being one of the finest and most terrible of all the dramas presented in the *Comédie Humaine*.

II

It is also (together with *La Cousine Bette*, *Le Père Goriot* and *Splendeurs et Misères des Courtisanes*) one of those in which we can best study Balzac's technique. The full title is *Histoire de la Grandeur et de la Décadence de César Birotteau*. These upward and downward movements in the destiny of an individual are peculiarly suited to Balzac's talent. He finds an especial pleasure in first satisfying the desires of his central figure and raising him to the summit of social eminence, only to precipitate him, step by step, into the deepest hell of degradation. Like Baron Hulot, Birotteau is shown to us, at the beginning of the book, as an honourable and honoured member of society. The ball, the cross of the Legion of Honour, the new enterprise on which he is about to launch, are the culminating points of his career. It is on such heights that we find the Devil watching and waiting. Balzac is about to withdraw, relentlessly, one after the other, all the stays and supports which have so far kept the wretched perfumer steady and upright on the precipice. For the conquering heroes of trade, as for those of Rome, the Tarpeian Rock is uncomfortably close to the Capitol. These quick and headlong falls fascinated Balzac.

He prepares the ground for them while the predestined victim is still happy and successful. While he stands triumphant on his peak in full enjoyment of his fortune, the stage is already being set with slippery stones, camouflaged holes, and all the paraphernalia of a landslide. Round the unfortunate Birotteau squat the bandits, alert, concealed. Balzac has his bullies ready to his call. The reader of the *Comédie Humaine* knows them well, and trembles at the very sound of their names. Birotteau is to encounter all of them: Palma, Gigonnet, Werbrust, Gobseck, the money-lenders: the men of straw, of whom Claperon is the type: the crafty lawyer, Roguin, who

brings Mme Descoings, too, to ruin in *La Rabouilleuse*
as well as Guillaume Grandet, Eugènie's uncle.

But the money-machine, like all machines, is, in itself,
neutral. It becomes hostile only when long-simmering
hatred employs it against a victim. The Birotteau
brothers (César and the curé Tours) are involved in
disaster as the result of cunning plans prepared by
implacable enemies. In the case of the perfumer it is
Ferdinand du Tillet, his former assistant who had been
caught red-handed in a theft, and could never forget or
forgive his master's kindness to him on that occasion.
Du Tillet is an adversary to be feared, because he is
intelligent, shrewd, perverse and unscrupulous. It is he
who, in association with Nucingen, will, later, "skin"
Philippe Bridau. He has, as mistress, Carabine, a "walker
on" at the Opera, and as wife, Marie-Eugénie de Gran-
ville who makes of him a familiar figure in the Faubourg
Saint-Germain.

In this way is the story of the perfumer closely knit
into Balzac's world. The ball given by Birotteau serves
the same purpose in the *Comédie Humaine* as the Prince
de Guermantes' reception in *A la Recherche du Temps
Perdu*. It is an occasion which the novelist-demiurge
uses, with justifiable pride, to bring together on the stage
all the creatures to whom he has given life. Balzac could
not include among the perfumer's guests the whole of
his fictitious aristocracy. Its members have their place in
the book as part of the clientèle of *La Reine des Roses*.
"Heavens above, César!" says Constance, "not a single
invitation must you send to anyone you know only in the
way of trade. Don't tell me you're thinking of asking
the two Vandenesse brothers, M. de Marsay, M. de
Ronquerolles or M. d'Aiglement—in fact any of your

customers? . . . You must be mad—success has turned
your head . . ." All the same, Félix de Vandenesse
comes on the scene later, as the King's private secretary, bringing Louis XVIII's congratulations to the
rehabilitated César after his discharge from bankruptcy.

For the book is as firmly set in the history of France
as it is in the *Comédie Humaine*. It is a novel of the
Restoration. Birotteau has been a monarchist during the
Revolution, partly by temperament, partly by chance.
Because his first patron, M. Ragon, was a fanatical
royalist, *La Reine des Roses* has served as a veritable
headquarters of conspiracy. To it went "les Georges, les
Billardière, les Montauran, les Bauvan, les Longuy, les
Manda, les Bernier, les du Guénic and les Fontaine".
We have met the du Guénic at Guérande and the Comte
de Fontaine in *Les Chouans* under the name of Grand
Jacques. The citizen Ragon and his wife play a part in
Une Episode sous la Terreur. César himself has been
slightly wounded while fighting against Bonaparte on the
steps of Saint-Roch, and this unimportant incident has
determined the direction of his life. To it he owes his
success after the Restoration, his position as a Municipal
Councillor, and that cross of the Legion of Honour which
is to be the cause of his downfall after having been the
symbol of his greatness. Much taking of sides in politics,
seemingly determined by ideas and doctrines, is in fact
due to some chance meeting or fleeting impulse. But for
Mme de Berny, Balzac might not have been a monarchist:
but for the episode of Vendémiaire, Birotteau might
have remained a humble purveyor of scents without
any ambitions beyond those of trade. So wags the
world.

III

One of the dangers to which, by the very nature of his subject, Balzac might have been exposed in writing *César Birotteau*, was that of succumbing to the contempt felt by the artist for the philistine. He might have painted not a portrait but a caricature of his bourgeois tradesman. There was a strong temptation to follow the example of Henri Monnier, and that he was aware of this is clear from the following passage in a letter he wrote to one of his friends:

"For six years I kept *César Birotteau* as a rough draft only, because I despaired of being able to interest anybody in the story of a rather stupid, rather feeble little shopkeeper whose misfortunes are of the most commonplace kind and who does little more than symbolize the type at which we are always poking fun —the small Parisian retailer. But one lucky day I had an inspiration: what I'd got to do was to transform my little man into an example of complete integrity."

It was a stroke of genius. The central character of a novel should almost never be a mediocrity. That is where so many modern novelists fail. Flaubert, it is true, made of *Bouvard et Pecuchet* a bitter and dazzling caricature: but his heroes are saved from insignificance by the burning sincerity with which they conduct their researches. Madame Bovary is by no means mediocre. Old Grandet achieves greatness, as does old Goriot. César Birotteau, nondescript so far as culture and background are concerned, becomes great by reason of his uncompromising honesty. There is a touch of sublimity in the way he abandons to his creditors everything that he possesses, "even down to the engraving of *Hero and Leander* given him by Popinot, his personal jewelry, his shirt-pin, his gold shoe buckles and his two watches which any normally upright man would have secreted without feeling that, by doing so, he was guilty of a dishonest act." Our emotions are touched when he refuses to wear that cross of the Legion of Honour which had been such a source of pride to him, so long as he is an undischarged bankrupt. The honour of a tradesman is worth no less than the honour of a soldier. Birotteau dies a martyr's death.

On the central figure depends the whole composition and tone of the picture. Having transfigured Birotteau, Balzac found himself obliged to use a loving brush when it came to depicting those members of the humbler bourgeoisie "who have a little house in the country, who would like to be thought distinguished, and dream of attaining to municipal honours. This section of the population is envious of everyone and everything: at the same time it is good-hearted, obliging, loyal, sensitive, compassionate. It is the victim of its own shortcomings and jeered at by a society which, in every way that matters, is its inferior . . . This virtuous class brings up its daughters to be honest, hard-working and generously endowed with good qualities which contact with their 'betters' debases so soon as they have personal relations with them. They are just the sort of not very intelligent young women from among whom Chrysale[1] would have chosen a wife . . ." Very few of Balzac's aristocrats have anything like the true greatness to be found in Constance Birotteau, Anselme Popinot and Uncle Pillerault.

These noble characters are never insipid. Their pro-

---

[1] A character in Molière's *Les Femmes Savantes*. (Translator.)

found humanity marks them out from their fellows. Pillerault is sensible and wise; he charms us by the simplicity of his most generous actions. "Dear Uncle," says poor Birotteau, "how simply you say the most wonderful things! You touch my heart." But Pillerault is no stained-glass saint. He is a shrewd man of business and familiar with the tricky ways of crooks and money-lenders. He does not hesitate to advise bankruptcy when he thinks it necessary. He can be churlish and exacting when occasion demands. In the same sort of way Constance Birotteau is a perfect wife. Her common sense has warned her of catastrophe, but her good heart prevents her from saying "I told you so". All the same, she has her secrets. There was a time when du Tillet had tried to seduce her. But she had never mentioned this matter to her husband and had merely urged him to get rid of the odious assistant on some trumped-up excuse. Nevertheless, she kept the letters which were so full of the things that Birotteau had never said to her: "You know that I adore you, my angel. . . ." She is an honest woman who scorns so vulgar a rake, but a good-looking one, too, who takes pleasure in the knowledge of her power. It is because of their complexity that Balzac's characters are three-dimensional, and that his world has the solidity of real life.

IV

Balzac observes his characters: he rarely judges them. He knows that Roguin would never have been a dishonest lawyer if his breath had not smelt. His affliction had turned his wife against him. Despised and deceived by her, he had turned for consolation and reassurance to mercenary mistresses, and as a result of being in constant need of money, had turned crooked, and ultimately taken to flight. But Roguin, being physically what he was, could only with the greatest difficulty have been saved. Alain has pointed out that Balzac's characters are never false to themselves. Each one of them expresses his point of view with passionate sincerity. Gobseck feels no compunction at being Gobseck. "Their besetting fault is in believing that what they think at any one moment is the whole truth. Simple-minded and incomplete they may be, and therefore wavering and non-existent, but Balzac presents them in the round and they become eternally real because no one of them could ever be anybody else . . . because they are not interchangeable."

Unlike Dickens, he feels no desire to reward virtue and punish vice. Birotteau makes a good death, but so does Gobseck. Du Tillet works hard to make a tremendous success of his life. Pillerault is powerful though virtuous, and it is by prudence and shrewdness, rather than by sermonizing, that he saves the situation. Anselme might well have ruined himself by being over-generous, had not Pillerault and the judge Popinot acted as his guardian-angels. The novel teaches, not a moral lesson but a technique—the technique of trade and business. For the bad, who know it inside out, there is no punishment, but only contempt: for the good, who neglect it, no reward, but only esteem. Anselme, who can combine technique and morality, becomes (in *Le Cousin Pons*) Count Popinot and a Peer of France, after having, several times, held the post of Secretary of State. But the vanities of the bourgeois Court of Louis-Philippe do no harm to the heart of the former Minister. Differing from Birotteau, Anselme Popinot remains modest and enjoys a stable happiness.

The great fault, in Balzac's eyes, is the failure to understand that in the ocean of the world, moved by so many currents and lashed by so many thousands of waves—interests and ambitions—the man who thinks that he can settle comfortably into happiness and stand firm against the fury of the billows, is lost. It is essential to reckon with the interests of others, for only so can one work upon them. The simple-minded Birotteau thinks that a Keller or a Nucingen will allow him credit out of pity. The wise Pillerault knows only too well that the lender is too strong to be sensitive, but that, on the contrary, the creditor is too vulnerable not to be indulgent. Hence the necessity of being a declared bankrupt. From that moment the bankrupt becomes the master. "The debtor is in a stronger position than the creditor." Alain has said that Balzac should be required reading in all commercial colleges; and he is right. From him can be learned the laws of credit, selling and publicity. *César Birotteau* is the best novel ever written on the subject of business technique. It was true for Balzac's day: it anticipated our own.

This attitude of the technician led certain contemporary critics to say that Balzac was immoral. This reproach made him indignant, and quite rightly. The simple truth is that he did not believe in the morality of existence. Human societies are compounded of thousands of strands, classes, the relation of masters to servants, of tradesmen to customers, of creditor to debtor. These natural bonds are above the law. Like the haggling of peasants, the activity of banking is a fact of nature. It is impossible to live without taking this reality into account.

He who neglects it plunges headlong to disaster. But morality, on its own level, is also a natural tie. That is the lesson of *César Birotteau*, though it is never made explicit. Balzac was too great an artist not to despise the crossing of t's and the dotting of i's.

CHAPTER VI

GUSTAVE FLAUBERT
Madame Bovary

I

MOST CRITICS, not only in France but throughout the Western world, consider this book to be a perfect work of art. What are the reasons for its tremendous reputation? Some are of a purely technical nature. Never was a product of the human mind constructed with such deliberate care. The subject is simple and well defined. The setting—both topographical and social—is one with which the author was thoroughly familiar. The great scenes are skilfully handled and distributed. The details are precise and perfectly adapted to their purpose. As to the style, we know with what intensity Flaubert worked at it, and how the placing of a word, the music of a phrase, the choice of a tense were for him matters demanding prolonged study and profound meditation. There were times when it took him three days to compose a single page, or even a few lines. So carefully was the balance of his periods constructed, that the change of a single vowel sound could spell disaster. When, so as not to cause offence, he found it necessary to find an alternative title to substitute for the *Journal de Rouen*, he consulted his friends with tears in his eyes. *Progrès de Rouen?* That would have involved the presence of too many consonants in a sentence which had not been arranged in such a manner as to carry the extra weight. He at last decided on *Fanal de Rouen*, not that he felt any enthusiasm for it, but, at least, it did not destroy the musical quality of the rhythm. The famous episode of the Agricultural Show is a true exercise in counterpoint. The Normandy wedding puts the reader in mind of a picture by one of the Dutch masters. All his life long, Flaubert had been in search of an inhuman perfection. In *Madame Bovary* he achieved it.

But this technical perfection does not alone account for the book's high reputation nor for its long life. One might even go so far as to say that it makes them more surprising. It is not, as a rule, the most perfectly constructed books that mark a date in the history of literature but those which, by reason of their novelty, stand as milestones on the high-road of letters. Merimée's novels are deliciously composed, but they are very far from ranking in importance with *A la Recherche du Temps Perdu*, which is an overwhelming, and, at times, a monstrous edifice, but amazingly original. *Don Quixote* is a book of capital importance, even what Proust would have called *capitalissime*, but it is not well constructed.

The universal and still undiminished prestige of *Don Quixote* helps us, however, as Thibaudet so clearly saw, to explain that of *Madame Bovary*. It is worth noting that both these outstanding books are anti-romantic in content. *Don Quixote* appeared after a long succession of tales of chivalry, and killed the fashion for such things stone-dead with ridicule. *Madame Bovary* is a cynical book, not by reason of any direct comments made by the author, who imposed upon himself an attitude of complete detachment, but because of the hard realism of its characters, and of the way in which they speak.

"*L'Hamour*", as Flaubert derisively wrote the word,[1] had been exalted by the romantics. Flaubert set himself the task of "debunking" their excesses of sentiment. That is why the young men of his own day regarded him as a "modern". If we are to understand the place occupied by *Madame Bovary* in literary history we must first study the alternating movement of romanticism — realism.

2

Love, in its origins, is just as much a human instinct as hunger and thirst. For this specific variant of desire which, in the animal world, is wholly sexual, to become first a passion, then a sentiment, it must assume an individual quality. Once a man starts craving, not for just any woman but for one woman in particular who, in her turn, is a being endowed with freedom of choice, then, and then only, are the conditions present for the operation of what Stendhal called the process of *crystallization*. That is what happened in the Middle Ages when Christianity turned women into human beings whom confession taught to analyse their feelings. A further element was added by the fact that the Lords —their husbands and masters—were frequently absent on expeditions to the Holy Land, leaving their Squires alone with the "Ladies" whom they both adored and respected. This situation was sufficient in itself to give birth to tales of chivalry, with the result that over a period of two centuries the rough outline of sentimentalism took on a definite form.

But the realistic animal who still lived on under the

[1] Or, as we might say, "lurve".

knight's armour and the burgher's gown grew tired of
so much courtesy. Man is neither wholly angel nor
wholly beast. After every sentimental epoch literature
has always veered to something not far removed from
brutality. Why? Because "gallantry" in love gives rise
to irony. Elegance of feeling is fine and noble when it
is the spontaneous reaction of superior individuals. It
becomes ridiculous only when men formed in a lesser
mould make a pretence of experiencing similar feelings.
The language of passion, which was sublime in the days
when poets invented it, tends to harden into a formula
the triteness of which is in absurd contrast to the violence
and ardour which it claims to express. The men of the
seventeenth century, whose emotional responses had not
yet been disciplined and domesticated, could still find
tremendous things to say about the ravages of passion.
Those of the eighteenth treated love more lightly. For
them it was no more than a game which was soon to
become a joking matter.

The natural debasement of language has a way of
corresponding to the alternation of tempo in historical
events. In the days of civil strife or barbarian invasion,
the manifestations of love could not but be both brutal
and hasty. The woman, at such times, becomes a prey,
and there is no time for the romantic approach. When
peace and order return, and leisure is again possible, the
arts of love come into their own once more. Brantôme
lived in a gross and vigorous period. At the Court of
Louis XIV, the tone was chaste, though men's desires
were still the same. Phèdre wanted precisely what
Rabelais' merry wives wanted: she merely expressed it
differently and disguised it in abstract terms. All the
same, one has the feeling that in *Phèdre* "passion still

shows with undiminished ardour". In the eighteenth century the French aristocracy had forgotten the grandeur which had been its strength. Because it was bored it welcomed the cynicism which, in the end, destroyed it. Very soon, however, love in its more brutish form returned with the Revolution and the Directoire.

Flaubert came to maturity at the tail-end of a romantic period. Between 1815 and 1848, all the novelists — Stendhal, Balzac, George Sand—had been romantics. Stendhal, who would have liked to be a cynic, though the tone of his writing was classic, gives us romantic heroes all of whom (even Count Mosca, even Julien Sorel) end by believing in passionate love. No great artist can ever be wholly classic or wholly romantic. The classic paints reality as it is; the romantic runs from it. He takes refuge either in the past, as in the historical novels of Vigny and Hugo, or in space, by producing exotic tales of adventure, or in dreaming, like George Sand whose books are filled with the heroes for whom women long, but who exist, alas! only in their imagination. Balzac was both realist, as when he describes Mme Marneffe or Baron Hulot, and romantic, as when he idealizes Mme de Mortsauf.

Round about 1848, a popular form of romanticism arose in France. Sand titillated bored patrician ladies by presenting them with the love of sturdy peasants. Then, with Louis-Napoleon a period began of utter lassitude and of distaste for romanticism in all its forms. The coup d'état was the triumph of the machiavellians over the heroes of fiction. A disillusioned public was ripe for a book which would tell the truth about love, stress the mediocrity of human responses and burn what once it had adored, just as Spanish readers, in the time of

Cervantes, had acclaimed the revelation of an anti-romantic spirit. The cynic (or the seeming cynic) had a great opportunity to attract and to endure when, just at the right moment, he set himself to undermine a political and sentimental system which threatened to bring disaster in its train. He would go down in literary history as the man who destroyed a world already in decay. Not that his experiment would be any more durable than the sentimentalism which it attacked. The see-saw would continue with its ups and downs. But the sentimentalism which returned after the fifties was different. Certain forms of escape and dreaming were no longer possible for women after the appearance of *Madame Bovary*. Flaubert shaped not only the outlook of the upper classes of his own day, but that of the masses of our own. For that reason his novel takes rank as an event of the first importance.

3

Why should Flaubert have been precisely the right man to write the great anti-romantic novel of his age? The answer to that question is—because he was both romantic and anti-romantic in temperament, or, more accurately, because he had been madly romantic and, at the same time, had realized the absurdity of romanticism. There was in him something of the Viking as well as of the bourgeois of Rouen, of the disciple of Hugo and of the ancestor of Maupassant.

"I am, quite literally, two different persons," he wrote in a letter of the 16th January, 1852, "one of whom is intoxicated with bombast, lyrical outpourings, eagle-sweeps, high-sounding phrases and noble thoughts; the other a person who burrows into the truth as persistently as he can, who loves to unearth little facts no less than great ones, who wants to make you feel, almost physically, the objects which he brings to light. It is the latter who enjoys laughing, and takes pleasure in the animality of mankind."

Flaubert the romantic had once made himself drunk on Goethe and Hugo. The reading of *Faust* had produced one of the great emotions of his youth. He had read it at Rouen, in the open air. The sound of the church bells had mingled with the poetry of Goethe. "Oh, deep-toned bells, are you already proclaiming the first hours of Easter? Celestial music, so powerful and so sweet, why do you seek me in the dust?" His head was in a whirl, and he went home like a man distracted. But Flaubert the realist had, from childhood, been in revolt against the universal stupidity of the human race. In association with his friends he had invented a sort of loud-mouthed Gaudissart, whom he had christened *Le Garçon*, a foolish vulgarian into whose mouth each of them in turn had put the most idiotic commonplaces. Masochist that he was, he had revelled in the very folly that he hated. He had dreamed of compiling a *Dictionnaire des Idées Reçues*, which he one day roughed out, and later embodied in *Bouvard et Pécuchet*. The Romantic was perfectly capable of being in love platonically with Mme Schlesinger and carnally with Louise Colet. The Realist was without mercy for the absurdities of his mistress, and made use of them in *Madame Bovary*.

Flaubert's dream was to bring together the two lobes of his brain, and he tried to do so in *l'Education Senti-*

mentale. "That", he said, "was an attempt to fuse the two sides of my nature (it would have been easier to put the human reality into one book and the lyricism into another). It is a failure. . . ." *La Tentation de Saint Antoine* was another, this time a purely lyrical experiment. The Romantic had revelled in the work. "Never again shall I indulge in those ecstasies of style which I allowed myself through eighteen tremendous months. With what love did I shape the pearls of my necklace! There was only one thing I forgot—the thread!" That was what his friends, Maxime du Camp and Louis Bouilhet told him when he read the *Tentation* aloud at Croisset. The scene, as recorded by Maxime du Camp in his *Mémoires*, has often been described since. The two judges advised Flaubert to choose some down-to-earth subject, one of those episodes of which middle-class life is full, and to treat it straightforwardly.

The advice was followed because it was in agreement with Flaubert's own line of thought. He had realized the weakness of the romantic-realist mixture. He had already tried his hand at unadulterated romanticism: there remained unadulterated realism. "What seems to me truly worth doing, what I want to do, is to write a book about nothing, a book without external attachments, which can stand firm on the internal solidity of its style, as the Earth keeps its place in the air without any visible means of support, a book which shall have practically no subject, or in which, at least, the subject shall be almost invisible, if that be possible. All the finest works of literary art are those in which there is a minimum of matter." Such a book was *Madame Bovary*. Tolstoy, speaking contemptuously of *Anna Karenina*, said: "It is nothing at all: just the story of a married woman who falls in love with an officer." The subject suggested to Flaubert by his friends was also "nothing at all"—the story of a romantically-minded woman who is married to a dull husband, deceives him, ruins him, and ends by killing herself. But, far from regretting the poverty of the subject, Flaubert at once exclaimed with delight: "What a splendid idea!"—for he had seen the possibility of using this thin and commonplace theme as an excuse for expressing passions which were his own.

4

"*Madame Bovary, c'est moi.*" What does that celebrated statement really mean? Precisely what it says. Flaubert chastises his own failings in the person of his heroine. What is the fundamental cause of Madame Bovary's catastrophe? It is her misfortune to expect from life, not what life can give, but what the novelists, the poets, the artists and the travellers had promised her. She believes in blissful happiness, in passion, in intoxication, words, all of them, which had seemed so lovely on the printed page. She had read *Paul et Virginie* and dreamed of love in a bamboo hut. She had read Walter Scott and filled her imagination with a vision of crenellated towers. She could not see the beauty, real though it was, of the Normandy countryside. The world after which she hankered was the sort of world we find in the pictures of the Douanier Rousseau.

"And sultans, too, there are, lying enraptured under leafy bowers, puffing at long pipes, or in the arms of beautiful nautch-girls; giaours and Turkish scimitars and Greek caps, and wan scenes in dithy-

rambic lands which show to our delighted eyes, at one
and the same time, palm-trees and pines, a tiger here,
a lion there, Tartar minarets on the horizon and, in
the foreground, Roman ruins and squatting camels,
the whole framed in neat and virgin forest, with a
great perpendicular sunbeam quivering in water on
which white swans swim, here and there, against a
steel-grey background."

Escape of this kind, in both time and space, this
craving for the exotic, is the very essence of the romantic,
of the disease of which Flaubert had only recently been
cured. He, too, had believed in nautch-girls and all the
wonders of the Orient, and it had needed a journey into
Egypt, the squalor of its prostitutes, the filth of their
huts with floors of beaten earth, the lowering melancholy
of night at Kuchouk-Hanem, to convince him how vain
were his desires. For Flaubert romanticism had brought
defeat on more than one level: on that of love (Louise
Colet's stupidity) no less than on those of travel (the
poverty of the East) and of art (his distaste for the
Tentation). By imprisoning the unhappy Emma within
the horrors of reality, he was purging his own passions.

M. Jules de Gaultier has coined the word *bovarysme* to
describe the state of mind of those who "see themselves,
in imagination, as other than they are". Almost everyone
has a touch of bovarysm in his or her make-up. Emma
is, by definition, bovarysm in its pure state. She *could*
have found a hum-drum but genuine happiness in looking after her little girl, in being a good housewife, and
in gradually moulding her husband who loved her well
enough to be malleable. She *could*, since she loved poetry,
have discovered for herself the poetic aspects of the

countryside in which she lived. But she refuses to see the world around her. She *dreams* a totally different life instead of *living* the life she has been given. That is her vice: it was also Flaubert's. It is yours, too, dear hypocrite, dear reader.

But Flaubert had had the good sense to see that romanticism must always end in disaster for the simple reason that it is always seeking the unattainable. "The real subject of *Madame Bovary* is the ever-widening gap between the circumstances of real life and those of a dream world." Emma dreams of loving a Tristan or a Lancelot: she is thrown with Rodolphe, who is a poor fish, then with Léon, who is worse. She ends up in the clutches of Lheureux, the pedlar, who represents reality in its most squalid aspects. Flaubert punishes her, not so much for having dreamed, but for trying to make her dream come true. So long as she does no more than *long for* lovers *à la* Walter Scott, and for wonderful clothes, she is only a poet, and sends Lheureux packing. But, as soon as she tries to reconcile dream and reality, as soon as she allows the ideal lover to be made incarnate in a coarse exterior, as soon as she starts buying real clothes for imaginary journeys, she is lost, and becomes Lheureux's victim. Her dream resembles the Zaïmph of *Salammbô*. It is permitted to adore the sacred veil, but he who touches it dies of the contact.

What, then, is the solution, since mankind cannot keep from dreaming? For Flaubert there was only one: to give up any attempt to live life, and to rest content with describing it. Like the great mystics, Flaubert held the world to be an illusion from which one must free oneself if one is to find salvation. His adventure is that of Proust's hero who does not find Time Regained until he accepts the necessity of living outside time. No man can imagine what he possesses. The only real paradise is Paradise Lost. "You can paint the delights of wine and love and glory only, my dear sir, on the condition that you are not a drunkard, a lover or a soldier."

This is the remedy for Flaubert and for every artist, but it cannot be one for the average man who, incapable of creating life, must live it. For him there will always be less unhappiness, less maladjustment, if he accepts life as it is. That is the lesson of *Madame Bovary*. To this, I imagine, the Romantic in Flaubert never ceased to answer: "But how can a man be expected to give up his attempts to shape life more in accordance with his dreams?" The argument can go on for ever. "Madame Bovary is me." She is, in fact, each one of us. Flaubert made a statement: he did not hope to reach a conclusion.

That the novel defends no thesis was consistent with Flaubert's aesthetic doctrine. He loved the final words of *Candide*, which are tranquil, as stupid as life, and a proof, if ever there was one, of supreme genius.

"What seems to me to be the highest achievement of art, and the most difficult, is not that a writer should make his readers either laugh or cry, but to do as nature does, in other words, to set people dreaming. All the greatest works have this character. They give the appearance of serenity, but how they do so is incomprehensible. They are as immovable as cliffs, as stormy as the ocean, as full of foliage, of greenery, of murmurs as forests, as melancholy as the desert, as blue as the sky. Homer, Rabelais, Michael-Angelo, Shakespeare and Goethe seem to me to be inexorable. This quality in art is unfathomable, infinite, multiple.

[127]

Through small openings we get a glimpse of precipices. The depths are lost in darkness, and we have a sense of dizziness. Yet, over all there broods something which is curiously intoxicating—an ideal radiance, the sun's smile, and tranquillity: something calm and strong."

Such is *Madame Bovary*. For almost a hundred years it has set people dreaming. What precise meaning has a girl sitting at a window with her sewing, by Vermeer, or one of Corot's landscapes? None and all. They *are* and that is all that one can say of them. "Free yourself more and more, when you write, from everything which is not pure art. Keep your eye upon the model: nothing else matters. Art is representation: we should be concerned only to represent." Flaubert does not ask us to share his heroine's horror of Yonville, nor yet to defend Yonville. Because a very great artist has painted its picture, we can look at the little Normandy market town and find it "unfathomable, infinite, multiple". Like the great religious mystics, Flaubert, a mystic of art, found his reward in a vision which lies outside of time. Like the believer who, because he humbles himself, shall be saved, so Flaubert the romantic, because he one day accepted the humblest of subjects, wrote the most famous, the most deservedly famous, of all French novels.

5

No writer has ever suffered greater anguish in giving birth to the child of his imagination. Flaubert's letters, from 1851 to 1856, bear witness to his labours; scenarios, rough drafts, passages scored through and rewritten six or seven times.

"Bovary is not moving quickly: two pages in a week ! ! ! It is enough to break one's heart. . . . How it is going to turn out, I have no idea, but written it shall be, that I warrant you. . . . One pays a high price for style. I've started all over again what I did the other day. Bouilhet thought that two or three of my intended effects hadn't come off, and he was right. Once again I shall have to set about tearing all my sentences to pieces."

What exactly was it that he wanted to do and found so difficult? He has himself given us the answer to that question. He wanted to "rid his sentences of fatty deposits so as to leave them all muscle". This meant getting rid of all author's "asides" and of all abstract phraseology. He must record only the impressions and the words of his characters. A good example of what he means is to be found in the description of Emma's ride with Rodolphe:

"Les chevaux *soufflaient*. Le cuir des selles *craquait*. . . . Le ciel *était* devenu bleu. Les feuilles ne *remuaient* pas. Il y *avait* de grands espaces pleins de bruyères tout en fleurs; et des nappes violettes *s'alternaient* avec le fouillis des arbres, qui *étaient* gris, fauves ou dorés, selon la diversité des feuillages. Souvent on *entendait*, sous des buissons, glisser un petit battement d'ailes, ou bien le cri rauque et doux des corbeaux, qui *s'envolaient* dans les chênes. . . . Ils *descendirent*. . . ."[1]

Proust, in his essay on Flaubert's style, has many

[1] The italics throughout this passage are mine. It had to be given in the original French since, not otherwise could the critical point be made. We do not use the imperfect to the same extent in English, which is one of the reasons why it is difficult to translate Flaubert. (Translator.)

admirable things to say about the moving-staircase effect of his sentences, about the continuous, monotonous, gloomy march of imperfects to the point where a past definite (. . . Ils *descendirent* . . . they dismounted . . .) breaks the rhythm and indicates action.

Flaubert's deletions had the effect of breaking up his periods and giving them a curiously clumsy quality. The elaborate style never flows freely except when it drops into poetry. More often than not it seems craggy and abrupt. That is because the objects in the composition have had their positions changed by an exacting landscape painter. "A navvy's style," Proust called it. Here is an example: "Something too strong to be resisted drove her towards him, so compulsively that, one day, seeing her turn up unexpectedly, he frowned as though annoyed." Then, two pages further on: "Whereupon, the tax-collector tried to conceal what he had just been feeling because of an order which had recently been issued from the Prefect's office to the effect that duck-shooting was forbidden except from a boat, and M. Binet therefore found himself guilty of an offence. He had been expecting a gamekeeper to appear at any moment." Yes, the style of a navvy working away in a stone quarry. The image is good, and fair.

And what a number of grammatical oddities noted by Proust have, because of Flaubert, become part and parcel of current usage. I need only mention, as an example, the *and* with which I began this sentence. Flaubert's *and* (contrary to what Proust says) is often used as a conjunction terminating an enumeration, but it is also, at the beginning of a descriptive passage, an indication that another part of the picture is about to begin, that the ebbing wave is now going to form again.

I have known good judges of literature (Alain is one of them) who do not like Flaubert's style, and I am prepared to agree that there is more charm to be found in Stendhal's free-and-easy methods. I do not greatly admire the Flaubert who recalls Gavarni and Henri Monnier, the Flaubert of *Le Garçon*, who, for instance, finishes *Madame Bovary* with the words: "He had just been awarded the Legion of Honour." On the other hand, I have a fondness for that noble melancholy which is so frequent in him, and those abrupt, almost artless touches, like: "She said, 'Oh Dear God!', sighed, and lost consciousness. She was dead! How astonishing!"

6

Something must be said about the famous trial. Extraordinary though it may seem, when the *Revue de Paris* serialized the book in 1856, Flaubert was prosecuted for offences against public morals and religion. All his fellow writers were on his side, and defended him (though cautiously) because they felt that his cause was also their own. Women, and, in particular, the Empress, spoke up for him. But the Emperor said, "Oh, don't bother me!"—and the trial took its course. Flaubert to Dr Jules Cloquet:

"I write to inform you, my dear friend, that tomorrow, the 24th January, I shall honour with my presence the dock of the Sixth Court of Summary Jurisdiction, at ten o'clock in the morning. Ladies are admitted. Quiet and decent dress is obligatory . . . I do not expect justice. I shall probably be sentenced to the maximum penalty, a pleasant reward for all my work, and a wonderful encouragement to literature."

The prosecution was lavish in its use of points of exclamation. "The lovers indulge in the grossest excesses of carnal pleasure!" The offence against public morals lay, according to the Public Prosecutor, in the frequency of lascivious descriptions. He regarded as highly equivocal a reference to the newly-married husband who, on the morning after the wedding night, "might have been thought to be as virginal as on the day preceding it", who started out on his rounds "with a heart still filled with the joys of the night just past, his mind at rest, his body contented, dwelling on his happiness like those who, when dinner is over, still savour the taste of the truffles which they are busy digesting."

"The author," said the Attorney-General, "has concentrated all his efforts, and employed to the full the magic of his style, on painting a portrait of this woman. Has he treated her as an intelligent being? Not once! Has he dwelt upon her heart? No! On the spiritual side of her nature? Still less! On her physical beauty? Not even that! Oh, I am well aware that we are treated to a glittering picture of Madame Bovary after her adultery, but it is a lascivious picture in which all the poses of the model are voluptuous. Madame Bovary's beauty is essentially provocative."

A strange and comic prosecution, indeed!

Four passages were held to be especially incriminating. The first had to do with Rodolphe's activities as a lover: "What was it that he found so alluring?—the billowing of Madame Bovary's dress, and the way in which it moulded her figure." The second had to do with the author's treatment of religion. The third concerned Léon's love-making, and the drive through Rouen in a cab, "with nothing described, but much suggested". Last of all, the scene of Emma's death which "is a hideous mixture of the sacred and the voluptuous".

Flaubert's Counsel, Maître Sénard, had an easy task. He drew a sympathetic picture of Flaubert's father, a surgeon much respected through the length and breadth of the province: "A great name round which many memories have clustered. . . . M. Gustave Flaubert is a man of serious outlook, by nature inclined to the consideration of grave and melancholy matters. He is far from being the man whom the prosecution, on the strength of fifteen or twenty lines chosen haphazard, has presented to the Court as a painter of lascivious pictures . . ." *Madame Bovary* contained, to be sure, instances of adultery, but these were but a succession of anguish, regret and remorse. The Rouen cab? Merimée, in *La Double Méprise*, had described a similar scene in a post-chaise. Emma's billowing dress?—but not once had Flaubert described his heroine in the nude, as Chénier, Musset and all the poets had done. As to lascivious pictures, Flaubert had done no more than copy descriptions in a book which was one of his favourite companions, Bossuet's *Discours sur les Plaisirs Illicites*. Must Bossuet, then, be forbidden reading?—and the *Lettres Persanes?*—and the *Confessions* of Jean-Jacques Rousseau?—though they contained passages infinitely more lascivious than any to be found in *Madame Bovary*.

The verdict was a masterpiece of compromise. The Court could not approve of the book, but "in view of the fact that it was a work to the writing of which prolonged labour had been devoted . . . that the passages quoted, reprehensible though they might be, were few in number . . . that, from what M. Gustave Flaubert had said, it was clear that he had the greatest respect for sound morals and for religious teaching . . . there was no reason to suppose that his book, unlike many others, had been written for the sole purpose of gratifying the sensual passions, or of encouraging licence and debauchery, or of holding up to ridicule matters which should be regarded with universal respect. His only fault had been sometimes to lose sight of those rules which no self-respecting writer should break, and to forget that literature, like art, if it was to achieve those noble ends which it should ever have in view, must be chaste and pure in form and content. . . ." In view of all these considerations, the Court acquitted the *Revue de Paris* and the author of the offences with which they had been charged, and dismissed the case without cost to the accused.

All the same, Flaubert was bewildered and disgusted by all this uproar which had nothing to do with Art. "Besides, the future frightens me. How can I write anything that will be more inoffensive than my poor Bovary who has been dragged by the hair, like a common strumpet, through the courts?" He knew that Art and Morality are two distinct categories. He was in a hurry to get back to his house in the country, far from his fellow men, and to fit new strings "to that poor guitar of mine which has been so bespattered with mud"—an image which goes to show that the great destroyer of romanticism was still a romantic at heart. "You, sir," Victor Hugo wrote to him after the trial, "are one of the leading spirits of your generation. It is for you to keep the torch of art burning, and to hold it high before our eyes. I am now in the shadows, but the love of light is still alive in me. By which I mean that I love you."

This must have made Flaubert smile, but not without a certain feeling of satisfaction.

CHAPTER VII

PROUST

A la Recherche du Temps Perdu

BETWEEN THE YEARS 1900 and 1950 there has been no body of fiction more outstanding than *A la Recherche du Temps Perdu*. This is not only because Proust's achievement, like Balzac's, is gigantic in terms of mere bulk. There have been other novels running to fifteen or twenty volumes, some of which give evidence of a considerable talent, but they do not have upon the reader the same effect of a revelation, of a self-sufficient whole. Their authors have been content to work seams already familiar and exploited. Marcel Proust opened up entirely new deposits. The *Comédie Humaine* had taken the external world as its field of manoeuvre. It had made its own, finance, newspaper offices, judges, lawyers, doctors, tradespeople and peasants. It was Balzac's purpose to portray—and, in fact, he did portray—a whole society. Part of Proust's originality, on the other hand, is a complete indifference in the choice of his material. He was less interested in the nature of the activities to be observed, than in observing all activities in a special way. Thus, like certain philosophers of his own time, he operated "a Copernican revolution in reverse". He restored man to his old central position in the universe, and the whole intention of his novel is seen to be that of describing a world reflected and distorted in the mirror of a human temperament.

To define Proust in terms of the events and characters presented in his book would be no less absurd than to define Renoir as a man who painted women, children and flowers. What distinguishes Renoir from his contemporaries is not the nature of his models, but of the special iridescent light in which he set them. Proust himself, when writing of Bergotte, laid it down that the raw material of a work of genius is of very little importance. It is the function of the artist to transform matter. The circumstances in which Bergotte grew up were, to all appearances, devoid of charm and interest. Nevertheless, he used them in such a way as to produce a masterpiece, because the little camera of his temperament could disengage and reveal the secret beneath appearances, much as the airman flying above a desert sees the walls of ancient cities buried in the sand, though from ground-level they are invisible. For this reason it is necessary, before speaking of *A la Recherche du Temps Perdu*, to explain how it came about that Proust, better than anybody else, could stand aloof from a world with which he seemed to be so closely involved.

I.

What were the elements of this world to which he belonged? A small town in La Beauce, Illiers, where, as a child, he had spent his holidays in the family circle consisting of his grand-parents, his father, mother and brother, his uncles and aunts, and their country neighbours. Next, the world of Paris; his schoolfellows at the

Lycée Condorcet, his father's friends, and a few women
—Laure Hayman, Mme Emile Straus and the Comtesse
de Chevigné; the *salons* of Mme Arman de Caillavet,
Mme de Beaulaincourt, the Comtesse Greffuhle; through
Robert de Montesquiou, the whole of the fashionable
world; through his mother's family and his Weil uncles,
the upper strata of the Jewish community; through
Cabourg and tennis parties in the Boulevard Bineau, a
number of young girls; the "people" scarcely more than
represented by a few servants, a few "lift-boys" and
hotel porters; some memories of army life; a scattering
of Illiers tradesmen; writers and artists with whom he
became acquainted through Anatole France, Reynaldo
Hann, Madeleine Lemaire and Helleu. All this amounted
to no more, perhaps, than a small cross-section of French
society, but what did that matter? Proust was to work
the seam, not in extent but in depth.

Many of his characteristics predestined him to become
a writer. He was highly-strung and morbidly sensitive.
He was watched over with brooding intensity by a
wonderful mother whom he adored. Where she was concerned he suffered agonies from the slightest suggestion
of friction, and painfully registered the faintest waves of
hostility or ridicule. Incidents which would have left no
lasting scar on a thicker-skinned boy became permanently
fixed in his mind, and haunted him like souls in torment
begging to be saved. (*Examples:* an evening when his
mother refused to go to his room and give him her
customary good-night kiss, and then repented: a night-
walk through Paris in search of someone dearly loved:
social snubs, the traces of which are to be found, first
in *Jean Santeuil* and, later, in *la Recherche*.) "A writer
finds what recompense he can for the injustices of fate."

This particular one was in sore need of compensation, explanation and consolation.

While still quite young, as the result of chronic asthma, he became, if not an invalid, partially incapacitated by delicate health. At certain times of the year he had to cut himself off entirely from social life, and this recurrent withdrawal was of great assistance to him in transmuting life into art. "The only true paradise is paradise-lost." Proust expressed this idea in many different forms. "The years of happiness are the years that have gone: only suffering can make it possible for a writer to work." Driven from childhood's Garden of Eden, he set himself to re-create the happiness which was no more.

He suffered, too, from an emotional flaw which was more serious than his physical ailments. While still an adolescent, he had made the discovery that the only form of love to which he was susceptible was generally considered to be a perversity. He was not, as Gide was, the sort of man to take up an attitude of defiance. So challenging a statement as *Familles, je vous hais* was entirely alien to his nature. It is not difficult to imagine the many long and painful struggles from which he emerged defeated: his efforts to get the better of his desires, the relapses and, finally, the certainty of failure. There is no greater mistake than to think of Proust as being amoral. Immoral, yes, but suffering profoundly from his immorality, and standing in especial need of confession and analysis, which served the novelist well.

And so it came about that this young man for whom writing was so overwhelming a necessity found himself marvellously well-equipped for the task. Not only was he possessed of a keen and highly-strung intelligence which provided him with precious material, but also of an immense culture which taught him how to use it. His mother, who had a passionate love of the classics, English as well as French, had communicated her enthusiasm to him. Few men of our times have had a better knowledge of Saint-Simon, of Mme de Sévigné, of Sainte-Beuve, Flaubert and Baudelaire. His *pastiches* prove how completely at home with them he was. He had studied the working of their minds, their methods and their style. Had he not been the greatest novelist of our day, he would have been its greatest critic. The English had brought him the benefits of cross-breeding which can enrich a mind no less than a racial strain. He, himself, pointed out how great was his debt to Thomas Hardy, George Eliot, Dickens and, most of all, Ruskin.

Fortunately for us, though he was well-equipped to become a writer of the traditional school, authoritative and slightly pedantic, he refused to take that easy road, influenced, perhaps, in part by what he had learned from his mother with her high standard in matters of taste. "In the cooking of certain dishes, the playing of a Beethoven Sonata and the manner in which a hostess should receive her guests, one could always be sure that she had a precise idea of perfection . . . and in all these three activities, perfection meant almost always the same thing—a sort of simplicity in the means to be employed, moderation and charm." Such, too, was Proust's attitude to style. The virtuoso in him did, it is true, sometimes yield to the temptation of over-elaboration (the young ladies at the telephone exchange—the flowering hawthorn trees—the Princesse de Guermantes' box at the Opera). But, at his best, when he was most truly himself, he achieved a perfect unity of naturalness and style. No one has ever better established the music of the spoken word, and differentiated the special intonations of various social classes.

For a long time he hunted in vain for a subject which should enable him to give expression to the many things of which he was full to bursting. When, as a child, walking along the bank of the Vivonne, he had had a confused feeling that there were truths imprisoned under the tiles of a roof or the branches of a weeping willow which he must find words to release, so now, at twenty-five or thirty, he kept turning over, again and again, the rich treasures of his memory without finding what he wanted. In 1896 he had ventured into print with *Les Plaisirs et les Jours*, a collection of stories and poems. It was a *fin de siècle* work of the decadence, packed with echoes of *La Revue Blanche*, Jean de Tinan and Oscar Wilde. Nobody reading it then could possibly have guessed that its author would one day be the greatest of all literary discoverers. Then, secretly, between 1898 and 1904, he filled a number of note-books with the draft of an auto-biographical novel, *Jean Santeuil*, written straight off the reel and never corrected. It was not published in his lifetime. A great number of pages were torn up, and he almost certainly intended to destroy it. We, today, find in it most of the qualities which we so much love in *A la Recherche du Temps Perdu*. It foreshadows many of the scenes which had an obsessional hold on Proust and were, later, to be given their final form. The profundity of its analytical passages, the poetic tone of its descriptions, and a Dickensian zest and humour all combined to announce the coming of a great writer. All the same, he was right not to publish it *just then*. Had he done so, he would have been prevented from handling the same themes with an infinitely greater mastery. Since, too, the book was written while his parents were still alive, who would certainly have been among his first readers, he had found it impossible to treat frankly of certain matters which he felt to be essential. *Jean Santeuil* is a thrilling book for us who are already Proustians, though too little transposed to be an altogether faultless work of art.

The observer in *Jean Santeuil* was already, quite clearly, a master. But to observe was not enough for Proust. Beauty, he held, is like the princess in the fairy-tale who has been shut away in a castle by a formidable magician. We try, in vain, to force a thousand doors in an effort to release her, and most men, in their haste to enjoy life, abandon the attempt. But Proust was prepared to give up everything in his determination to reach the prisoner. Then, suddenly, a day came, a day of revelation, of illumination, of certainty when the secret and dazzling reward was put into his hands. "One had knocked at all the doors, only to find that they opened on to nothing," he says, "and the only one through which one could enter, and had tried for a hundred years without success to find, one bumped into without being aware of its existence, and it opened."

2

Whither did this "only" door lead? When it suddenly flew open, of what work was it that he caught a glimpse which should be "as long as the *Arabian Nights* and the *Mémoires* of Saint-Simon"? What was it that he had to say which was so important that he must sacrifice everything else in life to it? What were going to be the themes of Proust's gigantic symphony?

The first, with which he began and ended his book, is the theme of Time.

"If only I could be given time enough in which to carry my work to its conclusion, I would not fail to mark it with the seal of that time which, just then, was forcing itself so powerfully on my attention, and I would describe men in it, monsters though some of them might be, as occupying in time a place as large as their situation in space was limited."

He was obsessed by the perpetual flow and disintegration of everything around us. "Just as there is a geometry in space, so there is a psychology in time." The whole life of a human being is a battle against time. He longs to cling to a love, to a friendship, to convictions: but out of the depths oblivion slowly mounts, and hides away his loveliest and dearest memories."

The philosophy of the schools assumes "that our personalities are made out of one unvarying belief, which takes on the form of a sort of spiritual statue" standing firm as a rock against the assaults of the external world. But Proust knew that the *Self*, plunged into the sea of time, disintegrates. Very soon a day will come when there will be nothing left of the man who has loved, suffered or made a revolution. In the novel we see Swann, Odette, Gilberte, Bloch, Rachel and Saint-Loup pass successively under the projectors of age and feelings, and taking on their colours like those dancers whose dresses are really white though they seem, turn and turn about, to be yellow, green or blue. Our self when conditioned by love cannot imagine what, a few years later, that self will be when cured of love's poison. "Houses, streets and roads are as fugitive, alas! as the years." We return in vain to the places we have loved. We shall never see them again, for they were situated not in space but in time, and the man who goes back to them is no longer the child or the youth who dressed them in the colours of his passion.

Yet, our former selves are not wholly lost, since they can live again in dreams and even in our waking state. It is not by chance, but quite deliberately, that Proust introduces the theme of waking into the first movement of his symphony. Every morning, after a few blurred moments of uncertainty, we recover our identity, and this proves that we have never wholly lost it. Marcel, towards the end of his life, could still hear, deep in himself, "the jerky, metallic tinkle, shrill and clear, of the little bell" which, in his childhood, used to herald Swann's arrival at the garden door. The sound, therefore, must have lived on in himself. It follows from this that time past is not entirely dead, as it seems to be, but has become incorporated with us. This is the creative idea at the root of Proust's book. We set off *in search* of time which is seemingly no more, though actually it is still present and merely waiting to emerge once again into existence.

The search cannot be conducted in the world which men call *real*, though in fact it is *unreal*, or, rather, unknowable, since we see it only as distorted by our emotions. But there is not *one* universe; there are millions of universes, "as many as there are human eyes and human intelligences which come to life every morning, on waking". What matters, therefore, is not that we should live in, and for, these illusions, but that we should search out in our memories the paradise lost which is the only paradise known to us. In each one of us there is something permanent, namely, the past. By recapturing it we are enabled, at certain privileged moments, "to have an intuition of ourselves as absolute entities". And so it is that to the first theme—*Time* the destroyer, an answer is given by a complementary theme—*Memory* the preserver. But not just any memory will do. Proust's basic contribution was to teach mankind a *certain manner of evoking the past*.

Are there, then, several manners of doing that? There are at least two. We can try to reconstitute the past by using our conscious intelligence, by reasoning and the use of documents, and other types of substantial evidence. But no deliberate act of memory will ever give us that sensation of the past breaking through into the present which alone makes the permanence of the self perceptible. Only if involuntary memory comes into play can we recover lost time. How, then, is this set in motion? By the coming together of a present sensation and a memory. The past goes on living in tastes and smells. "It must not be forgotten that there is a recurring motif in my life," wrote Proust, "more important than the love of Albertine—the motif of recollection, a matter for the dedicated artist . . . a cup of tea, trees seen on a walk, church towers, etc. . . .", and here he gives us the famous example of the *petite madeleine*.

No sooner has the narrator tasted the little cake shaped like a cockle-shell, than Combray, whole and complete, emerges from the cup of tea, fully charged with the emotions which gave it so powerful a charm. The linked pair, present-sensation/memory-reborn, is to Time what the stereoscope is to Space. It creates the illusion of three-dimensional time. At that precise moment time is recovered, and, also, overcome, since one whole segment of the past has become a segment of the present. Such an occurrence gives to the artist the feeling that he has conquered eternity. Nothing can be truly savoured and preserved *except* under the aspect of eternity which is also that of art. This is the essential, the fundamental and *new* subject of *La Recherche du Temps Perdu*. Other writers (Chateaubriand, Gérard de Nerval) had had a glimpse of it, but they had not got to the bottom of their intuition, had not flung the magic door wide open. Only Proust saw that, in association with a first memory, and as though coupled to it, a whole world which had seemed to be buried in oblivion, could be made to come from a cup of tea.

Fundamentally his novel is the adventure story of an abnormally intelligent and painfully sensitive human being, who sets out in childhood in search of absolute happiness, which he finds, not in his home life, not in love, not in the great world. He is driven to the conclusion, like the religious mystics, that such an absolute can be found only outside time. He discovers it in art, so that the novel merges into the life of the novelist, and ends at the point at which the Narrator, having recovered lost time, can start on his book, which becomes, as it were, a long snake turning back upon itself, a gigantic wheel that comes full circle.

3

And now that the past has been evoked by the magic spell of involuntary memory, what is it that the Narrator sees? In the centre of the stage the house at Combray, with those who live in it: his grandmother, his parents,

Aunt Léonie (tremendously influential and deeply comic in a manner all her own), the servant, Françoise (a superb portrait), and a number of "supers". The house has a garden of the kind to be found in country towns, where, on summer evenings, a neighbour, M. Swann, is entertained by the Narrator's parents, though without his wife. Combray lies at the centre of a familiar, though, at the same time, a mysterious world which, for the child, is divided into two *ways* which determine his daily walks: *Swann's Way* towards Tansonville, a property belonging to the Swanns, and the *Guermantes' Way* which leads to the country mansion of a noble family of almost fabulous lineage, the members of which Marcel occasionally sees coming out of church after Sunday Mass. To him they seem to be unapproachable and almost mythical creatures. He has been told that they are descended from Geneviève de Brabant, and he thinks of them as living in a sort of fairy world. And so it is that his life begins with the *Age of Names*. The Guermantes, Madame Swann and her daughter, Gilberte, are scarcely more than *Names*.

These names are replaced, one after the other, by beings of flesh and blood. The Guermantes, when the Narrator, as he grows older, penetrates into their world, still fascinate him, though they lose their superhuman prestige. The Duchesse de Guermantes, whom he had once seen as a figure in a stained-glass window, becomes his friend, and he realizes that, apart from the fact that she has a keen though superficial mind, there is nothing in her but egotism and aridity. Other Guermantes, the Baron de Charlus, the fascinating Robert de Saint-Loup, emerge in turn from the flattering dusk of the background into the harsh glare of the footlights. Little by

[147]

little, the Narrator discovers that the names of these men and women whom, once, he had seen as figures on a magic-lantern slide, merely serve to disguise a reality which is sometimes cruel and sometimes colourless. Romance is not a quality of the real world, but exists in the difference between the real world and that of the imagination.

In love, too, there is an *Age of Words*, at which a man, deceived by the classic or romantic portrayal of that emotion, pursues the mirage of an impossible communion. But, "nothing is more different from love than the idea we have of it". Proust set about revealing, with more truth than the traditional novelists, the phenomena of first meeting, choice, absence, and ultimate indifference. Eve, created out of Adam's rib, is a true symbol. The women whom we love are dream-figures who haunt our sleep for no better reason than that we are lying uncomfortably in bed. The beloved object, who was the product of our own imagination when first we met her, has no connexion with the real person to whom we shall be united for life. Swann marries an Odette whom he has seen in dreams, only to find himself in the presence of an Odette he does not love, who is not "his type". The Narrator, Marcel, comes to love Albertine whom, at first, he had thought vulgar and almost ugly, but to whom he has grown to be attached because she is an "evasive creature" and so keeps about her an aura of mystery.

Love survives possession so long as uncertainty remains a powerful force. The revelation of the utter nothingness of what one has set on so high an eminence is not enough to cure us, so long as jealousy lives with us in the desert. But, fortunately, "with the troubles of memory are linked the heart's intermissions. After a long absence, forgetfulness dissipates the mists of love". Abnormal love, described at length in *Sodome et Gomorrhe*, follows the same general curve as its normal brother. It matters little who or what the beloved is—coachman, waistcoat-maker, prostitute or duchess, since the essential fact of love, according to Proust, is that the beloved exists only in the imagination of the lover.

He has now explored the two "ways" of his childhood, Swann's Way and the Guermantes' Way. They had once seemed to Marcel to lead into two unknown, secret and alluring worlds, but he now realizes that he has found in them nothing worthy of intense and durable interest. Society, like love, is a disappointment. Swann had once passionately longed to be "accepted" by the Verdurin "clan", and Marcel to have the entry to the Guermantes' *salon*. But once known, once conquered, both clan and salon turn out to be nothing. The only worlds that keep their attraction are those into which one has not yet penetrated. Everything is simpler and more commonplace than it appeared to the eyes of childhood. Seen from Combray the two "ways" had seemed to be separated by an abyss: but now they come together and form, above the whole work, a gigantic arch. Swann's daughter, Gilberte, marries a Guermantes, Saint-Loup. So, the opposition of the two "ways" was itself a lie. Reality is unveiled, but in the selfsame moment it disintegrates.

I have deliberately used the word *arch*. When Proust's book began to appear, the critics completely failed to see the plan on which it was constructed, which, in fact, has the grandeur and simplicity of a cathedral. Of this Proust was, himself, fully aware.

"You have used the analogy of a cathedral in what you say to me, and I cannot but be deeply moved by this evidence of an intuition which has enabled you to guess at something which I have never mentioned to anybody, and now set down in words for the first time. It is this, that I originally intended to give architectural names to each part of my novel: *Porch*, *Windows in the Apse*, etc., for the purpose of replying in advance to the foolish criticism which is sometimes levelled at me, to the effect that the book lacks construction, whereas, as I will show you, its sole merit lies in the solidity of each part, no matter how small."

In the completed work there is, indeed, so much conscious symmetry, so many echoes in matters of detail, so many toothing-stones inserted in the very first pages in preparation for the erection of future vaulting, that the reader is overcome by sheer wonder that so gigantic a work could have been so scrupulously planned. Some character, who makes only a fleeting appearance in *Du Coté de Chez Swann*, turns out later to be one of the protagonists of the main drama—like musical themes, stated in a prelude, which are amplified at a further stage in the composition until they dominate the score with a blare of brass. (*Examples:* The Lady in Pink, seen for a moment by the young Marcel in his uncle's house, turns out to have been Odette de Crécy, who was to become Mme Swann, and to end up as Mme de Forcheville: the painter Biche, something of a "butt" in the Verdurin circle, develops into the great Elstir: the young woman encountered by the Narrator at an "accommodation address" turns out to be no other than Rachel, Saint-Loup's adored mistress.)

[150]

And, just as the gigantic arch, bestriding the years, ends by uniting the two "Ways", so, too, is the theme of the *petite madeleine* echoed in thousands of intervening pages by other sensation-memory groups (an uneven paving-stone which transports the Narrator to Venice: a starched napkin which brings Balbec into the Prince de Guermantes' library). The keystone of the whole work is, undoubtedly, Mlle de Saint-Loup, the daughter of Robert and Gilberte. She is scarcely more than a tiny sculptured figure high up on the façade and barely glimpsed from the ground, though in her "time, colourless, intangible" is materialized. The arch is firmly anchored, the cathedral completed.

In this way does Proust's novel show as an affirmation, a deliverance. In Vinteuil's Septet there are two contrasted themes: Time the Destroyer and Memory the Preserver, "but," says the Narrator, speaking of that work,

> "in its final passages, the motif of joy emerged triumphant. It was no longer an almost timorous appeal sounding from an empty sky, but a cry of ineffable delight which seemed to come from Paradise, of a delight as different from that of the Sonata as is an archangel by Mantegna, clothed in scarlet and blowing on a trumpet, from one of Bellini's grave and gentle angels plucking at a lute. I knew then, most certainly, that never again should I forget this new modulation of joy, this summons to a superterrestrial happiness . . ."

Claude Mauriac, in his excellent little book on Proust, rightly insists upon the eminently Proustian notion of *joy*. "Even more than the intermissions of the heart, we have, in Marcel Proust, the intermissions of happiness. Whence come these gusts of joy?" From this: "that a great artist partially draws aside for us the veil of ugliness and insignificance which leaves us incurious before the spectacle of the universe". As Van Gogh, from a straw-bottomed chair, as Degas or Manet from an ugly woman, created masterpieces, so does Proust take an old cook, a smell of damp-mould, a room in the country, a hawthorn tree, and says to us: "Look more closely: beneath these simple things lie all the secrets of the world."

4

But the moments of ecstasy, the chance occurrence of a present sensation which makes possible the rebirth of the past, and give us the joyful sense of our own permanence, come but rarely to any man. How, then, can a writer, on each page of a book, bring imprisoned beauty into the light of day? It is here that style plays its part:

"One can enumerate indefinitely, in a description, the objects of which a given scene is composed: truth will begin to emerge only when the writer takes two different objects, establishes their relationship, analogous in the world of art to the unique relationship of cause and effect in that of science, and encloses them within the necessary setting of a fine style, or when, like life itself, by stressing a quality common to two sensations, he can disengage their essence by reuniting them, and so remove them from the accidents of time, by linking them in a metaphor through that close alliance of words which it is impossible to describe."

It is the function of metaphor to help both author and reader to evoke something unknown, or a feeling difficult to describe, by underlining their similarity with objects known already. Needless to say, Proust was not the first writer to have recourse to the "image". It is a mode of expression common to even the most primitive of men. But he understood, better than any other writer of his time, the "capital importance" of the image: what a lively intellectual pleasure the reader can enjoy who can make out, in an analogy, the incipient formulation of a law, and how essential, too, it is to breathe new life into it.

Since its object is to explain the unknown by the known, it is necessary for the second term of the comparison, the one that is seen behind reality as through a transparency, to be linked with a sensation which is familiar. Homer was right to describe someone as being *like a furious lion* because he was speaking to men who had fought with lions. Proust has made it plain that our modern metaphors must seek out behind things, either the elementary sensations of taste, smell and touch which are eternally true, or the images of plants and animals which are the most primitive elements of all art (the transformation of Charlus into a great bumble-bee, of Jupien into an orchid, of the Guermantes into birds), or, finally, the images of actual life borrowed from the experiences of our own day. Hence, the scientific, physiological and political comparisons with which his pages are sprinkled.

Here is a whole bunch of new images drawn at random from the book. The Narrator's mother tells Françoise that M. de Norpois has expressed the opinion that she is a cook of the very first order, "like a War Minister, after a review, passing on the congratulations of a visiting

Sovereign, to the Commanding Officer." Marcel, in the full flush of his calf-love for Gilberte, looking on everything to do with the Swanns as sacrosanct, flushes with horror when his father speaks of their apartment as nothing at all out of the ordinary:

> "I felt instinctively that I owed it to the Swanns, and to my own happiness, to make all necessary sacrifices, and, by a great effort of the will, in spite of what I had just heard, to put away from me, as a devout Catholic might put away Renan's *Life of Jesus*, the undermining thought that an apartment of theirs could possibly resemble any that *we* might have inhabited."

The Narrator's mother compares Mme Swann's campaign for the extension of her zone of influence among the higher ranks of society to a colonial war: "Now that the Tromberts have handed in their submission it will not be long before the neighbouring tribes will abandon the struggle. . . ." Whenever she had met Mme Swann in the street she would tell us, on returning home: "I noticed that Mme Swann was on a war-footing. She must be planning a promising offensive against the Massechutos, the Cingalese or the Tromberts." Mme Swann sends an invitation to a boring but kind-hearted lady who has an extensive visiting list because "she knew what an enormous number of bourgeois flowers this active worker-bee must see in the course of a single afternoon, when armed with her aigrette and her card case."

Another of Proust's favourite methods is to evoke the real through the medium of works of art. For it is true that in these days the fine arts provide the cultivated with terms of reference which are generally intelligible.

Thus, he conveys the quality of Odette's beauty by invoking the name of Botticelli, and Bloch's foreign appearance by comparing him to Bellini's portrait of *Mahomet II*. He likens Françoise's conversation to a Bach fugue, and the glances directed by M. de Charlus at Jupien to Beethoven's broken phrases. The great painters and the great musicians enable us to penetrate into a world which lies beyond the power of words to describe, to which, without their aid, we should find it impossible to attain. Proust reaches metaphysics by way of aesthetics. There are worse roads.

Metaphors, in his work, serve as sacred vessels in religious ceremonies. The realities with which he is concerned are all spiritual, but because human beings have both souls and bodies, they need material symbols in order to establish a link between themselves and the inexpressible. Proust was one of the first to realize, not instinctively, like Victor Hugo, but by the use of intelligence and method, that all valid thought has its roots in daily life, and that the use of metaphor gives strength to the Spirit by forcing it to make contact with the Earth, its mother.

5

Alain has argued that the novel should be, essentially, a halfway house between poetry and prose, between appearance and a practical and, as it were, a workaday reality. Proust is a novelist in the pure state. No one has better helped us to grasp in ourselves that passage from childhood to maturity, and ultimately to old age, which is what we mean by living. For that reason his book, from the very first moment of its publication, took its place among the bibles of humanity. Few things could be more impressive, more truly deserved than the enthusiasm aroused all over the world by this simple, highly personal and strictly localized story. As a great philosopher can epitomize all thinking in a single thought, so can a great novelist, by exploring one single life, and fixing his attention on the humblest objects, bring into the light of day the lives of each and all of us.

CHAPTER VIII

GOETHE

A Decisive Turning-Point in His Life or
Destiny, Two Women and a Carriage

1775. FRANKFURT. Young Wolfgang Goethe, son of
the Imperial Councillor, Johann Kaspar Goethe, has just
returned, at twenty-six, to the place of his birth. He has
genius, and he knows it. Ever since childhood he has
had faith in his destiny. "The stars will not forget me,"
he had said at the age of six. Always, too, he has known
that he has been made to dominate and to observe. "The
Genius of Nature shall take you by the hand, lead you
through many countries, and show you life—that strange
restlessness of men—as a whole. You shall watch them
in their aimless wanderings, for ever seeking, herding
together, thrusting, elbowing. All the strange bustle of
the human breed shall be displayed before your eyes.
But it shall be as though you were looking at a shadow-
show."

As though you were looking at a shadow-show. . . . What
did that mean? It meant that his daemon (for Goethe,
like Socrates, believed that he had a familiar spirit who
directed his steps) had laid it down that he should never
be wholly caught up in human affairs. Only he who
keeps freedom of mind can grow into *a poet*, a creator
of worlds. But for a young man of twenty-six so high a
degree of detachment was not easy. Goethe was hand-

some. He was attractive to women and had need of them. "The Eternal Feminine leads us on." Unless he were in love he could not create. Furthermore, he had a violent temperament, and his recklessness made him a fine game-bird for the Devil to bring down.

At eighteen, this young Faust had already fallen in with his Mephisto, the student Behrisch of Leipzig. "Damme, if I am not now of an age to seduce a young woman," wrote the youthful Goethe to this diabolical character. "In a word, sir, you will find in me all the zeal and all the diligence which you have a right to expect of your disciples." It was not long before Faust had found his Gretchen, and had broken more than one heart. In Alsace, the charming Frederica Brion made a conquest of him. But her he threw over without a twinge of remorse. "Providence has willed it that trees should never reach to the sky," he said with perfect composure. In other words, a passion, when the right moment comes, must cease to grow. More precisely, Goethe's daemon was determined that he should not stray from the path marked out for him.

There was, however, one occasion when he nearly paid for an unhappy love affair with his life. The marriage of Charlotte Buff, whom he adored, to his friend Kestner, plunged him so deep in despair that he contemplated suicide. For several nights he went to bed with a dagger within reach. But he never inflicted upon himself even the slightest of wounds. Was the flesh weaker than the will? No, it was the will that said "live". Instead of killing himself he wrote the story of his love—and of his suicide. As soon as he had finished *Werther* he awoke to the fact that the chains which once had bound him to Charlotte were broken. "After much suffering," he said,

"I am myself again. But what self do I find that to be? —an artist." The shadow-show. But this agonizing experience had turned him into an enemy of the gods. There was something of Prometheus in this young man.

It was the age, in Germany, of *Sturm und Drang*, that literary movement which preceded, and resembled, romanticism. The aim of its disciples was to show giants in revolt against society. Goethe played a part in it, and produced its masterpiece. He was in rebellion against the "reason" of eighteenth-century France, and exalted the dark powers of the spirit. He identified himself with the Titans and called down curses upon Zeus.

> "Behold! I am he who makes men—in his own image, a race like to himself—a race that shall weep and suffer—that shall know enjoyment and rejoice— that shall, as I do, hold Thee in contempt . . ."[1]

There were those among his friends who were frightened by this attitude of revolt, and said that he was "possessed" of the demon of pride.

It is true that to rebel against the gods is dangerous since such a challenge can lead to nothing. The world is as it is: the gods are as they are. It is for the strong man to transform the world, not to curse it. Goethe at twenty-six was handsome, unique, inspired, but there was reason to fear that he might dash himself to pieces against the obstacles that stood in his way. Lavater, who was fond of him, was astonished and disturbed by so much ranting. "Goethe is all power, sensibility and imagination. He acts without knowing why, nor how. It is as though he were being swept forward on a mighty river." Of himself, Goethe said: "Am I not the Inhuman one who, without

[1] Goethe: *Prometheus*.

goal or pause, flings himself into the abyss, like the torrent that roars from rock to rock?"

But his watchful daemon was now, by devious ways, to lead him to a crisis as a result of which the Inhuman would draw closer to the Human. For this purpose it made use of a young girl, a prince, a carriage and a great lady. No one can foresee what the chosen instruments of Destiny will be.

The young girl was called Anna-Elizabeth Schönemann. She was the daughter of a great Frankfurt banker who had died some years before Goethe discovered Elizabeth, generally known as Lili. This was at the beginning of January 1775. *Werther* and his poems had already made him famous, and the *salons* of Frankfurt were hot on his trail. But the young Titan fought a hard defensive battle. He did not want to let himself be tamed. The more he played the savage and the bear, the greater grew the general curiosity about him. One evening, however, a friend, on the spur of the moment, suggested taking him to a concert at the house of a family of Calvinist bankers, and he accepted. He loved doing things on the spur of the moment. It meant taking a ticket in the lottery of life.

He was shown into a great *salon* in the middle of which stood a harpsichord. The only daughter of the house, seventeen years of age, fair, charming and a flirt, played upon it. She played fluently and with a light touch. Goethe, who was sitting opposite her, admired in Lili a natural, childlike quality. When he complimented her, nothing could have been prettier than the way in which she answered. He noticed that she looked at him with pleasure, as though he were a show. This did not surprise him, for he knew that he was both handsome and famous. He was ravished by the spectacle presented to him, and felt that a mutual attraction was in its early stage. A crowd surrounded them, and they had no opportunity to talk. But when the time came for him to leave, both mother and daughter expressed the hope that he would visit them again.

He took frequent advantage of this invitation, and spent many charming hours with Lili. Then, all of a sudden, their talks grew intimate and confidential. She told him how she had grown up as a rich young girl among all the pleasures of society. She did not hide her weaknesses from him, the chief of which was flirtatiousness, a gift of making herself attractive. "I tried it on you," she confessed, "but I have been punished for doing so, because I am now attracted by you." He soon found that he could not do without her, and this completely changed his way of living, for this great heiress spent almost all her time in a social whirl. So as not to lose a moment of her company, the Solitary had to compromise with his principles.

As always, he hovered above the scene and described it, with a touch of self-mockery, to his friend Augusta von Stolberg, on the 13th February, 1775.

"Imagine me, my dear, in an embroidered coat, under the commonplace illumination of chandeliers and candelabra, held for a moment at the gaming-table by two enchanting eyes, then moving from the babble of voices to a concert of music, and, finally, allowing myself to be drawn away to the ballroom, all the time paying court to a graceful, golden-haired beauty—and you will have a picture of that carnival Goethe who, not so long ago, acquainted you with certain profound and nebulous sensations." Then, he added: "But there is another Goethe, wrapped in a grey cloak, with a brown silk neckerchief, already catching in the sharp February air the first heraldings of Spring, and seeing a vast and darling universe again opening before him . . ."[1]

In this Goethe-Symphony there are two contrasted *motifs*: Goethe in love and, for the first time, held a prisoner in the shackles of society: Goethe, independent and creative, who has need of the whole universe and of all mankind. *Liebe, liebe, lass mich los!*—Love, love, leave me alone![2]

Therein lies the drama. There are two Goethes: the one who carries the whole world within himself: the other, who spent the night of Shrove Tuesday, 1775, dancing—far from nature, far from work, far from himself. Doubtless, there had been other loves which had torn him to pieces, but over those he had triumphed, either by the conquest of the beloved, or by flight. This time no conquest would be possible without marriage. The Schönemann family was powerful and respectable. Lili was no Gretchen whom he might seduce. The only alternative was flight. But he was happy with his charmer. Even in that smart world, the influence of which he dreaded, he found pleasure in watching her unfolding so gracefully and with so precocious a self-assurance. Then, in March, when he saw her again, in the country, he knew an unmixed happiness, for he had

[1] Goethe: *Briefe an Augusta von Stolberg.*

[2] Goethe: *Neue liebe, Neues Leben.*

Lili to himself and the "golden hours were full to over-flowing".

Love, love, leave me alone! Goethe seems, at that moment, to have been perilously near to losing his freedom. To be sure, the two families showed no great enthusiasm at the idea of a marriage. The Goethes were of the Lutheran middle class, the Schönemanns, Calvinist patricians. Goethe's sister, Cornelia, who, like all the overbearing sisters of men of genius, kept a jealous watch upon her brother in the hope of saving him from himself, was firmly set against this marriage in particular, and marriage in general. But events were precipitated by yet another influence. In April, a lady from Heidelberg suddenly turned up in Frankfurt, Fraülein Delph — an auspicious name indeed for Goethe, who had a taste for Delphic Sibyls and Oracles!

The Sibyl saw the two families, and after considerable difficulty got their consent. A very decided woman was Fraülein Delph and she promptly took matters into her own hands. She sought no material advantage for herself: to have arranged a marriage was her sufficient reward. It gave her a sense of power. She had known Lili since childhood, and was fond of her. She proceeded to study the two young people, saw that they were in love, and decided that the right and proper conclusion had been too long delayed. One day she came upon them by surprise, when they were alone together, informed them that she had obtained the consent of their respective parents, and said: "Take hands." Goethe was standing opposite Lili, and held out his hand to her. Slowly, but without hesitation, she gave him hers. Then, after a moment's pause, they threw themselves into one another's arms. Sheer strength of will on the part of

Fraülein Delph had brought about their engagement. Was the Sibyl going to overcome the Daemon? The ever-to-be-admired Goethe put a different interpretation on the event. "It was a strange decision of the Supreme Being that, in the course of an eventful life, I should add to my experiences the feelings of an affianced lover."[1] In other words, Providence, determined to form a perfect writer, was seeing to it that the young man should have a taste of everything.

He found his position as a *fiancé*, which was new to him, only too pleasant. The barriers were down. The impulses of nature and the wisdom of the Law had been reconciled. He now saw his beloved under a double aspect. He still found her beautiful and graceful, but, in the knowledge that she was to be his wife, he took pleasure also in her dignity, and in the dependability of her character. In short, all would have been calm happiness and delight had not his presiding genius continued to grumble and mutter. The Daemon saw only too clearly what would happen to the tamed bear. He would sit up and beg when his mistress told him to: he would purr with pleasure when she stroked his back with her foot. He would live a family life in a fine Frankfurt "palace". He would be a faithful husband and an excellent father. But Goethe, Goethe!—where would Goethe be?

> And I!—dear gods in your hands does it lie
> To put an end to all this dark enchantment;
> How I would bless you if you set me free!

In May he attempted to escape. With three friends he set off for Switzerland. The trip was full of interest and

[1] Goethe: *Dichtung und Wahrheit IV*.

gaiety. The four handsome young men bathed naked in all the streams they came to. Goethe saw Lavater, boated on the lakes, grew drunk on nature. His friends tried to take him on with them to Italy. But the Daemon had its eyes open. The time when Italy would be necessary to Goethe had not yet come. He felt a little golden heart that Lili had given him dancing against his breast, and he wrote for her lines which have become famous:

> Wenn ich, liebe Lili, dich nicht liebte,
> Welche Wonne gäb mir dieser Blick!
> Und doch, wenn ich, Lili, dich nicht liebte,
> Wär, was wär mein Glück?

(If, Lili dear, I loved thee not—What pleasure would these scenes bestow!—Yet, Lili, if I loved thee not—where should I find my joy?)

From this it is plain that the bear had not yet broken his silken cord. Goethe turned northwards, and, at the end of July, returned to Frankfurt. To all appearances the two young people were as fond as ever. During his absence, Goethe's future parents-in-law had been working against him. But Lili remained faithful. She expressed her willingness, should her liberty-loving poet fear the fashionable life of Frankfurt, to go with him to America. Still, it is difficult to believe that the prolonged absence of her betrothed, an absence of his own choice, had not come to her as something of a shock, and made her sad.

As to Goethe, he had compared himself, in the course of his wanderings, to a bird who, having escaped from his cage and flown back to the forest, still carries with him, as a *token of the horrors of captivity*, a little piece of string. *He is no longer the bird he once was, a bird born to be free*. And now here was Goethe, back in the gilded cage. He chafed against confinement more and more. To his distant confidante, Augusta von Stolberg, he wrote: "Oh! if only I could tell you all. But here, in the room of this child with the soul of an angel, who makes me unhappy through no fault of her own . . . I am reduced to the simple level of a baby and as little free as a parrot on a perch . . ." When Lili was not there, he flirted with another girl, just to prove to himself that he was still independent: but he found no pleasure in it: "All the time I was like a rat which has eaten poison: it runs into, and drinks any liquid it can find, but there is a mortal and inextinguishable fire burning in its belly."

A man who could write like that had already, in his heart of hearts, made the fatal break. He told himself, and he meant it, that to do so in fact would be impossible; that he could not inflict such torment on an angel. But in his unconscious he already knew that all was over. In September he could stand the situation no longer. On Wednesday, the 20th, he spoke "seven words to Lili", and the rupture was complete. It was not only from her that he wanted to break free, but from Frankfurt-am-Main. It was now that ever-watchful Destiny gave him the chance he needed to start his life over again in a wider and more active field, by making him acquainted with the young reigning Duke of Saxe-Weimar, a youth of eighteen, who, by the death of his father, had recently inherited a small independent State, complete with chateau, subjects, a court, a cathedral and the university of Jena. The new monarch prided himself on being progressive. He had ideas about reform. His meeting with Goethe filled him with enthusiasm.

Their very first talk together turned on politics. Goethe, who had thought much on most subjects, gave forceful expression to his views on government. The young Duke, Charles-Augustus, was amazed to find in a writer so great a taste for an active life, and such a wide knowledge of facts. *What a minister this poet would make!* he thought. Since, too, he had found in Goethe a charming companion for his hours of leisure, and a wonderful interpreter of human feelings, he told himself that no mentor could be more worthy, or more suitable to accompany a youthful sovereign through life. What joy to have at his side, instead of old and obsequious courtiers, a young and handsome companion with a brilliant intelligence! To cut a long story short, Charles-Augustus invited Goethe to Weimar as his personal guest. There was, as yet, no question of an official post. In what guise, then, should Goethe visit him, and for how long? All that was left unsettled, and it was better so. When one has just opened the door of one bird cage, one must not frighten the inmate away by showing him another.

The only arrangement made was that, on a certain day, the Duke should send his carriage to Frankfurt, and that Goethe should get into it. What obstacles was he likely to encounter? Lili was no longer one. She had been sacrificed. The part she had been called upon to play was ended. *Der Lebenskünstler*, the artist in life, knew why Destiny had stationed Lili on his path. It had been necessary, at a moment when Goethe was in great danger of dissipating his energies in aimless revolt, to restore him to a life among his fellows and, after the torments which had produced *Werther*, to give him renewed confidence in his power to make himself beloved. There had been a serious risk that the rebellious Titan might provoke the gods into striking him down with their

lightnings. It had been Lili Schönemann who had cured
Goethe of his ragings. But an excess in the other direction
would have been no less dangerous. If he was to become
an Olympian, he must be free, yet conscious of certain
necessary ties. His presiding genius had been careful to
assure this equilibrium. The Lili episode had been useful, but its usefulness was now over. He must move
forward now on the further side of love.

But there was a very present obstacle in his father.
The Imperial Councillor warned him not to stake his all
on the friendship of a sovereign-prince. Such men, he
said, were, all of them, superficial and changeable. The
favourite of a few months must expect to be cast off as
easily and quickly as he was taken on. But Goethe was
conscious of a genuine fellow-feeling between the young
duke and himself. He was sure that he could dominate
him. On the day named, however, the carriage did not
come. There was no message. What had happened?
Goethe was in a somewhat embarrassing position. He
had informed all Frankfurt of his impending departure
for Thuringia. So as not to lose face, he shut himself
away, let it be known that he had started off, and set to
work on his play: *Egmont*. Still no carriage. Had his
daemon deceived him? Sick of his father's jokes at his
expense, he took flight to Heidelberg. There he waited,
not doubting that the coach of destiny would appear at
the moment laid down for it in the stars.

And, sure enough, one day at Heidelberg, when he
was deep in argument with Fraülein Delph, the match-
making Sibyl, he heard a postilion's horn. The ducal
carriage was in the street. The prince's envoy explained
the delay. There had been an accident, but his master
was expecting Goethe. The latter bid a hasty farewell to

the Sibyl, giving her, as a parting present, some lines
he had just composed for *Egmont*:

"Whipped by invisible spirits Time's horses of the
sun make off, in spite of us, with the airy chariot of
our destiny. It is left for us manfully to hold the reins
and guide the wheels, here round a rock, there on the
brink of an abyss. Whither are we bound? No man
can tell. Only with difficulty can we remember whence
we have come . . ."[1]

With the swift drive to Weimar the turning-point
was rounded. Goethe had been torn free of his family
and of Frankfurt society. In the new world, over which
he was quite soon to reign, his genius could unfold
more freely. The carriage had played the rôle for which
it had been cast by Destiny. In order to complete the
Goethe whom we know, the gods now called to their aid
a prince and a lady.

Charles-Augustus was eight years younger than
Goethe. The two men were to spend fifty years together.
The Duke was a fine man. He was concerned for his
subjects' welfare, and longed to accomplish great things
in many fields. Goethe's wide-ranging mind enchanted
him. Here was someone capable of improvising sublime
poetry, of taking part in all the exercises of the body, of
dealing with matters pertaining to science, administration, art and much else. If ever the word *genius* had a
meaning, it was when applied to Goethe. The influence
of the poet on the prince was tremendous. He formed
his mind, imbued him with a love of ideas, and taught
him so to use his absolute power as to make of Weimar

[1] Goethe: *Egmont*, Act II.

an intellectual and cultural capital, without in any way neglecting the material interests of the poor.

For Goethe this school of action was no less essential. The Duke lost no time in making him a Privy Councillor, and charging him with a hundred varying missions. Then he appointed him to the position of his First Minister, which meant that he was the second man in the State. This naturally aroused lively jealousies. The older courtiers frowned upon the novelties which Goethe introduced. But he, his sovereign's master, was master of the situation, too. "It is very probable", he wrote on the 14th February, 1776, to Johanna Fahlmer, "that I shall remain here. I shall play my part to the best of my ability for just so long as I find pleasure in so doing, and as Destiny wills." Remain he did, and grew in power and wisdom. Nothing is more stimulating to the mind than having to grapple with those obstinate things known as facts. In the course of his duties, he was led to study the sciences. Since he had to deal with mining problems, he must inform himself about minerals. Since he was concerned with forestry and cattle-breeding, it was necessary for him to study the species of the animal world. His activities ranged from superintending roads to directing the theatre: from administering the army to reforming the fiscal system. In this way did he enlarge the base of the pyramid of his life and was able to raise its apex higher. At Weimar he gathered the materials for the Second Faust: "In the beginning was Action."

But action alone would not have sufficed to achieve that masterpiece of the human race—Johann Wolfgang Goethe. Action, left to itself, tends to absorb the energies, and to keep the intelligence at ground-level. If the proper balance was to be established, it was necessary for Goethe that *das Ewig Weibliche*—the Eternal Feminine—should intervene. Man is active: Woman affective. It was Charlotte von Stein who saved Goethe at Weimar. But for her, the turning-point would not have been decisive. The Baroness von Stein was an aristocrat, the daughter of a former Marshal of the Court, and wife of the Master of the Horse. Married without love she had born her husband eight children. Her difficult pregnancies and laborious accouchements had exhausted her. "My time of labour has been most painful," she wrote to a friend. "Why has nature condemned one half only of the human race to endure this agonizing experience?" She was resigned, wise, noble and sensitive. Goethe was attracted to her almost at first sight, but she was frightened by the ardent courtship of a man so fiery, so widely admired, whose declarations were "like a burning torrent". She was proud to know that she had been picked out by a great man, and determined, at least in the first years of their relationship, to "sublimate" his passion. She was very pious, and, until she met him, had enjoyed the *peace of God*. She tried hard to retain it.

This gentle feminine genius, "peaceful and pacifying", imposed on Goethe (at first) her own standard of purity. She accepted the homage he paid her, consented to see him every day, even received him in her château of Kochberg, but "insisted upon a discipline of heart and senses which brought about a complete metamorphosis in Goethe". Like a rushing stream foaming down the mountainside, which, when it falls into a great lake, mingles its tumultuous waters with the quiet depths, soon ceases to leap and boil, and assumes the appearance of the smooth and tranquil surface in which it is lost, so did Goethe, mingling his turbulent thoughts with those of the Appeaser (*Besantfgerin*) share in her serene dignity and lunar calm. Self-mastery was, in Charlotte's eyes, the greatest quality a man could have. She taught it to Goethe, and, from then on, he was, thanks to her, to rise to the level of that Olympian wisdom which was a greater and a nobler thing than the Titan's rage.

Goethe at Weimar. An example, almost unique, of a poetic genius at the head of a State. It was a time for him of power and achievement. "My daily task demands my constant presence. It is by carrying out those duties which I have grown to love, more and more, with each day that passes, that I hope to prove myself the equal of the greatest of men, and by that alone. Besides, the talisman of Frau von Stein's dear love protects me with its sweet odours." The turning-point had been rounded. Goethe had become Goethe.

There was to be one more, lesser, turning-point in his life, and that was the moment (in September, 1786) when he set off from Weimar for Italy. A corner, when taken by a *Lebenskünstler*, a driver of genius, may well let both vehicle and life go too far. It needs a light touch of the hand to restore the balance. Weimar had led the artist too far along the road of action. Charlotte had instructed him, only too well, in the sacrifice of body to spirit. Goethe, a mystical German, bound now for a strange land, had need of the lessons which the South could give. He found them in the land where "the orange-tree blooms", and returned to Weimar, after an absence of two years, strengthened and more supple. But this "rectification" was all that he had asked from Italy. He went back there once, but only once (in March, 1790), to wait in Venice for the Dowager-Duchess Anna-Amelia, whom he was to conduct back to Weimar. The great turning-point, the determining influence, had been when he had broken free from Lili Schönemann, when he had answered the summons from Weimar in 1775, when he had met the Baroness von Stein. For its task of shaping one of the greatest of human beings, Destiny had made use of two women, a Prince and a carriage.

CHAPTER IX

GIACOMO LEOPARDI

The songs of despair are the loveliest songs
And some, now immortal, the purest of sobs.

PAUL VALÉRY, who had no liking for Musset, was
severe in his criticism of these two lines. "A sob", he
said, "is not a song: it is, in fact, the very reverse." He
was right. Every song is an ordered whole. But when,
beneath the purity of the song one can still catch the
echo of the lamentation which sets its tone, it is then
that the poet touches the sublime. Wordsworth defined
poetry as "emotion recollected in tranquillity". There
must first be the living, poignant emotion, then the time
of gestation, and finally the remembered experience in
disciplined form. That is the Proustian theme of *Time
Regained*: it is also the secret of Leopardi's poetry.
Giacomo Leopardi had endured much suffering, and
this he sublimated in a few short lyrics which are among
the most perfect in the whole world. By natural inclina-
tion, and by reason of the time at which he lived, he was
a romantic. He had been nourished on the culture of the
ancient world. He expressed new thoughts in an antique
mode, and recovered the gracious rigour of the Greeks.
In this he resembled Shelley.

My purpose here is not so much to make his work
known—for it must be read in Italian, because translation
distorts its purity—as to recall the strangeness of his life.
The story has often been told in France, first and fore-

most by Sainte-Beuve in his *Portraits contemporains*. But a great number of publications, journals, letters and biographies have, in the course of the last thirty years, brought to light many of Leopardi's writings, and several facts relating to his life which had remained unknown. For the present study I have made extensive use of the latest edition of Iris Origo's *Leopardi*,[1] a book well informed about recent Italian works on the subject, which tells the sad and lovely story with a simple dignity worthy of its hero.

I

"I was born of a noble family in an ignoble Italian town." The adjective here applied to Recanati is unfair. It is a small town in the Marches, built on one of the most easterly spurs of the Apennines, not far from the Adriatic, and no more "ignoble" than a hundred other such places. The blue sky, the hills crowned with vine and olive, the sea and the high mountains provide a setting of perfect beauty. The dark and narrow streets are lined with *palazzi* which, in the days of Leopardi's childhood, were occupied by some forty or so aristocratic families. "All of them kept a carriage, entertained several times a year, put their footmen into liveries, and maintained, as part of the household, one, or two, priests who superintended the education of the children." They were circumspect in their behaviour and kept a jealous eye upon each other. The lower orders of the town put up with them, hated them, and laughed at them.

[1] Iris Origo: *Leopardi: a study in solitude*. (London: Hamish Hamilton, 1953.)

Since the thirteenth century, the *gens Leoparda* had maintained its social position and produced its fair quota of soldiers, magistrates, bishops, Knights of Malta and nuns, of no very great distinction. The family *palazzo* was not lacking in dignity, with its double staircase, its wrought-iron balconies, its gallery of portrait-busts and its vast range of bookshelves, all evidences of a long and noble line by no means destitute of culture. Count Monaldo Leopardi, the poet's father, took a manifest pride in his rank, his *palazzo* and his town. He would be first in Recanati rather than last in Rome. He revered the government of the Holy See, and looked upon the invasion of the Papal States by French troops as sacrilege. In more than one way he resembled Stendhal's Marquis del Dongo, not least in his refusal to show himself at a window when Bonaparte had ridden through the town. "That", he said, "would have been doing too much honour to the rascal." Having lost his father when he was five, Monaldo had been brought up by his mother with unyielding severity. His education had been entrusted to the family chaplain, Don Vincenzo Ferri, and a Jesuit, Don Giuseppe Torres. Even when he was eighteen he was never allowed to leave the house unless accompanied by one or other of his tutors, so little confidence did his virtuous mother have in the power of virtue.

As head of the family, Monaldo Leopardi was well intentioned but blundering, convinced of his own importance, at once rigid and weak. He was always dressed in black. He wore knee-breeches and an embroidered coat from morning till night, and a sword. "In full-dress, and with a sword at one's side," he said, "it is impossible to fall very low, even if one wants to"—a statement which proves the strength of his temptations and his determination not to yield to them. His patience was tested to the full by his marriage, in 1797, to the Marquise Adelaïda Antici. His mother had wept when he announced his intention of taking this step, and had tried to dissuade him. "I was proof against her tears, and for that I have suffered a terrible punishment," he says in his autobiography. "The arsenals of the divine vengeance are inexhaustible: let those tremble who provoke it! My wife's temperament was as far removed from mine as the earth is from the sky. Every married man will know what that means."

The Countess Adelaïda Leopardi was perfect in the worst sense of the word. She was a woman of character, but the character was bad. The Count, from a wish to be useful and a hope of making money, had embarked upon a project to get part of the Roman Campagna back into production by employing new agricultural methods, with the result that he ruined himself no less successfully than if he had been a gambler or had run after women. From that moment his wife took charge, and kept the purse-strings so tightly fastened that, though she managed to maintain appearances, she did so at the cost of depriving her husband of comforts and pocket-money alike. She reduced him to stealing from himself if he happened to need a couple of shillings. There is a story to the effect that being filled with pity, one winter evening, for a half-naked beggar, and having no money to give him, he withdrew into the shelter of a carriage entrance, took off his breeches, and made a present of them to the poor wretch. But such intermittent acts of generosity had to cease when his wife intervened.

Nevertheless, the Countess Adelaïda produced a show

of decorum. She steadfastly refused to put down so much as a priest, a coachman or a lackey. "Throughout her life," wrote her husband, "she recognized no interests other than those of her family and of God." She demanded of her children not only a strict adherence to all their religious duties, but also a complete contempt for all worldly matters. She condemned all pleasures and distractions which might come between them and God.

"I once", wrote her son Giacomo at a later date, "was intimately acquainted with a mother who not only refused all sympathy to parents who had lost children in infancy, but deeply and sincerely envied them, because those children, escaping so soon from the perils of life, had gone straight to Heaven, and because their parents had been spared the anxiety of rearing them. Whenever her own children were in danger, as happened more than once, she did not actually pray that they might die, because her religion forbad her to do so, but, in her heart, she rejoiced. . . . The death of one of them brought her great happiness, and she completely failed to understand how her husband could mourn its loss. . . . She regarded physical beauty as a terrible misfortune, and thanked God when any of her children turned out to be crippled or ugly . . . She never missed an occasion of pointing out to them how ill-favoured they were, and dwelt with merciless frankness on the inevitable humiliations to which their physical defects would expose them. . . . And all this she did in order to chastise in them the curse of original sin. . . ."

Did these terrible parents, one wonders, conceal, deep down, a tenderness for their children? Their father was most certainly fond of them, but fear compelled him not to give expression to his affection. As to the Countess Adelaïda, if ever she felt an impulse of maternal love, she immediately suppressed it. There were times when she was seen to burst into tears, but, when that happened, she would at once withdraw into her bedroom. We should, perhaps, see in this a proof of pent-up sensibility. Undoubtedly she tortured herself—and others. A prayer, found among her papers, gives us the clue to her behaviour: "Thou, O God, art the first father of my children. Grant that they may die rather than be a cause of offence to Thee." She was haunted, for herself and for her family, by the terror of sin.

The eldest son of this lugubrious couple, Giacomo Leopardi, was born on the 29th June, 1798. He had eleven brothers and sisters, seven of whom died at an early age. He was brought up with a brother, Carlo, and a sister, Paolina (a slight age difference divided these three from their two youngest brothers, who were virtually brought up separately). The room in which the two boys slept was in full view of their mother's. They never went out alone. "Her eyes were constantly upon us," Carlo said. "Their watchfulness was her only form of caress." When they were of an age to make their confessions, she always stationed herself near enough to the confessional to hear everything they said. This almost divine "omnipresence" had an overpowering effect upon the children. They were thirsting for love, but at the slightest demonstration of emotion on their part they were brought up dead by the icy stoicism of their mother, and the timidity of a father who had been reduced to the position of a slave. Nurses' stories about Hell, and the sight of penitents moving in procession, filled their nights with terrors. Giacomo's imagination was obsessed with ghosts, phantoms and devils. He would lie awake listening to the creaking weathercocks and chiming bells of Recanati.

Never was severity less necessary. Intelligent, gentle and docile, Giacomo believed everything his parents told him, showed a sincere piety, and was never so happy as when serving Mass. He dreamed of becoming a saint, though, in actuality, sanctity attracted him less than fame. He longed for the day when he should be a figure of renown, acclaimed, like St Louis, in the streets. At that time he was a pretty little boy with a serious and melancholy expression. His tiny universe consisted exclusively of the house, the garden and the church. From an attic window he looked at the moon and the star-spangled sky. He invented fantastic tales in which, under a number of fictitious names, the tyrant Monaldo tried in vain to overcome the eloquent and gallant heroes who were his sons. "What happy times those were," he said later, "when one had only to use one's imagination to give life to creatures of fantasy, when one was quite convinced that fauns and dryads haunted the woods; when, with arms round a tree-trunk, one could almost feel the pulsing life within." Such were Giacomo's earliest years. The two resident priests taught him Latin, and a refugee, the abbé Borne, French as well, which he learned with staggering ease. In his hours of freedom he played with shadows or counted the stars.

By 1808 the Leopardi boys had shown themselves to be so precocious and altogether remarkable, that their father invited, not only the family, but some of their Recanati neighbours as well, to be present at a series of examinations in which the youngsters engaged in a public discussion with their masters on many different subjects. "30th January, 1808. The three Leopardi children—Count Giacomo, nine years of age, Count Carlo, eight, and Countess Paolina, seven, will engage in an exercise dedicated to the memory of their dearly loved great-uncle, Count Ettore Leopardi, in which the two boys will answer questions in grammar and rhetoric, and the Countess Paolina those relating to Christian doctrine and the history of the world, to the fall of Carthage." The last of these examinations took place when Giacomo was fourteen (in 1812). For the last two or three years he had been released from the custody of his tutors, who had nothing more to teach him, and his father had turned him loose in the library there to pursue his studies without supervision.

Count Monaldo was justifiably proud of this library. It contained fourteen thousand volumes accommodated in fourteen long galleries, the walls of which were entirely covered with shelves. He, himself, had enriched the collection of his ancestors by purchasing, from time to time, books left behind by some erudite priest, or works brought there by Greek monks who had been driven from Corfu. He had been forced to employ countless shifts so as not to arouse the anger of the Countess Adelaïda, such, for example, as selling a sack of corn which he had stolen, under cover of darkness, from his own granary.

The library was well planned and arranged. Above each section there was a title in gilded lettering: *Philosophia, Historia Profana, Historia Sacra, Jurisprudentia,* etc., and there Giacomo undertook his own education. He taught himself the ancient languages. He read, without a tutor, the Greek and Latin texts, to which he later added the Hebrew works collected by his father. Methodically, pen in hand, he made abstracts of the poets, the historians and the Fathers of the Church. Sainte-Beuve compared him with Pascal who, from childhood, had displayed a genius for mathematics. The young Leopardi had a similar aptitude for philology. At an age when others are stumbling through the rudiments, he was already possessed of real learning, and was one of the foremost of Italian scholars.

Thus was this growing youth, who lived a life so cloistered that he was not allowed to leave the house alone, and knew nothing of the world around him, left free to explore the past history of mankind. "The world with which he was familiar was that of two thousand years ago." His mastery of Greek was soon so complete that he could write a letter in that language, and later, composed a *pastiche* of Anacreon which deceived even the most erudite. "It was equipped with a commentary and notes designed to throw dust in the eyes of the learned." Winter and summer, Giacomo lived in the library, ruining his eyesight as a result of so much reading by candle-light, and, by an excess of writing, giving himself severe curvature of the spine. He had a presentiment that his life would be short, and strove to achieve a precocious fame. Having read and translated so many poets, he had acquired considerable skill in the techniques of Latin, Greek and Italian verse. But it was not by employing such facility that he expected to establish the reputation for which he longed so eagerly. He dreamed of becoming a great scholar, and that dream was already beginning to take on form and substance. He translated the lesser-known Greek authors. He wrote commentaries on the Greek Fathers of the second cen-

tury, and the ecclesiastical historians before the time of
Eusebius. It made Monaldo very proud to hear his son
carrying on discussions, in Hebrew, with Jewish scholars
from Ancona. When the abbé Angelo Mai, Keeper of
the Ambrosian Library in Milan, discovered a hitherto
unknown fragment of Fronto, it was Giacomo who made
the first translation of it, without a single mistake.

How was it, then, that he passed from scholarship to
poetry? His own answer to that question was, "By the
Grace of God", though, no doubt, the awakening of his
emotions had something to do with it. Round about his
eighteenth year, he began to realize that Homer, Virgil,
Ariosto and Dante aroused in him feelings of delight
such as he had never previously known. As he read these
authors, a whole new world was revealed to him. Sometimes tears would come into his eyes. He translated the
second book of the *Aeneid*, parts of the *Odyssey*, and
other classical writings, into Italian verse. From books
he learned about the passions. So far, Giacomo, in the
quiet refuge of the library, had enjoyed a tranquil happiness, the happiness of a young intelligence for the first
time becoming aware of its powers, and discovering the
ancient world. But he now began to wonder whether
there was not something absurd in burrowing endlessly,
like a mole, among old books. For seven years he had
been living within the same four walls. He had weakened
his eyes: he was bent and twisted. His deformed body,
deprived of all physical exercise, was incapable of responding to the slightest call made upon it. "What an
existence!" said the ladies of Recanati. "What a way to
spend his youth!"

The awakening was painful. The thought of so many
lost years made him rage and fume. "I have miserably

and irremediably brought ruin on myself by making my outward appearance odious and contemptible . . . for it is appearances, only, that count with the majority of men." But this verdict on himself was too severe. There was something fine, something even beautiful about his face, with its large melancholy eyes. The nose was delicate, the features well formed. "His smile had an indescribable, an almost other-worldly quality." But this impressive head was deeply sunk between his shoulders. The cruel truth had to be faced: he was going to be a *gobbo*, a hunchback. What woman would ever love a man whose soul, alone, was beautiful? "What does that matter?" the Terrible Parents would have said. He had been made to wear a priest's soutane ever since the age of eight. His father was insistent that he should be ordained. The churchman's cloak would hide the scholar's hump. But Giacomo abandoned himself to gloomy meditations. Leaning over the rim of a well, he thought of death with a bitter longing.

For a shy and ill-favoured youth the dawning of the age of love can well be a tragedy. For a whole year now Leopardi had dreamed of being like other men, of talking to pretty women, of bringing a fleeting smile to their lips, in short, of being pleasing. But, living, as he did, in complete solitude, what chance was there that such experiences would ever come his way? He was nineteen when an elderly cousin, Count Lazzari, spent three nights with his young wife at the Palazzo Leopardi. The Countess Gertrude was beautiful. For Giacomo it was love at first sight. Gertrude Lazzari's rôle was completely passive. She was resigned to being the wife of an old fogey, and scarcely so much as noticed the young man's existence except to play at cards with him, to give him an occasional smile, because smiling suited her, and also because she was good-natured and felt sorry for the poor boy. Not a word of love did he utter, but this visit completely knocked the ground from under his feet. On the very first evening he fell madly in love, and suffered the tortures of the damned at the thought that she whom he loved would so soon be gone. For weeks after the visitors had left, he cultivated and observed his emotions. He fed them on a course of Racine, Goethe, Byron and Chateaubriand. He kept a "lover's journal". He had spoken scarcely a word to Gertrude Lazzari. What could he have said? He knew nothing about her. But she served as an object round which his feelings could gather. "I have experienced one of those attachments without which no man can be great." His journal was not really concerned with this one specific case of love, but with love in general.

Desire, and the ability to suffer, are emotions which, in all young men, exist in a diffused state, and are for ever on the look-out for some object on which they can be employed. The imagination clothes with charm and beauty any unknown female casually met with. Like many of his own age, Leopardi was in love with *la donna che non si trova*—the undiscoverable she. When the Countess Gertrude vanished into the mists of oblivion, two young women were called upon to share between them the part of the Beloved. One was the daughter of a coachman, Teresa Fattorini, the other, Maria Belardinelli, whose origins were no less modest. Giacomo never saw them except through an open window, and sometimes heard them singing. He gazed from afar upon the pretty pair: "the cloudless sky, the orchards, the field-paths, golden in the sunlight, the distant sea and the hills: no human tongue can tell what thoughts then filled my heart". The only words he ever exchanged with the two girls were passing greetings. Nothing more was needed. They were to become the Nerina and the Sylvia of his poems. Poetry can take root in the thin soil of an uneventful life, like a flower in the hollow of a rock.

2

The Italy of Recanati, bigoted, reactionary and anti-French, had its opposite in the Italy of Stendhal's friends, and Byron's, anti-clerical, all of them, liberal and anti-Austrian. Milan sheltered a considerable number of these rebels, who were also, for the most part, men of letters. When, in 1817, Giacomo completed his translation of the second book of the *Aeneid*, he sent it, not only to the abbé Angelo Mai of the Ambrosian Library, but to Vincenzo Monti and to Pietro Giordani as well. Monti, a man given to recantations, had abandoned the creed of liberalism after the fall of Napoleon. But Giordani stood firm. He was forty-three years of age, and had spent some time in a seminary (he was known as the abbé Giordani) from which, however, he had emerged as an intransigent anti-clerical. His political friends spoke of him as one of the leading Italian writers. He had become a hero to Giacomo Leopardi who, in the letter which accompanied the *Aeneid*, expressed himself as follows.

"If it be a crime for a mere nobody to write to a great man of letters, then am I much to be blamed . . . I have no excuse to offer save that I feel an incomprehensible need to make myself known to my Prince, for, in very truth, I am your subject, as must all be who have a love of literature."

Angelo Mai and Vincenzo Monti sent polite acknowledgments. Giordani was, at first, repelled by the excess of his correspondent's praise, but, having heard how incredibly young he was, sent a reply, by express, to *il Signor Contino*: "It is happiness for me to know that, in the twentieth century, Count Leopardi (whom I already love) will be ranked among those who gave back to Italy her lost honour." As was only natural, Leopardi was intoxicated by this communication, and the long pent-up flood of his confidences burst over Giordani. "I have a great longing—perhaps immoderate and insolent—for fame." He wished for guidance. Monti had written that his work was not without faults. "But it is useless to tell a blind man that he has lost his way if one does not indicate the direction in which he should turn". Giacomo admitted that he wanted to leave Recanati. "What beauty is there in Recanati? What is worth seeing or learning there? Nothing. . . . God has filled the world with so many marvels, yet I, at eighteen, must face the fact that, in this hole I have to live, and to die where I was born."

Giordani advised patience, and promised to pay him a visit. It was long delayed. Leopardi was eaten up with restlessness. "Solitude is not good for those who have a fire within them." At last, Giordani was as good as his word. He stayed for five days, and in that space of time, the whole direction of a man's life was changed. The visit began badly. For the first time Giacomo took his courage in both hands, and went out alone. On his way to the inn at which his unknown friend was lodging, he ran into his father. Because Giordani was an abbé, Count Monaldo allowed himself to be persuaded. He even authorized his son to make a whole day's excursion with the visitor. How deeply he was to regret that decision! "Since Giordani's arrival, a complete change has come over my two sons. Until that moment they had never, literally never, been far out of sight of my own eyes or their mother's. I gave them permission to consort with Giordani, believing in his friendship and his honour." Poor Monaldo never knew what was said in the course of those meetings: complaints about the pettiness of life in a small town, plans for the future, political and religious revelations, encouragement to correspond with the leaders of the movement for Italian liberation. "When Giordani left", concluded the Count, their father, "he took with him the secrets of my children . . . how they hate their father's house in which they feel themselves to be strangers and prisoners. Perhaps they even hate *me*. I, who am so brimful of love for them, am become in their corrupt imaginings an implacable tyrant."

It is true that Giordani's influence would not have worked so quickly, had not the educational methods of the Casa Leopardi prepared the way for rebellion. Ideas of liberation were in the very air breathed by the two young men. All over the country the *carbonari*, and other conspirators, were plotting to free Italy, not only from the Austrians, but from the Papal Power as well.

"Today", wrote Leopardi, "I have reached my twentieth year. What have I achieved so far? No great action . . . O! my country, my country! I cannot shed my blood for you, since you no longer exist. . . . To

what object, to what person, to what land am I to
devote my work, my sufferings, my life?"

Ever since Giordani had opened his eyes, Leopardi had
realized that he was an Italian patriot, and, on the 1st
of January, 1819, he published two *canzoni* : *All' Italia*
and *Sopra il Monumento di Dante*. A third patriotic
poem, *Ad Angelo Mai* (on the fragments of Cicero's *De
Re Publica*, brought to light by Angelo Mai), appeared
at Bologna in 1820.

It is the formal beauty of these poems, rather than the
sentiments expressed in them, that appeals to the modern
reader. They are a prolongation of "that perpetual indict-
ment, that sense of desolation" which we find in Dante,
Alfieri, *Corinne* and *Childe Harold* on the subject of Italy
stripped of her ancient glory. "O my country! I see the
walls, the arches, the columns, the statues and the
ruined towers of our ancestors. Their glory I do not see,
neither the laurels nor the steel which once our fathers
wore." They are poems in the classic mode, imitated
from the ancients, and, in particular, from Simonides.
"Messenian", Sainte-Beuve called them, and they are
disfigured, here and there, by an academic rhetoric. But
the vigour of their form shows the mastery of this young
beginner. They are certainly as good as Victor Hugo's
earliest political odes. Leopardi's passionate outbursts
against the France of Napoleon echo those of Kleist. By
a miracle, the little volume received the *imprimatur*, and
Leopardi distributed three hundred copies. They caused
his father much painful anxiety. "I am not a competent
judge in these matters, but I cannot approve this admiration for Italy in its days of battle and glory. Speaking
for my own part, I consider obedience to be necessary,

and see little difference between a sovereign born on this side of the Alps and one born on the other." One might be listening to Ascagne del Dongo! The sarcastic Carlo Leopardi wrote later: "Terror has made our father lose almost all his hair."

Recanati, like the whole of Italy, was torn between two factions. On the *carbonari* side, as on that of the *sanfedisti* (the Congregation), the flames of fanaticism burned high. In every family the young and the old were in conflict. It was a time of plotting and concealed weapons. Byron's letters give us a vivid picture of armed horsemen riding through the night. Is it surprising that Monaldo should have been terrified at seeing his son's poems turned into the battle-hymns of the guerilla troops?

"O, Giacomino," wrote Giordani to his disciple, "what a great man you are already! . . . Your *canti* run through the city like trains of burning powder: everybody wants to have them. . . . I have never known poetry, nor prose, to be so praised, so much admired. You are talked of as a miracle."

This same Giordani wrote to a third person as follows: "If only he be granted ten years of life and good health: if only he can be torn free of the appalling conditions in which he has to live, then call me the worst fool in Italy if, in 1830, it is not being said that few Italians, in the greatest centuries, deserve comparison with Leopardi." This is reminiscent of what Fontanes said of Chateaubriand when he was just beginning, and proves that though Giordani may not have been a good writer, he was certainly a good judge.

The young, now famous, man remained a prisoner, completely cut off from the world. His mother still refused to give him any pocket-money, his father, any liberty. For some time an ophthalmia, brought on by too much reading, had deprived him of the company of his beloved books. What was he to do? His father would, at a pinch, have agreed to send him to a seminary, but, as the result of his close study of the profane authors and of Giordani's influence, Giacomo had lost his faith though he still loved the ceremonial of the Catholic Church. He could not, without sacrilegious dishonesty, have entered the priesthood. His last hope was his maternal uncle, the Marquis Carlo Antici, who lived in Rome and had considerable influence there. Leopardi tried to get a passport for Rome and almost succeeded.

Thinking that he was about to leave Recanati, he had written a letter to his brother Carlo, which he meant to leave behind him. "I have taken my departure without telling you of my intentions, so that no one should hold you responsible for my going. I have been influenced in my decision by two main reasons. The first is that I find it impossible to continue my studies: the second you can guess, though I would rather not put it into words." This second reason was the need he felt to love and to be loved. The deliberate policy of depriving him of all feminine society, which his parents in their foolishness pursued, drove him to despair. To his father he had written:

"In the interest of something I know nothing of, but which you call home and family, you have demanded of your children the sacrifice, not only of their physical well-being, but also of their natural inclinations, of their youth and of all their lives."

At the last moment his plan of escape was brought to

nothing, because Count Monaldo intercepted the passport. His love for his sons was greater than they knew. He shared their taste for reading, but, as Carlo said, "he very early in life got himself entangled in his wife's apron-strings and never afterwards succeeded in freeing himself."

On the day when he learned the truth about the passport, Leopardi lost all confidence in his father. He refused to go on wearing the soutane. Unable, any longer, because of his bad sight, to take refuge in books, and completely out of touch with life, he had ceased to hope for anything, not even for death, not even for happiness. "I abandoned myself to the terrible and barbarous joys of despair." He quoted a saying of Petrarch: *Ed io son di quei che'l pianger giova* . . . "I, too, am of those who find delight in weeping." Here, again, one is tempted to recall Kleist and Chateaubriand. Certain spirits there are who, having found themselves in suffering, fear that, by escaping from it, they may lose their characteristic "tone". They cultivate with care a melancholy which is productive of poetry. In order to see nature with the artist's eye, they must rise above it and look down. Turning his back on action, the unhappy man can give himself up wholly to analysis. The year 1819, so tragic for Leopardi, was the one in which he wrote his *Idylls*, which, of themselves, would give him the right to be called a great poet. What are they? Brief instants of emotion caught and noted down in a few minutes, then, slowly given their final form. All through his life Leopardi kept a journal, the *Zibaldone* or *Medley*, a collection of thoughts, and of notes on his reading, in which are to be found first sketches, sometimes no more than a single line, for his poems:

"A peasant at his cottage door, speaking out loud, just for himself alone, the *Ave Maria* and the *Requiem aeternam*, and looking at the moon hanging low above the trees. . . . Two young men sitting on the deserted, moss-grown steps of a church, joking and nudging one another under the great tower. . . . The carter's daughter, leaning from a window and calling down to others below, at their supper: 'It's going to rain good and proper! What a night! black as your hat!' Then a voice: 'Ah! here comes the rain.' A gentle spring rain. Then all go indoors. I hear the sound of doors being shut and bolts shot."

A rough sketch, but jotted down by a master, which gives one the feeling of a profound thought not put into words—such is a Leopardi idyll. Nature becomes one immense metaphor, the felt image of a secret truth. It takes the mind back to the Greek Anthology, to Shelley's sweet and bird-like notes: also, perhaps to a few exquisite poems by Hugo, and certain lines by Valéry. But Leopardi's simplicity is inimitable. His vocabulary is at once rare—in so far as he likes to revive archaic words so as to give new life to the language—and poor, because he refuses to use words which are merely erudite. Like every great poet he attached supreme importance to the music of language:

> The heart grows tired of everything,
> Song, sleep and roses and the dance's ring,
>   Even love's fever;
> But the sweet pleasure of a perfect tongue,
> The perfect loveliness of words, lasts long,
>   Perhaps for ever.

The welcome extended by Monaldo to his son's first

poems was frigid in the extreme. The patriotic ones reeked of revolt, and round the idylls hung the odour of sin. Was it to such frivolous and blameworthy trivia that a man should devote his whole life when he was capable of attaining to a high position in learning and philosophy? Count Leopardi put every possible difficulty in the way of their publication: they might, he argued, be thought to have been "inspired by a faction", and, in any case, the Austrian police authorities disapproved of them. Giacomo's despair reached new depths. Even Giordani admitted that there seemed to be no way out of the situation. "I see", he wrote, "that your misfortunes are never-ending, without remedy, or hope of alleviation. All I can say is that if God sends you death, it should be accepted as a blessing. . . . To lose your life is to lose nothing worth the having." This letter had the curious effect of making Leopardi determined to go on living.

For a whole year he wrote no more poetry, but filled eleven hundred and sixty-seven pages of that wonderful "breeding ground", the *Zibaldone*, with scraps of everything: philosophy, philology, science, history, criticism and quotations. Here and there one finds a perfect line: *And hope reborn each day before the sun. . . . Beside me I can see the travelling moon. . . .* It is in this journal that the true Leopardi is to be found, the reader fed on all that the classics can most exquisitely provide. In the following summer he resumed his work and composed a number of poems which, though they do not have the fleeting purity of the *Idylls*, take the form of painful and vigorous confessions: *Sappho's Last Song*, for instance, in which he expresses the misery of a gentle, noble spirit imprisoned in a misshapen body.

He had come to think, with his darling Greeks, that

physical ugliness is a crime. Because of his deformity he
had grown to hate himself. In a poem on Brutus, *Bruto
Minore*, he painted the picture of a man who found a
cure for his wretchedness in suicide. The longing for
death, which had haunted him since childhood, was
gaining strength.

3

During the winter of 1822–1823, the door of the tomb
in which he was buried alive opened just far enough to
show a crack of daylight. His uncle, the Marquis Antici,
moved by a sense of pity, offered to take him to Rome.
To the arguments of this much respected relative, the
Terrible Parents yielded. All Leopardi's life was wrapped
up in ancient Rome. Of this visit he expected much: the
revelation of an almost divine beauty, but also of a living
world where lovely and brilliant women would at last
understand that he had genius and was deserving of love.
He was disappointed. To Carlo his brother: "I take no
pleasure in all the great things that I see. I *know* that
they are marvellous, but I *feel* nothing . . . I swear to
you, Carlo mine, that my patience and my self-confidence
have not only been defeated but destroyed." At Recanati
he had been blamed: in Rome nobody seemed even to
notice his existence. He had detested the little town and
its triviality: he now discovered that it had at least one
good quality: its scale of values was human. "In a great
city there is nothing to relate a man to what surrounds
him." He had hoped that great scholars like Angelo Mai
—now Monsignor Mai—would seek him out. He went
to see the great man. Mai was friendly, but his friend-

liness was distant, worldly and superficial. What it all amounted to was that he was incapable of recognizing a man of outstanding distinction. "To attract the attention of others in a great city is a heart-breaking business."

There was, of course, his uncle's house where he was now living, but the Antici family seemed to him to be no less provincial than his own. He had hoped that, freed from the stern supervision of his parents, he might, in Rome, make easy conquests in the field of love. Alas! his timidity and his misshapen body were obstacles harder to overcome than paternal vigilance. "It is as difficult to approach a woman in Rome as it is in Recanati, more difficult in fact, because of the extreme frivolity of these female animals, who are quite devoid of interest into the bargain. They are a mass of hypocrisy, and think only of amusing themselves." The indifference of the young women he met, and the conviction that, all his life long, he would be deprived of love and beauty, served to discourage him. Yet, the Rome of that time was the Rome in which Stendhal found such lively pleasures. But, then, Stendhal was neither bearish nor thin-skinned. Leopardi exaggerated his ugliness. He despaired of being liked, and this very despair made of him an unsympathetic figure. "This is the most painful and mortifying period of my life . . . For God's sake, love me!" he wrote to his brother, "I am hungry for love, love, love, for ardour, enthusiasm and life. This world, it seems, is not made for me, and I find that the Devil is blacker than he is painted!"

Gradually, however, the world of learning opened its doors to him. But he looked upon the archaeologists, who valued more highly the discovery of an inscription than the composition of a fine poem as solemnly ridicu-

lous. They made Stendhal laugh: they made Leopardi's
blood boil. The erudite foreigners he found less displeas-
ing. With them one could talk intelligently in French. The
Prussian ambassador to the Holy See, Berthold Niebuhr,
an eminent scholar, recognized the prodigious learning of
this ill-favoured young man: "Read his Annotations on
the Chronicle of Eusebius—what penetration! I have
found nothing to equal it in this country." He went to
see Leopardi in his attic room, and came away from the
visit, saying: "At last I have found an Italian worthy of
ancient Rome!" Niebuhr warmly commended Giacomo
to the attention of Cardinal Consalvi, who seemed
disposed to help the ambassador's protégé, provided
Leopardi should consent to assume the *manteletta* (short
cape) of the Roman Court. This would have opened the
way to ecclesiastical preferment. For some weeks Leopardi played with the idea, but decided that his lack of
faith demanded that he should retain his liberty, and left
Rome for Recanati after an absence of five months. It
was an heroic refusal.

The atmosphere of the *Palazzo Leopardi* had not
changed. It was still divided into two camps: the parents
and the priests were, as they had always been, champions
of paternal authority, political subservience, and aus-
terity. The children built all their hopes on liberty,
independence and love. Carlo and Paolina, exasperated
beyond bearing, dreamed of making their escape. The
former succeeded, through marriage. This, the sister
never managed to achieve (a marriage was, indeed,
arranged, but it fell through at the last moment).
Giacomo, shut away in the library, wrote a number of
Operette Morali, which contain, in the form of essays,
dialogues and discourses the essence of a philosophy, or,

rather, of a state of mind. The theme of all these pieces is the same: life is bad: only death is good. . . . An itinerant vendor offers an Almanack for the New Year to a passer-by, who asks: "Is it going to be a happy year for me?" The hawker says that he hopes so. "But has any year of your life ever been happy?" asks the other. "Would you be willing, your life having been what it has, to live it over again? Have you ever known anyone who would? The life that we call good, is not the life we know, but the life we have never had. It always lies in the future, never in the past. . . . So, give me the most hopeful of your almanacks . . . here is your sixpence." The happy life, like the beloved woman, was always, in the poet's eyes—*La Donna che non si trova*.

Many of these dialogues, imitated from Lucian, are fragile, but always perfect. Manzoni himself said of them: "There is probably nothing better in the whole range of Italian prose." The thoughts expressed in them were wholly subjective, though Leopardi was always annoyed when anyone told him that his pessimism was nothing but the voicing of his own unhappiness. It was because of cowardice, he said, and of a refusal to recognize the horror of existence, that people chose to consider his philosophic opinions as the result of his personal sufferings. He claimed that he was giving an outline of a universally valid philosophy, the main tenets of which were: that the universe is incomprehensible: that human life, seen in the light of that immensity, is nothing: that action is pointless, that it is our realization of the truth that causes our boredom and our misery. Here he makes contact with Byron and Chateaubriand, but in him the evil lies deeper. Byron and Chateaubriand, for all their theorizing, took their stand on love and action. Leopardi,

all through his life, was the "Outsider" who refuses to
abide by the rules of the game, or can find no partner
with whom to play it. But no one can judge action who
remains aloof from it.

In 1825 it looked as though Fortune might favour him
at last. A Milan publisher, Antonio Stella, was planning
to bring out a complete edition of Cicero in an Italian
translation, with notes. He suggested that Giacomo
should superintend the work. What was more surprising
still was that Count Monaldo agreed to the arrangement.
He thought that the strict police administration of Milan
would keep his son in the straight and narrow path, and
compel him to show proper respect for the authorities.
Leopardi set off, and, on the way, stopped at Bologna
where, for the first time, and with Giordani's help, he
found himself surrounded by friends who esteemed and
loved him. So happy was he there, that, when he found
Milan no less disappointing than Rome, he hurried back.
All he had to live on were the twelve crowns paid him
monthly by Stella, and the proceeds of occasional Latin
lessons. But he was with friends.

This was much to the credit of the people of Bologna.
It was not easy to remain faithful to Leopardi. As a
result of having lived for so long a time in seclusion, he
had become a creature of fads and fancies. It was
necessary to put up with his headaches, his constipation
and his insomnia. The house in which he happened to
be was always either too hot or too cold; the light too
strong or too weak. His friends consented to sit with him
in the dark so as to spare his eyes; to keep all the windows
shut because he could not bear the thought of draughts;
to satisfy his perpetual craving for sugar. He would put
six pieces into a cup of coffee, and, in addition, was for

THE ART OF WRITING

ever demanding ice-cream. His visitors had to endure the sight of food stains on his clothes, his long silences, his habit of taking snuff, and the extraordinary manner in which he cracked his finger joints. But, in this atmosphere of warm companionship, he let himself relax. His suspiciousness melted away and he displayed his true nature, which was gentle and engaging.

At Bologna, too, he experienced other pleasures which, for him, had the charm of novelty. One of the local academies asked him to give a public reading of his poems. His impression was that they had produced a great effect. A fairly well-known poetess, Teresa Malvezzi, opened her *salon* to him, and even received him *tête-à-tête*. She was thirty-nine and had never been beautiful, but Leopardi, who lacked experience in such matters, was easily taken in. Very soon he was devoting all his evenings to this amiable blue-stocking. There was no hint of anything more serious between them. "We never spoke of love, except jokingly, but lived in a tender and mutually sympathetic relationship." But the lady's husband protested. He regarded as ridiculous her intimacy with a scruffy little hunchback. A woman finds it easy to sacrifice an adorer who is not her lover. Giordani to Brighenti:

> "Have you any news of Leopardi? . . . Is it true that he is seeing a great deal of that Malvezzi woman, who likes to think herself a literary pundit? Is it true that she has given him to understand that she can no longer endure either the frequency or the length of his visits? Is it possible that Giacomo can go twice to the house of such a person?"

So was Leopardi's first friendship with a woman rather

ungraciously broken off. The last words he ever wrote on the subject of Teresa were: "I have seen the Mal-vezzi's poem. Poor woman!"

He had been away from Recanati for fifteen months when he received a rather pathetic letter from his father. The poor man assured him of his love, offered to send him a little money, unbeknownst to his wife, and begged him to return. Leopardi, moved to pity, agreed to go back to the family home. He found a certain degree of pleasure in taking up his old habits again. But the atmosphere of the house remained suffocating. The urchins of Recanati, with surprising cruelty, ran after Giacomo in the streets, throwing snowballs at him and shouting "*Gobbo!*" He made a small sum of money by editing an anthology for Stella and decided to go to Florence, which had the reputation of being an intellectual capital. The reading room, run by a Swiss called Jean-Baptiste Vieusseux, was much frequented by literary-minded aristocrats, artists, and famous foreigners who happened to be passing through the city. The Marquis Capponi had been brave enough (in those days of strict censorship) to launch a periodical: *L'Antologia*. Mazzini wrote for it, and Leopardi became a contributor.

As before, in Rome and Milan, he was disappointed by what he found. The men who now surrounded him were generous-minded and cultivated, it is true, but they were a local version of the English *Whigs*. They believed in progress through reform, and thought that a liberal aristocracy, by improving education and social institutions, could bring happiness to the people. They held the view that science would solve every difficulty. In short, they shared the illusions which were to be prevalent in France in 1848, and found a mouthpiece in

[201]

Renan. Leopardi had no false hopes. He expected
nothing to come of nothing. The ingenuous optimism
of the Florentines made him smile sadly. Of what use
were reforms? The root of the trouble lay in mankind,
in life, in the nature of the world. Evil was the product
not of institutions, but of a faulty humanity. A young
Catholic writer, Nicolo Tommaseo, was driven frantic
by his "black atheism", and began to attack him no less
brutally than the urchins of Recanati. "A little Count
has recently emerged from the watery flood," he wrote,
"the burden of whose song is *'There is no God because I
am a hunchback: I am a hunchback because there is no
God.'* " This brutal argument *ad hominem* was only too
familiar to Leopardi. Even the great Manzoni had used
it against him. Once more, he made up his mind to beat
a retreat. Besides, the bitter *tramontana* would have
made it impossible for so ailing, weak and chilly a subject
to spend the winter in Florence.

He took refuge in Pisa, which had a mild climate, and
lived there in solitude. He was not too unhappy. The
fields and paths of the neighbourhood reminded him of
Recanati. His landlord's sister-in-law, Teresa Lucignani,
a girl of fifteen, became for him what once those barely-
glimpsed young women had been who had inspired his
earliest idylls, *La donna che non si trova*. Seventy-seven
years later she was questioned about the famous poet
whom she had known so well. She admitted that he had
made a bad impression on her. "He was deformed," she
said. "He scarcely ever changed his shirt, and he let his
chocolate run down his chin." But he had never tried
to please her. What did he ask of Teresa?—nothing,
except to be there. A note written by Leopardi on leaving
Pisa: "In her face, in her movements there was some-

thing hard to define, something almost divine." Watching this young creature live so freshly and so naturally, he was inspired to write a beautiful poem, *Il Risorgimento*, in which he expresses the joy of once more feeling the sap rising in his veins:

> The woods, the sea-shore and the hills
> With me return to life.
> The running waters speak to me,
> And to me speaks the sea.

The evocation of the past through the medium of a present sensation (O Proust!) moved him, both at Pisa and at Recanati, whither he later returned, to write idylls no less pure and touching than those he had composed in earlier days. He recalled the Sylvia and Nerina who had set his young heart beating. He loved to recover "time lost" and sang: *Il rimembrar delle passate cose*. The death of a twenty-four-year-old brother, Luigi, and the supplications of an afflicted father, had taken him back, yet again, to the gloomy family house. He lived there for the last time, shutting himself away so as to see nobody, taking his meals in solitude. "The sight of a man indulging in physical pleasure is disgusting to others," he said. For sixteen months he tried in vain to produce work of an ironical nature: *An Encyclopaedia of Useless Knowledge: The Art of being Unhappy*. But all that rose in him from the bitter depths of desolation was the pure, the airy, the discarnate note of the idylls. It was at this time that he wrote *Le Ricordanze*, *La Quiete Dopo la Tempesta*, *Il Sabato del Villaggio* and *Canto Notturno di un Pastore Errante dell' Asia*:

> What are you doing up there in the sky,
> Tell me, what are you doing,
> Oh silent moon? . . .

Yes, what was that eternal and silent pilgrim doing? Did she know the meaning of death and the wherefore of things? But no answer came from the white moon, nor from the heavens. Perhaps the truth lay in the last line of the poem:

Fatal indeed to a man is the day on which he is born.

4

Just as he was falling back into that sense of utter despair which the house at Recanati always produced in him, a generous offer came. General Pietro Colletta wrote to him from Florence, in the name of a group of friends who were prepared to make him a monthly allowance which would enable him to live and work in that city. It would involve no obligation of any kind. Colletta carried tact so far as to tell him that the money had been provided by an anonymous admirer. Into Leopardi's darkness this offer came like a ray of light, "more blessed than the first gleam of dawn after the polar night". He accepted. For two years (1830–1832) he was to remain in Tuscany where his life, always precarious, was given a fresh lease by two great passions: a friendship and a love.

The friend, Antonio Ranieri, was a tall and handsome young Neapolitan with a great devotion to literature, a rather vulgar Don Juan, who, from their first meeting, was flooded by an admiration half mixed with love. For the romantic Ranieri, the appalling moral and physical state of Leopardi, almost blind, very ill and utterly disconsolate, was a reason the more for developing an attachment for the unhappy genius. Exiled from Naples for his political opinions, and cast off by his father, his resources were reduced to a low level. A wonderful sister who, like Leopardi's own, was called Paolina, did her best to help him. He went often to Rome to see a young actress, Maddalena Pelzet, known as *Lenina*, whose lover he was. As soon as he realized the full extent of Leopardi's distress and loneliness, he suggested setting up house with him.

The question has often been debated whether this impassioned friendship had a sensual origin. The letters exchanged between the two men are unusually emotional. It needed considerable courage on Ranieri's part to link his life with that of Leopardi, who was the most unsociable of men. The passionate tone of the letters proves nothing. It was typical of the period. We know that Leopardi, where women were concerned, was timid and very conscious of his inability to please, and also, that he needed affection. That he should have sought it in friendship is not surprising. What is certain is that Ranieri, and, later, his "angelic sister", Paolina, remained loyally devoted to Leopardi until his death. Not that Ranieri was intellectually worthy of Leopardi's companionship. His writings show that he was vain and, in the last analysis, mediocre. But it is not hard to imagine what the enthusiastic warmth of a younger man's admiration must have meant to a little hunchback who firmly believed that he was an object of scorn to others.

Ranieri's fidelity touched him the more, because, at the end of the year, Colletta's little group discontinued the promised allowance. At that time, the two friends were spending the winter in Rome, where they lived in a small apartment in the Via Condotti. Ranieri wanted to be near "Lenina". As for Leopardi: "The affection which binds me to Ranieri", he said, "is such that our destinies are henceforward inseparable." And again: "I am living with Ranieri from whom only Jupiter's lightning can tear me." Another friend, Louis de Sinner, was doing everything he could for him. This young Swiss philologist, to whom, in 1830, Leopardi entrusted all the philological writings dating from the first part of his life, was trying to get them published in Germany. Sinner devoted himself entirely to furthering the prestige of his friend, and it was he who drew Sainte-Beuve's attention to him.

As to the love: the last woman who inspired that emotion in the poet was an extremely pretty, but frivolous and sensual, Florentine girl, Fanny Targioni. She was the wife of a doctor interested in botany, and was commonly believed to have four lovers "of whom two were imaginary". Leopardi was introduced to her. She saw the advantage of adding to her court an admirer who was without good looks, without danger, but not without genius. "*Il mio gobbetto*," she called him, while Leopardi named her *Aspasia*. She may have had the charm of the original bearer of that name: she probably had the "salon"; she most certainly did not have the intelligence. But Leopardi never saw women as they were, and made of her, for a time, *la donna che non si trova*. His love began like Sainte-Beuve's for Adèle Hugo. He went to see her in her home, and found her surrounded by flowers and children. "From that moment, a new heaven, a divine radiance were revealed to me."

It was not long before la signora Targioni, and the whole of Florence, knew that he was in love with her. It gave rise to a great deal of amusement. Only Ranieri understood. He had had his fill of women, and realized that the poor fellow was the more violent in his feelings since he was fated to die a virgin. In Leopardi, fear was still stronger than desire, and, besides, he dared not run the risk of being repulsed. The beautiful Fanny infinitely preferred the virile Ranieri to the melancholy *gobbetto*. Leopardi, all humility, soon came to see that the rôle of confidant between his friend and the woman he loved, was better suited to his weakness than that of lover. A shared jealousy of Ranieri's mistress, *Lenina*, became a link between him and *Aspasia*. It did not amount to much, but "love and death", as he wrote to Fanny, "are the most beautiful things in all the world, and alone worthy of our desires. Farewell, my charming and delicious Fanny. I scarcely venture to ask what orders you would give me, knowing, as I do, that I am good for nothing."

These lamentable loves were sublimated by Leopardi in tragic poems: *Il Pensiero Dominante: Amore e Morte* (translated by Sainte-Beuve) and *Consalvo*, in which the sad adventure with Fanny Targioni is thinly disguised. Its end was sudden. The plot hatched between Giacomo and Fanny to detach Ranieri from Lenina had resulted in a few small favours being granted to the poor hunchback. Leopardi to Ranieri: "Fanny is more than ever yours . . . She has taken recently to giving me a little fondling, so that I may plead her cause with you—for which task *sum paratus*." Then, all of a sudden, complete silence, final rupture. What had happened? Had a definite liaison between Fanny and Ranieri been established, or had the latter stormed off in a rage because all Florence was laughing at this three-cornered situation? All we know is that there was an active correspondence between them, and that Fanny asked: "How is our poor Leopardi? I am in his bad books, am I not?"—and that Leopardi said good-bye to the romance in a poem: *To Himself*.

When Ranieri went back to Florence and saw for himself what a deplorable moral and physical state Leopardi was in, he declared that he would take him to Naples, whither he was now permitted to return. There the "angelic Paolina" would look after them: the sun would soon put Giacomo to rights, and a new life would begin. So far as the Ranieri brother and sister were concerned, the programme was duly carried out. For four years they surrounded the sick man with an atmosphere of tender solicitude. But it became more and more difficult to live with Leopardi. Owing to the weakness of his eyes he was for ever calling upon somebody to read to him. A victim to insomnia, he needed a companion to share his sleepless nights. His constant craving for sugar and ices made a heavy drain on the inadequate domestic budget. He insisted that his cakes should be supplied by one especial confectioner — Vito Pinto. Meanwhile, his various ailments, asthma, breathlessness, enterocolitis, were becoming more acute. The displacement of the thorax put a heavy strain on his already exhausted heart.

In 1836, Ranieri's brother-in-law lent him a villa which he owned on the slopes of Vesuvius, at Torre del Greco. Leopardi loved this landscape which the lava flow had made desolate. On the flanks of the formidable mountain grew golden broom. In the courage shown by this vegetation which flourished under the constant threat of eruptions, the poet saw a symbol of human life. Are we not, all of us, constantly clinging to the side of a volcano, exposed to the fierce hostility of nature? Does not man's greatness lie in looking his terrible destiny in the face rather than seeking comfort in illusions? That the poet, knowing himself to be under sentence of death, can still produce his golden blossoms shows a high degree of heroism. While at Torre del Greco, Leopardi wrote two great poems: *La Ginestra* (The Broom) and *Il tramonto della luna* (The Setting of the Moon):

> The moon sinks, and colour is drained
> From the world. . . .

These verses contain the essence of Leopardi: *Desire lives on though hope is dead.*

In 1837 an epidemic of cholera swept through Naples, but Leopardi, in his refuge at Torre del Greco, died of endocarditis. Speaking to Ranieri on the day of his death, he said suddenly:

"How is it that Leibnitz, Newton, Columbus, Petrarch and Tasso all believed in the Catholic religion, though to us the doctrines of the Church can bring no satisfaction?"

"No doubt", replied Ranieri, "it would be better to believe, but if our reason turns its back on faith, are we to blame?"

"But the reason of those great men did not turn its back," said Leopardi.

A silence followed. In a voice so weak that Ranieri could scarcely hear the words, he dictated the last six lines of *Il Tramonto della luna*. They were filled with a poignant beauty. That evening, while Paolina was holding his head in her arms, and wiping the sweat of the last agony from his face, he opened his eyes very wide, said "I cannot see you", and ceased to breathe.

5

At Recanati, the news of his death reached Count Monaldo at the moment when the *carabinieri* had just brought back his youngest son, Francesco, from an escapade which had taken the form of an elopement with the cook's daughter. It should not have been difficult to foresee that the educational methods in force at the Palazzo Leopardi would inevitably result in something of the kind. Monaldo ordered ten masses to be said each year for the soul of his eldest son, after which he never again mentioned Giacomo's name. As to the Countess Adelaïda, when, ten years later, one of Leopardi's admirers, after looking long at a portrait of the poet, said earnestly: "How happy must she be who gave him birth", she raised her eyes to heaven and murmured: "May God forgive him!"

Paolina Leopardi was the only one of the family who felt any real sorrow. As edition after edition of her brother's books was published posthumously, she had to hide them away in the "Hell" of the family library, the cupboard in which the "bad books" lived. Her parents brought all her marriage plans to nothing. Up till the age of fifty she was never allowed out of the house unless accompanied by a duenna and followed by a man-servant in livery. At seventy-seven, an orphan at last, she ventured to make the journey to Naples for the purpose of seeing Giacomo's grave. As an old woman she fell into her mother's cheese-paring habits, and used the same metal ring for measuring eggs. Carlo ended his life in a similar routine of squalid avarice, lending money at so usurious a rate of interest that his fellow-citizens stoned the coffin on the day of his funeral, took off the lid and pulled the corpse's whiskers.

As time went on Giacomo's fame shone with an ever-increasing radiance. His spiritual and physical agonies had inspired some of the loveliest poems in the world. "Sombre lover of death, poor Leopardi," wrote Musset. In 1848, the young Neapolitans, still suffering under the yoke of tyranny, visited his grave and, in hushed voices recited his hymns to Liberty. When Italian unity was at last achieved, it was those same poems that came to the lips of men like Carducci, who remembered how, as children, they had read them, trembling with emotion. The places which Leopardi had loved, and had celebrated in immortal verse, now bore the names that he had given them. One can still see at Recanati, the Hill of the Infinite, and, at Naples, the Villa of the Golden Broom. His body was moved from the church of San Vitale to a small Roman monument which, so tradition has it, is Virgil's tomb. There, on a high cliff, poor Leopardi found at last "the more than human silence and the profound repose" which he had valued more than life.

CHAPTER X

TOLSTOY
and Married Life

ONE COULD bring together in a single volume the stories in which, at two periods of his life, far removed from one another, Tolstoy embodied his views on the subject of conjugal love. True, in several pages of *War and Peace* and *Anna Karenina* also he dealt with this great subject. But it is the sole theme of *The Kreutzer Sonata* and *Family Happiness*, to the second of which he added a postscript which casts a harsh but revealing light on the nature of Tolstoy's sexual morality in his later years. To us it seems to have been exacting and inhuman, but before we can hope to understand how it came to be what it was, it is necessary to establish a relationship between fiction and reality, and to "place" these two books within the framework of the author's life.

If we try to imagine what Leo Nicolaïevitch Tolstoy was like as a young man, we have to take into account a number of characteristics the co-existence of which in a single human being is surprising. By instinct he was a moral man, or, rather, he wanted to be. But an exceptionally virile temperament made him feel a constant and frantic craving for sexual indulgence. In Saint Petersburg he spent his evenings in the company of beautiful gypsy girls. As an officer, he lusted after Cossack women, and, on his country estate, where he was lord and master, he seduced the peasant wenches. In his Journal the same entry occurs over and over again: "I must have a woman. My sensuality does not give me a moment's peace." But even when he was yielding to his fierce onsets of desire, the moralist in him was up in arms. He resented the influence which women had over him. Round about his thirtieth year, he began to think that marriage was the only way of reconciling his insatiable craving for the female body with his horror of sin.

Could he hope to attract a young girl? He was not good-looking. There was something faun-like about his face, and his rather loutish behaviour made him lacking in charm. He had the head of an Old Testament prophet, "the look of a man", said Suarez, "who has seen God in the burning bush." When he contradicted, which he seemed to do on principle, it was always with extreme violence. Fanaticism and good manners have always made bad bedfellows. He was passionate rather than polite, and his fits of rage were terrible. But he was Count Tolstoy, the owner of a great estate, Yasnaya Polyana, and, above all, he had genius. His first writings had astonished and enchanted the literary world. This combination of qualities might well tempt a woman. Nevertheless, the prospect of playing the part of a serious lover made him hesitate. At thirty he felt that he was already old. How could he offer a heart exhausted by a life of debauchery to an innocent young girl dreaming of a pure and uncomplicated happiness? How could he persuade her to live shut away with him in the country? If she should want to live in Saint Petersburg or Moscow, how could he bear to see her, without jealousy, surrounded by

THE ART OF WRITING

men with whose desires and habits he was only too familiar?

It was these fears that inspired him, in 1860, to write *Family Happiness*. The hero, Serge Mihailovitch, a man no longer young, falls in love with his seventeen-year-old ward. Masha, scarcely more than a child, and proud to think that she has inspired passion in a man whom she has always respected, leads him on to declare his love, and marries him. At first they are happy, but their happiness is selfish and they are completely forgetful of the duties which they owe to others. A little later, the young bride begins to find country life irksome, and complains that one whole side of her husband is shut away from her. In the hope of distracting her, he takes her to the city, where she has a tremendous success, for she is beautiful. Serge Mihailovitch grows jealous. His unwarranted suspicions are offensive to her. She begins to criticize him, and that is the end of their happiness. Each has formed a false idea of the other. He thinks that she is frivolous and needs to live a social existence. She thinks that he is absurdly irritable, and that she must handle him with care if she is to avoid rubbing him up the wrong way. From then on, there is no more frankness or gaiety between them, and a moment comes when, time and children helping, they forget the passionate love which once had brought them so much pleasure and so much pain.

"From that moment", says Masha, "our romance was at an end. . . . Love of my children and of their father meant the beginning of a new sort of life and of a different kind of happiness." This different happiness is family happiness, and Tolstoy is already coming to the conclusion that it must be cleansed of the poison of passion.

[214]

He thinks that this change from love to a conjugal companionship is possible. The man who now embraces Masha is no longer a lover but an old husband. She is conscious of a great sense of relief. She feels as though she has been liberated from a form of constraint which we are left to guess was sensuality, though Tolstoy, on the last page of the book, which is gentle, beautiful and resigned, does not say so, as he was later to do, so crudely, in *The Kreutzer Sonata*. The reason is that the two books were separated by twenty-five years of his own married life, which had been, if not a total failure, at least a painful and incessant struggle. "When", he said, "I speak of how two married persons ought to live, I do not for a moment claim that I have lived, or am capable of living, in that way. On the contrary, I know from personal experience how married life should be lived, just because I have lived it as I should not."

Leo Tolstoy had long known the family of Dr Behrs, to which Sonia Behrs belonged. She was at least sixteen years his junior. The Behrs had always hoped that her elder sister, Lisa, would be his choice. But it was not long before he fell in love with the younger girl, who was tall, dark, had a figure which was well set off by her close-fitting jersey, and seemed to be saying, "Take me and not the other." He has painted a self-portrait of the man he thought himself to be at that time, in three of his characters: Levin, in *Anna Karenina:* Bezoukhov, in *War and Peace*, and Posdnicheff, in *The Kreutzer Sonata*. Of the three, Levin, probably, is closest to the real Tolstoy, and the romantic scene of the betrothal of Levin and Kitty is an exact description of the author's own. Like Levin, too, Tolstoy, actuated by moral scruple and, perhaps, by an unconscious sadism, believed it to be his duty to give his affianced bride a Journal to read, in which he confessed the sins of his youth, with particular emphasis on his abandonment of a servant-girl who had been his mistress. Sonia Behrs cried a good deal and wondered how long she would be able to keep the love of such a man. The marriage, however, went forward.

In spite of the scenes and the dramas which must have been constantly blazing up throughout their married life, it would be far from the truth to represent that life as being a dead loss. Very soon a strong physical bond developed between husband and wife. In vain did each of them, though for different reasons, assert that sensual love is not love at all. Neither was ever unfaithful to the other, and Tolstoy, even at an advanced age, still found his wife desirable. Though she was sometimes frightened by the demands made upon her by so astonishing and lasting a virility, she was also flattered. In her Journal she wrote that the physical act of love never gave her any pleasure, but she showed too much jealousy for us to conclude that she was entirely apathetic. "I love to look at her lying with her head thrown back," says Tolstoy, "and to see her passionate face, the serious, frightened, passionate face of a child."

Work was another bond. Sonia Tolstoy was a wonderful source of inspiration to her husband, and it is to her that we owe the great masterpieces. Before her, and after her (for towards the end she lost her influence over him) Tolstoy had dissipated his energies in edifying tasks. It was she who made of him what he was, a novelist. She encouraged him to write *War and Peace* and provided him with much wonderful material for the book. With patience and courage she copied, many times over, the whole of that gigantic work, at a time, too, when she was further engaged in bearing and tending thirteen children, in running her house and in managing the estate. She was, as she said with an entrancing show of pride when her husband embarked on *Anna Karenina*, a true author's wife: "Yesterday, Levotchka suddenly started to work on a novel. . . . It makes me so happy."

That is enough to make us feel deeply grateful to her. In other ways, however, she was in a state of permanent conflict with him. Tolstoy thought that it was his duty as a Christian to live a life of poverty, to hand over his property to the peasants, and to refuse to copyright his books. He blamed his wife for making him live in luxury, with numerous servants, and for letting the children get up plays when the world was filled with slums and prisons and penal settlements.

"All this is very fine and noble," write the Countess to her sister, "and I cannot but feel how far below his level I am. . . . But, unfortunately, life makes demands upon us, and the disagreement between us is too fundamental to admit of remedy."

What remedy could there be? The children had got to be educated. Tolstoy was always filling his house with friends. Visitors became more and more numerous and Sonia had to provide them with beds and food. Sometimes he realized, for a moment, how unfair this double attitude of his was to her, and said: "I feel very guilty about the way I treat you, my dear." But more often than not he reverted to the view which he had held as a young man: that woman is the tempter who delivers man over to his worst instincts; that a married man is only half a man.

There was a further grievance. She was impatient, jealous and irascible almost to the point of madness. She several times threatened to kill herself. Then, after a succession of violent scenes, there was a physical reconciliation, as a result of which both felt ashamed. Tolstoy went so far as to wonder whether his wife's hysteria might not be due to a form of nervous exacerbation connected with too intense a sexual life. Was it reasonable to expect a woman who was always either pregnant or nursing, and weighed down by domestic responsibilities, to be a mistress as well? But that was what he had done all his life, and was still doing at the age of sixty. Was it not his duty to live with his wife in a state of chastity? It was over this question that he was brooding in 1888, and it was from these painful lucubrations that *The Kreutzer Sonata* emerged.

The subject of the novel is announced in the epigraph, taken from St Matthew: *I say unto you, that whosoever looketh on a woman to lust after her hath committed adultery with her already in his heart.* Even when that woman is his own wife. "The worst form of lust is married lust," he said, anticipating Bernard Shaw's epigram: "Marriage is popular because it combines the maximum of temptation with the maximum of opportunity." The postscript further presses the thesis which has been sustained throughout the book, for *The Kreutzer Sonata* is nothing if not a novel with a purpose. What Tolstoy says in it, in effect, is:

(*a*) That men argue wrongly when they say that an intense sexual life is necessary for the preservation of health. A wife should give herself only for the purpose of having children, that is to say (taking the nursing period into account) every two years. A man should, and can be, content with this without any damage resulting to his nervous and physical balance.

(b) That we do wrong to disguise in a cloud of poetry the animal side of physical passion: we are pigs, not poets, and it is well that we should recognize that fact.

(c) That the value attached to love and to woman in her rôle as an instrument of pleasure, is the principal cause of debauchery and idleness. There is nothing sublime about the physical act of love. On the contrary, it is an obstacle to the sublime.

(d) That the perpetual exacerbation of the senses produced by the reading of novels and poetry inevitably leads the wife into adultery and the husband into jealousy.

The Kreutzer Sonata is an illustration of these themes. The idea of it came to Tolstoy in 1887. At first the book did not bear this title, and the lover was a painter, not a musician. Was it a deliberate criticism aimed by Tolstoy at his own married life? This he denied. He says in his Journal:

"Many of the ideas to which I have given expression, are not mine at all. . . . The underlying idea of the novel came from a Slav lady who had written me a letter about the enslavement of women brought about by their sexual duties. My comment on the statement in St Matthew's Gospel about adultery, to the effect that it does not refer only to other men's wives, was supplied by an Englishman." It seems that he himself was surprised by the bitterness and cruelty of the story: "Now that I fully understand the ideas which it contains, they seem to me strange and unintentional.

I sometimes think that I hold these opinions only because I am an old man."

But he must, at least temporarily, have entertained such feelings. Otherwise he could not have depicted them so strongly.

Not unnaturally, Countess Tolstoy was horrified by the book. It was, she said, "disgusting". She found too much of their own life in it: and her modesty was outraged. In 1887, she got her husband to agree that it should be laid aside and not published. Then, one evening in 1889, the Tolstoys had among their guests a famous painter, Ilia Jefimovitch Repin, and the great actor, Andreyev Burlak. Tolstoy's eldest son (Serge) and a violinist, played Beethoven's *Kreutzer Sonata*. Tolstoy was completely bowled over, and said to Repin: "I am going to write a story about that sonata. You shall illustrate it and Burlak shall read it aloud." It was then that he changed the hero into a musician. The Censor forbade the publication of the book, but readings of it were given in Saint Petersburg and Moscow. They aroused tremendous interest. People said, when they met, "Do you know *The Kreutzer Sonata*?"

Sonia Tolstoy was afraid that the jealousy of the central character might be attributed to her husband, and thought it necessary to justify herself for the sake of her children. So she, too, wrote an autobiographical novel, *Whose was the Fault?*, in which a gay and pious young woman of noble birth becomes engaged to a prince who is a sensual brute. When he goes walking with his fiancée, he is continually gazing at her breasts and her legs, and undressing her in imagination. No sooner is she married than she is disgusted by the exclusively physical love which he demands of her. Then a painter appears on the scene who offers her love of a different kind, romantic and sentimental. The husband, a savage and jealous animal, kills the painter, although his relationship with the wife has been entirely innocent.

Friends of the family dissuaded the Countess from publishing the book. The affair caused her much suffering. She wrote in her Journal:

"I feel in my heart that it (Leo's book) is aimed at me. I have been deeply hurt and made to look ridiculous in the eyes of the whole world. All possibility of love between us has been destroyed. If those who read *The Kreutzer Sonata* had the slightest idea of the sort of erotic life he leads, which alone can make him happy and gay, they would throw down this little tin god from the pedestal on which they have set him. Yet, I love him best when he is like that, normal and weak. To be sure, it is not a good thing to be an animal, but it is even less good to preach principles which you cannot act upon."

Then, since people continued to see in the novel a picture of the Tolstoys' married life, she decided to seek an audience of the Czar, and persuade him to lift the interdict. "If the book had been really written about me, then, obviously, I should not have asked its publication to be authorized. My action will be interpreted as a denial." The Emperor received her politely. She told him that the interdict was preventing Tolstoy from working, and was therefore depriving the world of another *War and Peace*. Alexander III, who admired Tolstoy though he feared his influence, and would have much preferred him to write novels instead of pamphlets, gave his consent to the inclusion of *The Kreutzer Sonata* in the Complete Works. This success satisfied the wife's pride. But the author was annoyed. "I now feel only disgust for the book," he said. For a few days in December 1890 the Countess feared that she was again pregnant. Everyone, she thought sadly, will laugh, and say: "*That* is the real postscript to *The Kreutzer Sonata!*"

But Tolstoy's personal inability to observe the chastity which he preached, in no way weakened his beliefs. The compass shows the line a ship should follow. For accidental reasons, storms or damage, the ship may deviate from that line, but that does not mean that the compass was wrong and ought to be scrapped.

> "One should keep only one end in view, to achieve the greatest possible degree of chastity compatible with one's character, one's temperament and the conditions of one's life, past and present, not as other men see it, for they know nothing of the nature of the struggle, but as one sees it oneself, and as it appears in the eyes of God. . . . Then, the temptation and even the fall show only as stages on the road to an eternal goal—to get rid of bestiality and to draw nearer to God."

Let me conclude by summarizing these two books. Tolstoy, like Pascal, knew that men are neither wholly angels nor wholly beasts. We have a body, and to attempt, as certain religious sects in Russia have attempted, to suppress the sexual instinct by castration, is an act of cowardice (formally condemned by the Church). We must live in accordance with the human condition as ordained by God. But, if the mutual attraction of the sexes is a law of nature, it can assume a

[222]

spiritual form, and that is more valuable than the purely physical. When a man marries, he must ask himself: "What chance is there that this woman will help me to live a human and not a bestial life?" A woman in the state of matrimony must be a mother and not a mistress, except within certain strictly defined limits of passionate love. One must marry as one must die, since one cannot do otherwise. "His disciples say unto Him, if the case of a man be so with his wife, it is not good to marry." And He answered them and said: "All men cannot receive this saying, save they to whom it is given."

This is a mysterious and beautiful statement which is also perfectly applicable to the absolute, surprising and profound ideas held by Tolstoy on the subject of married life.

CHAPTER XI

THE ART AND THE PHILOSOPHY OF
ANTON TCHEKOV

THOSE WHO would understand Tchekov the man, should not think of him as he appears in his later portraits. The drawn, tired face, the lack-lustre eyes behind their pince-nez, the bourgeois chin-tuft, are not the real Tchekov but the physical consequence of exhaustion, sickness and approaching death. It is better that we should see him as he was at twenty, with frank and courageous eyes looking fearlessly at the world around him. He had already endured much suffering from which he had emerged considerably strengthened. No more honest mind has ever observed the spectacle of mankind. He was a great artist, one of the very greatest of all times and of all lands, admired by Tolstoy, and, by reason of the musical delicacy of his emotions, reminiscent of Chopin. But he was more than an artist; he was a man who, without being dogmatic, revealed, taught and practised a way of living and thinking which was heroic without ever being pretentious, and well suited to keep hope alive even in moments of despair. He read and admired Marcus Aurelius, and was worthy to be his disciple, though he would never have allowed anybody to tell him so. Modesty was his only weakness.

ANTON TCHEKOV

I

Anton Pavlovitch Tchekov had a childhood which was
no childhood. He was born in 1860 at Taganrog, a "dull
little town" which owed its existence to the thieving
nomads of the steppe and to a succession of Greek
pirates, where his father carried on business as a grocer.
His grandfather was a serf, and had been liberated in
1841. His father had been able, with his savings, to
set up shop, after first marrying the daughter of a
cloth merchant. She was gentle, melancholy, and was
adored by her children. He was a man who inspired
terror and asserted himself by beating his sons and his
assistants alike. But with his savagery he combined a
strong feeling for art. He loved music, conducted the
church choir, and painted icons. Tchekov said, later:
"We owe our gifts to our father, our capacity for feeling
to our mother."

The family consisted of five sons and a daughter.
When their father was absent, the sons had to look after
the shop. One day, Anton had just started on a piece of
Latin translation when the door opened. "I'm going out,"
said his father, "get down to the shop." The little boy's
eyes filled with tears: "The shop's icy, and I've got some
homework to do for tomorrow." "You can do it in the
shop: no dawdling!" He had to do as he was told, and
spent hours sitting on a soap box with a bottle of frozen
ink in front of him. In this way did the most honest
writer who ever lived learn, while still very young, and
by the big stick method, all the shifts and dodges of
small-scale commercial dishonesty.

Then there were the choir practices at which he had
to sing "Glory everlasting" and "Thy House, O Lord."

His father was very religious and was for ever crossing himself in front of the icons. Everyone trembled before him. When he beat the children, their gentle mother tried to protest. "It's how I was brought up," he would say, "and you can see for yourself that I'm making my own way in the world. A man who's been well thrashed is worth two of him as hasn't." From this form of upbringing Anton Tchekov also learned compassion. In the shop he got to know men of all races and all trades, and, at church, priests, whose special vocabulary he stored away in his mind. A precious apprenticeship, this, though he did not know it, for a writer of fiction.

Even slaves have their moments of gaiety, and the Tchekov children flourished, ill-treated though they were. They had the gift of mimicry (which is drama in an embryonic form) and a sense of humour. Even at the age of fifteen Anton was already contributing to the school magazine, and combining with his young friends in the writing of farcical sketches. In fact, like most people, he lived simultaneously on two levels, the comic and the tragic. In 1876 his father's business took a turn for the worse. The Taganrog house had to be sold, and the family moved to Moscow: all of them, that is, except Anton, who stayed behind to finish his schooling, paying the costs of his education by giving lessons. The sale of his childhood's home was a sad blow to him, and a distant echo of the pain he felt sounds in *The Cherry Orchard*.

Suffering breeds precocity. Anton ransacked the great books of the world in an attempt to find some reason for believing in his dignity as a human being, in spite of humiliations. At sixteen, he was writing to his brother:

"I have been reading *Don Quixote* (it is a splendid book and was written by Cervantes who is generally regarded as the equal of Shakespeare). I recommend our brothers to read *Hamlet* and Turgenev's *Don Quixote* if they have not already done so."

And again:

"Dear brother Misha, I have received your letter. . . . The handwriting is good and there is not a single mistake in grammar. But there was one thing about it that I did not like: why do you sign yourself 'your insignificant little brother'? . . . In God's eyes, yes, but not in the eyes of men. In dealing with one's fellows one should be conscious of one's own dignity—"

which shows that the adolescent Tchekov was already Tchekovian.

In 1879 he joined his family in Moscow, and began to work as a medical student. Things were in a bad way. There was no money. One of his brothers had become consumptive and was spitting blood. What was to be done? He tried his hand at writing comic stories for the newspapers.

"I wrote as naturally as a bird sings. I just sat down and the writing came. How, or about what, did not bother me. It just came of itself. To write an essay, a story, a short sketch, caused me no trouble at all. Like a calf or a foal let loose in a green and sunlit field, I jumped and sweated, flicking my tail and waggling my head in the funniest way. I laughed and made those round me laugh."

He did his writing in abominable conditions. In the room next door a child was squalling. There was a fellow-student sitting on the bed and talking medicine. In another room his father was reading aloud to his mother. But Tchekov sold his articles and stories. He did not get much for them, three or four roubles, and sometimes an editor would say: "There's nothing in the till: would you like a theatre ticket or a pair of trousers?" It was not long, however, before he was making a hundred roubles a month, and keeping the whole family. He signed his stories "Anton Tchekonté", not valuing them sufficiently to use his real name. When he tried to be more ambitious, the editors protested.

"You tell me," he wrote, "that my *Willow Tree* and my *Thief* are a bit too serious. . . . But I can't help thinking that something short and serious—a hundred lines or so—wouldn't do the readers any harm. To be perfectly frank I find it hard work always trying to be funny."

Meanwhile he was working hard at his medical studies. One can never too often stress the part played by medicine in Tchekov's life. It taught him to have a respect for facts. He always had a great contempt for writers who could not think scientifically, that is to say, who would not see things as they are, but only as they wanted to see them, or were frightened of seeing otherwise. If he had not been a great writer, he would have been an excellent doctor. He had a firm belief in medicine, and was angry with Zola for treating it with scorn in *Dr Pascal*. "This fellow Zola", he said to Kuprin, "knows nothing whatever about it. He just sits in his study and invents. I wish he'd come here and see how our country doctors live and what they do for the poor." Later on, there were always overworked and sympathetic doctors in his plays.

But, above all, he made a man of himself.

"Somebody ought to write a story about a young man, the grandson of a serf, who has served in a shop, sung in the choir and been brought up to kiss the priest's hand and to be grateful for a scrap of bread, who has been beaten, and has enjoyed dining with his rich relations, and has lived as a hypocrite in the eyes of God and men—and then show how that young man forces out the slave in himself, drop by drop, and then wakes one fine morning with the consciousness that he no longer has the blood of a slave in his veins, but only the blood of a real man."

In 1884 he got his medical diploma. His stories were now having a genuine success. Then, suddenly, in 1886 an incredible and wonderful surprise came his way. A letter reached him from a writer who enjoyed a high reputation, Grigorovitch. The letter was full of praise: it was fine and generous.

"You have a real talent which sets you high above the writers of the younger generation. I am sixty-five, but my love of literature is still so strong, that, having come across someone with a gift that is genuinely alive and vigorous, I could not resist the temptation of writing to you, and extending the hand of friendship."

Tchekov replied at once. "My wonderful, my dearly loved bearer of good news, your letter made me feel as though I had been struck by lightning. I very nearly burst into tears." He went on to explain that he had been scribbling away too quickly for the newspapers,

THE ART OF WRITING

because he had had no faith in his own work. "And then came your letter, and I suddenly felt how important it was for me to get out of my rut without losing a moment." Both the letters should be read in their entirety. There is nothing finer than an elderly master without jealousy, and a young master without presumption. Like Tchekov, I feel as though I could cry from sheer admiration. There is nothing I love more than proof of generosity of mind.

Grigorovitch had spoken about Tchekov to Suvorin, the editor of the *Novoié Vremya*, who not only published him, but became his friend, and strongly urged him to give up medicine.

Tchekov to Suvorin: "You advise me not to hunt two hares at the same time, and to think no more of my work as a doctor. But I really do not see why one should not hunt two hares at the same time, even in the quite literal sense. I feel more confident, and more satisfied with myself when I think that I have two professions instead of only one. Medicine is my lawful wife, literature my mistress. When I am tired of the one, I spend a night with the other."

In 1885 he was living in a village and actively working as a doctor in a local hospital. There, as formerly in his father's shop, he made contact with patients of every class and every calling. The profession of medicine, like that of a lawyer's clerk (Balzac) or a newspaper reporter (Dickens) is of great benefit to the novelist. "Medicine has had a great influence on my literary work. It has much enlarged my field of observation. . . . Familiarity with the natural sciences and with scientific methods has always put me on my guard against spurious inventiveness."

ANTON TCHEKOV

Since he had been working for Suvorin, whose paper was extremely influential, he had been not only better paid but better advised.

"We spent the whole day talking, and the whole night, too. . . . Suvorin is really *flair* personified. He is a great chap. He plays exactly the same rôle in literature as the setter who puts up grouse. What I mean is that he works with his diabolical *flair* and is always on fire with enthusiasm. . . . He is intuitive, and for that reason his scent is as keen as a dog's."

At twenty-eight, the grocer's son was already a famous writer. He had published several volumes of short stories, and had written a play, *Ivanov*. In 1888 he was awarded the Pushkin Prize.

Tchekov to Suvorin: "The news about the prize has had an extraordinary effect upon me. . . . For the last few days I have been like a man in love. My father and my mother are almost out of their minds with delight. My sister is for ever running round to all her friends, very ambitious and excited. Jean S—— talks about the Iagos of the literary world, and warns me that my five hundred roubles are bound to make me five hundred enemies."

Ivanov enjoyed a respectable success, but Tchekov was beginning to bring a stern critical eye to bear upon himself:

"The execution is worthless. I ought to have waited. I am glad that I did not listen to Grigorovitch when he advised me to write a novel. I can just imagine how much excellent material I should have made a hash of!

'Talent and freshness', he said, 'will carry everything before them.' But there's something else needed, which is no less important. One's got to be mature, and one *must* have a feeling of personal liberty."

About this time he went through a phase of Tolstoyan moralizing. In 1890 he paid a visit to the Island of Sakhalin to see for himself the conditions in which the convicts lived—a project with the true Tolstoy hallmark. He had to cross Siberia in mud and dust. He was appalled by what he found at Sakhalin. "This is a pilgrimage that everyone should make, as all Turks go to Mecca." If one is to remain wise and just it is essential that one should have first-hand knowledge of human suffering. But Tchekov was very different from Tolstoy. Tolstoy was always looking for scapegoats: Tchekov confined himself to saying, "That's how things are", and then looking for a remedy. He already knew that he was a very sick man. When he put his handkerchief to his lips it was often spotted with blood when he took it away. But he refused to see a specialist. Of what use would it be? He had made his own diagnosis.

Now that he had a little money he bought a property at Melikhovo, not far from Moscow, where he lived until 1898, working and coughing. His family joined him there. He doctored the peasants, had schools built at his own expense, and produced a great many stories. In 1892 he put up a brave fight against the cholera epidemic. Many charming women, actresses and poets, came out to see and make much of him. But their whims and fancies got on his nerves. To one of them he wrote: "You feel no need for regular employment. That is why you are ailing, why you feel fed up, and whine. The cholera is already in Moscow. Look after yourself, my little goldilocks, and don't irritate me with your laziness."

To Suvorin: "Friendship is superior to love. My friends are fond of me, and I of them. Through me they are fond of one another. But love makes enemies of those who love the same woman." Yet few writers have written better about love. Ill-health made it necessary for him to live a life of chastity, and his art to flee from those *misunderstood women* who are always such terrible time-wasters. At Melikhovo he enjoyed entertaining his pretty women friends who were brimming over with vitality, as actresses so often are. With them he planted and weeded, for he was a passionate gardener. He loved the sweet smell of flowers, the white and pink apple blossom and the songs of birds. Like all country houses, Melikhovo had two defects: family and guests. A third was added to these by the sick and ailing of the neighbourhood whom he treated free of charge. Nevertheless, while living there he produced a series of masterpieces: long short stories, short novels (*Three Years*, *My Life*) and plays (*The Seagull*, *Uncle Vanya*).

But, like one of the characters in *The Seagull*, he suffered from the feeling that he had got to go on writing, writing, writing. He took a few trips abroad, sold Melikhovo and bought, at Yalta in the Crimea, a plot of rocky waste-land on which he built a house and made a garden. The climate of the Crimea was generally considered to be good for consumptives. Tchekov had no affection for Yalta, but he was proud of his garden. Where once there had been nothing but stony earth and wild flowers, he had conjured into existence a civilized and lovely spot. "In three or four hundred years, you know," he said to Kuprin, "the earth will be transformed into a flowering garden, and life will be astonishingly easy and pleasant."

Nearly all his plays, in spite of their overriding melancholy, end with some such promise of a golden age. As the believer looks forward to a paradise in which all the injustices of this world will be redressed, so did Tchekov who, agnostic though he was, felt a strong nostalgia for the religious atmosphere of his childhood, look forward to a wiser race of men, and a future of reparation for all the miseries of which he had been the witness and the victim.

He had at last discovered a theatrical company capable of interpreting his plays—Stanislavski's Moscow Art Theatre. There, all of them, from *The Seagull* to *The Cherry Orchard*, were admirably mounted and performed. There, too, he found a wife, the actress, Olga Knipper, who had taken a leading part in all his productions, a wonderfully good and valiant woman from whom, however, he was constantly separated, because she had to play in Moscow whereas the state of his health kept him, except for a few short journeys, tied down at Yalta. "If you fear solitude, don't get married," he said.

To Yalta came a number of great writers: Tolstoy, Gorki, Bunin and Kuprin. When he went to Moscow he was fêted so often and so well that he was quite worn out. He always stayed at the Bolshoï Moskovsky Hotel, and the news of his arrival quickly spread through the city. He was invited to dinners and theatres, but the impression he always made on people was that of a remote spectator, of an adult playing with children. From behind the mask of his pince-nez and his humorous smile, melancholy and aloofness showed. He wore a charm on his watch chain inscribed with the following words: "For the solitary man all the world is a desert."

Once, when a birthday party was to be given for Grigorovitch, the old writer who had discovered Tchekov, the latter explained that he would be leaving Moscow before the time of the dinner. "But that's impossible! Think of it—Grigorovitch . . . the famous letter. . . . Your absence would be taken very badly!"

"Yet, it should be easy enough to understand," said Tchekov. "I was discovered by Grigorovitch, and so, shall be expected to make a speech. It would be in the worst possible taste if I did not. But if I did, my voice would be expected to tremble, and my eyes to fill with tears. . . . Then, Grigorovitch would get to his feet and come to me with his arms spread wide to embrace me, and crying with emotion. Like all old writers he enjoys crying. . . . That is his own affair. The point is that I should have to cry too, and I don't know how."

This was not just a joke: anything that was not perfectly natural caused him genuine pain. When, after the triumphal first night of *The Cherry Orchard* he had to submit to a spate of congratulatory speechifying, he was obviously suffering agonies of embarrassment. It was in 1904, and he was a dying man. His tightly buttoned overcoat, the brooding look in his eyes, his way of turning the conversation when it touched on his health, everything about him went to show that he knew how ill he was.

"It is terrible to become *nothing*," he said. "They take you to the cemetery and then go back to drink tea and say a lot of hypocritical things about you. . . . *They'll* all go on living—even that mangy dog, if the police don't pick it up. . . . And I shall be lying there in smug tranquillity. . . . You see, I do so want to live, to write something great, really great!"

In the spring of 1904, the doctors sent him to Germany, to Baden-Baden in the Black Forest. Olga Knipper went with him, and in her company he was almost gay. Only a few hours before his death he made her laugh with a story improvised on the spur of the moment, in which he described a fashionable watering-place full of fat, overfed bankers and red-faced, strapping English and Americans, all with thoughts for nothing but good living. One day, when they return from a walk, looking forward to a tip-top meal, they are suddenly informed that the cook has left, and that there won't be any dinner. He pictured the effect produced on all these pampered visitors by such a mortal blow aimed at their stomachs. "Curled up on a sofa," wrote his wife, "I laughed and laughed. It was a relief from all my recent anxieties. It never so much as occurred to me that in a few hours' time I should be looking at Tchekov's dead body."

He always liked to introduce some trivial detail into a story with a deep, tragic meaning. It was a recall to modesty. His coffin was transported from Germany to Moscow in a green-painted goods wagon with the single word "Oysters" in large letters on the door. This ending to his own story would have pleased him. But even more so, perhaps, a very simple incident recorded by Olga Tchekov.

"The doctor came to see him, and ordered champagne. Anton Pavlovitch sat down and, in a loud, solemn voice, speaking in German, a language of which he knew very little, said: 'Ich sterbe'—I am dying.

Then, raising his glass and turning to me with that wonderful smile of his, added: 'It's a long time since I last tasted champagne.' Then, very calmly, he emptied his glass, turned over on to his left side, and never spoke again. . . . The terrible silence of the night was broken only by a large black moth which hurtled into the room like a whirlwind, and fluttered about, bumping painfully against the electric light bulbs. The doctor went away. The cork shot out of the champagne bottle with a pop which sounded frighteningly loud in the airless, silent darkness. . . . The dawn began to break, and in the new day the chirping of birds and the notes of an organ from a nearby church seemed to be announcing a funeral service. There was a complete absence of human voices, and of all the trivialities of daily life. There was only the beauty, the stillness and the majesty of death."

Olga Knipper, when she wrote those words of perfect simplicity and dignity, showed how worthy she was to have been Tchekov's wife.

2

It is very difficult to speak about Tchekov's art when one has read, in the recollections of those who knew him, the severe things he said about his critics. At first he had been treated as a sort of minor Maupassant, and it is true that in those early days he was writing well-constructed short stories without much depth to them. When he became a great writer, there were many who refused to acknowledge him as such, and this hurt him. He had a complex and basically timid temperament, in addition to which, his finest effects were contrived without his ever "raising his voice", with the result that those who beat the big drum had the advantage of him. "It's always the same old thing," he said, "Korolenko *and* Tchekov: Gorki *and* Tchekov."

Then he got a reputation for gloom: he became the "poet of twilit moods". We know from Bunin how this infuriated him. "*Am* I gloomy? *Am* I a pessimist?"

"Nowadays", Bunin continues, "the exaggeration is all in the other direction. People never get tired of talking about Tchekov's tenderness, Tchekov's warmth. . . . I can just imagine his attitude to all this stuff about tenderness! It is a word that should very rarely be used about his work, and even when it is, only with the greatest caution. He would have found the 'warmth' and the 'melancholy' so often attributed to him, even more disgusting."

Pretentiousness always irritated him. When a friend, who was indulging in a regular bath of self-pity, moaned out: "Tell me, Anton Pavlovitch, what I should do— thinking is driving me mad," he answered: "Drink less vodka." One day, three richly dressed ladies came to see him. After first filling the room with the rustle of their silk skirts and the overpowering smell of their scent, they began to question him about politics. "Anton Pavlovitch, how do you think the war will end?" He coughed, and then said, with a gentle, serious look on his face: "Probably in a peace."

"Yes, of course: but who will win, the Greeks or the Turks?"

"My own opinion is that the strongest side will win."

"But which is the strongest side?"

"The one that is the better fed and the better educated."

"Which do you like best, the Greeks or the Turks?"

He smiled sweetly:

"Personally," he said, "I like stewed fruit . . . what about you?"

He could not bear words like "beautiful", "delectable", "colourful". The affectations of the Moscow modernists made his blood boil. "Decadents, indeed!—they're a lot of strong, healthy young men: what they need is to be sentenced to a few months' hard labour! This new-art business is just a pack of nonsense. I remember seeing a shop sign in Taganrog which said 'Artificial Mineral Waters', which amounts to about the same thing. There's nothing new in art except talent." He would have agreed wholeheartedly with Valéry's maxim: "Nothing ages more quickly than novelty." For the vanity of fools he shared Flaubert's horror, but, whereas Flaubert got angry, Tchekov brought a scholar's penetration to bear, and analysed the causes of stupidity and bombast. "The trouble with Korolenko is that he'll never write better unless he deceives his wife. He's too noble."

It was a favourite saying of his that a man who doesn't work is always conceited and lacking in talent. He himself was always working, even when he was only listening. His notebooks are crammed with subjects caught on the wing. Sometimes he would take one of these books from a drawer, look up with his pince-nez glittering, and wave it in the air: "Precisely one hundred subjects tucked away in here. I'm not like you young fellows. Would you like me to sell you a couple?"

For a subject to interest him, it had to be simple. "A

Professor learns that he has a mortal illness, and keeps a diary of his last months." Out of that he made a masterpiece (*A Dreary Story*). What he liked in it was the contrast between the tragedy and the commonplace nature of the dying man's last activities. Here are some other subjects from the notebooks. "A man who has been run over and lost a leg is worried by the fact that he had twenty-one roubles stuffed in the boot." "X, a former building contractor, sees everything from the point of view of repairs. He chooses a thoroughly healthy woman to be his wife, so as to be sure that he won't have to spend a penny on having her 'done over'. N . . . though enormously fat, takes his fancy because she has a slow and stately walk. All that matters is that she is solidly built." "Title: *Gooseberries*. X . . . works in one of the Ministries. He is a terrible miser and has saved a lot of money. His dream is to get married, to buy a country property, and to doze in the sun. Twenty years, forty years pass. At sixty he is a rich man living in retirement. Through an agent he buys a small property with a pond. Walking round the garden he has a feeling that something is lacking—a gooseberry bed! He gets some plants from a nursery. Two or three years later, by which time he has cancer of the stomach and is near death, he is brought a plateful of his gooseberries. 'How idiotic!' he says, 'to think that's all I've got out of life.' Already, in the next-door room, a niece with a voluminous bosom is ordering some for herself in a peevish voice."

Here are a few more that he used: "A cab-driver who has just lost his son, has to go on working just the same. He tries to speak of his grief to his fares, but finds only indifference." . . . "Some officers on manoeuvres are invited to a house where there are several young women.

One of them kisses one of the officers, a shy and reserved young man, in the dark. He looks for her, but in vain." ... "Some very old men meet. In the life of one of them there has been an extremely serious incident involving a breach of trust. It has been forgotten, and nobody seems to remember it." ... "A very rich woman, who has inherited a large factory, is unhappy and dis-contented. She tries to make contact with the workers, and even thinks that she has fallen in love with one of them. But it comes to nothing, and she takes up again the life she detests. Her young daughter, who is more courageous, runs away to Moscow."

These simple subjects were not invented. "There is nothing in Tchekov's stories", says Gorki, "which cannot be found in the real world. The terrible power of his talent lies precisely in the fact that he invents nothing." He could, like so many others (like Zola and Maupassant, whom in point of fact he admired) have dramatized. But piling on the agony sickened him. "A writer ought to be as objective as a chemist, and have nothing to do with the subjective approach which we most of us make in our every-day lives." He should never sit down to work "until he feels as cold as ice", until he has learned to realize that "manure heaps are perfectably respectable elements in a landscape" and that "evil passions are as integral a part of life as good ones".

Thanks to his labours as a doctor he had had many opportunities of seeing men in moments of crisis and horror. Sickness and poverty are serums of truth. A. Tchekov, the man, had the appearance of "a creature in pain, and often, in his abjection, very close to the animals". He had seen a moujik with his stomach ripped open by a pitchfork, a woman who had thrown boiling water over the child of a hated rival, a little girl who had been made to live in such a state of filth that her ears were full of worms. "When one lives quietly at home", he notes, "life seems ordinary enough, but one has only to go out into the street, to question the women one meets there, to see that it is terrible."

And if life is terrible, how is one to bear it, or make it bearable to others? First, by engaging in works of active compassion. No writer has ever *done* more to help those in distress than Tchekov the doctor and the counsellor. Love gives us some idea of what a better world should be like. The man or woman who loves ceases to be egotistical and self-centred. But there is something even greater than love, and that is truth. One must never lie, and we can only *not* lie if we keep a careful watch over ourselves.

To Bunin he said: "One has got to work, you know . . . without pause or rest . . . all one's life long." Then, after a moment's silence: "My own experience is that once a story has been written, one has to cross out the beginning and the end. It is there that we authors do most of our lying. . . . A piece of writing should be short, as short as possible." Then, suddenly: "It is very difficult to describe the sea. Do you know how I found it described recently in a schoolboy's exercise book? *The sea is big*— just that, and no more. It seemed to me quite admirable."

To somebody else he said: "One must always tear up the first half. I mean that seriously. Young writers begin by, as one says, 'placing the story'—whereas the reader ought, on the contrary, to be able to grasp what it is all about by the way it is told, without any explanations by the author, from the conversation and the actions of the characters. . . . One must ruthlessly suppress everything that is not directly concerned with the subject. If, in the first chapter, you say that there is a gun hanging on the wall, you should make quite sure that it is going to be used further on in the story."

The exacting standards which he applied to his literary work, and his determination never to write anything that was not true, even scientifically true, are very apparent in the relentless way in which he revised and deleted in the last years of his life.

"But," said his friends indignantly, "if one didn't snatch the manuscript out of your hands, there would be nothing left of a story but 'They were young, they were in love, they married and were unhappy'."

"But don't you see," he answered, "that's how things are in real life." He once said: "If I were a millionaire, I would produce works no bigger than the palm of my hand."

He liked to paint his characters and his scenes in a very few strokes. To an actor who was playing Lophakin, the merchant, in *The Cherry Orchard*, he said: "Now listen to me: he doesn't shout, he has yellow shoes": then, pointing to his inside pocket: "And plenty of money, *here*." Similarly, in his stories, he could bring a group of officers to life by giving a single sentence to each one of them. He could conjure up a whole landscape with one carefully observed detail. "You can get the effect of moonlight by saying that a scrap of broken glass was glittering like a tiny star on the path by the mill." Movie directors have made peculiarly their own this method of creating atmosphere by concentrating the camera on the unusual and significant detail.

Explaining why he so much admired and feared Tolstoy, he said: "Just think, it is he who wrote that

Anna felt, and seemed to see, her own eyes shining in the darkness. Quite seriously, he frightens me." Once, when he was getting ready to pay a call on Tolstoy, it took him a whole hour to make up his mind what trousers he should wear. He had taken off his pince-nez and looked much younger. As usual, he interlarded what was seriously on his mind with jokes, and kept on coming out of his bedroom wearing first one pair of trousers, then another. "No, these are almost indecently narrow. If Tolstoy were to see me in these he'd think me no better than I should be." Then he disappeared and emerged a moment later in another pair: "And these arc as wide as the Black Sea: he'd think I was a bit too full of myself" —which was all very Tchekovian, because he was attributing to Tolstoy, not without reason, his own way of interpreting detail.

When his descriptions are developed at greater length, they involve all the senses—sight, smell and hearing.

"In the light of the moon the lime-trees were casting deep shadows, so that the doorways were drowned in darkness. From them came the sound of women talking in low voices, of stifled laughter, of someone playing softly on the balalaika. The air was filled with the scent of limes and beechmast. The murmuring of all those unseen persons, and the smells, jarred on Laptiev. . . . When a man is unhappy, how trivial seem lime-trees and shadows, clouds and the beauties of nature, all of them so self-sufficient and so indifferent to humanity."

True to his principle of the economy of means, he was interested in scenery only as it was reflected in the consciousness of a character. He was concerned to depict, not reality but an impression of reality. Tolstoy, the Tolstoy who 'frightened' him, saw this clearly, as he saw everything.

"I have just been re-reading almost all of Tchekov's works. There is a touch of the marvellous in everything he does. He often says things that are not at all profound, but the effect of the whole is charming. As an artist he cannot be compared with any of the Russian writers of the past, not with Turgenev, not with Dostoievski, not with me. His manner is peculiar to himself: it is the manner of the impressionists. . . . When you watch him at his painting, his brush strokes seem to be entirely unrelated. But when you step back and look at the picture from a distance, the general impression is astonishing."

Fine creative writers are also fine critics. It was true that Tchekov painted, as he talked, by means of discontinuous touches, yet the finished picture was always luminous and irresistible. He was reproached by some for not trying his hand at full-length novels, and deeply regretted his inability to do so. "I have grown used to the short story, composed only of a beginning and an end. I get bored, and begin to repeat myself, when I reach the middle." But he was wrong. His long stories, *Three Years*, *My Life*, *A Sad Story*, are genuine novels, short but perfect. It has been said that they are badly constructed, but I do not agree. They show the gradual change brought about in a situation by time, and also the absurdity of life: one is unhappy, and one thinks that unhappiness will last for ever. Then, quite suddenly, without any explanation, comes happiness—or vice versa. The absurdity of events may be clear enough, but human wisdom tells us that they must be faced and accepted. Not that Tchekov tells us this in so many words: of course he doesn't, for the author has no business to intervene. All the same, the reader is left to guess, in a confused sort of a way, at what lies behind the stories, and that is what gives them their nobility.

3

Tolstoy did not like Tchekov's plays and, knowing this, Tchekov had but one consolation. Tolstoy had said to him: "As you know very well, I cannot stand Shakespeare, but your plays are worse even than his. . . . He does, at least, take the reader by the scruff of the neck and push him forward to a definite end, but where on earth *your* heroes are headed for I don't know."

In telling this anecdote, Anton Pavlovitch would throw back his head and laugh so loudly that the pince-nez fell off his nose.

"Tolstoy has been ill," he went on, "and I went one day to sit with him. Just as I was getting ready to leave, he took my hand, looked me straight in the eyes and said: 'You are a good man, Anton Pavlovitch, a very good man.' Then he smiled, let go of my hand and added: 'That doesn't alter the fact that your plays are bad.'"

Though I feel the highest possible respect for Tolstoy, I am pretty sure that he was wrong, and that Tchekov's plays are, I won't say better than his stories (they could scarcely be that), but just as good. Nor can there be any doubt that they have given an added splendour to his reputation because they have been performed all over

the world, and because the stage speaks more loudly than
the printed word.

The four best known, and deservedly best known, of
his plays are: *The Seagull, Uncle Vanya, The Three
Sisters* and *The Cherry Orchard*. All of them (except
The Three Sisters) are set in the world of country landowners. They present a picture of a bored and collapsing
society. The characters dream of making their escape and
going to Moscow, which they see as a promised land, or
(in the case of *The Cherry Orchard*) to Paris. *The Seagull*
is about art and literature. On the estate of a great actress
live two contrasted types of author: Trepliev, a young
man, searching for new literary forms, but inept and
vain; and Trigorin, an author with an established
reputation, who is a master of his craft, but does not
know how best to turn it to account. There is also Nina,
who feels for the older and famous man a sort of romantic
young girl's passion. She is symbolized as an injured gull
(this is the only Ibsen touch in all Tchekov). But the
gull, in other words Nina, does not die of her injury:
instead, she lives and becomes an actress. "I have come
at last to understand that what is really important in our
job is not the honour and glory I used to dream about,
but the strength to go on and endure. . . . One must
learn to bear one's cross and one must have faith. For
me, who have faith, the suffering is not so great, and
when I think of my vocation I am not afraid of life."

It is Trepliev, the young writer, who dies, by his own
hand, and it is probably true to say that the play is, in
part, autobiographical because there was a good deal of
Trepliev in Tchekov, though it did not outlive his
adolescent years, but was replaced, to some extent, by
Trigorin's technical skill, and by a great deal of Nina's

faith. *The Seagull* is not Tchekov's best play, good though it is: or, rather, it has never really appealed to the general theatre-going public for the simple reason that the discussion of aesthetic problems is not altogether suited to the stage. But artists, and art lovers, have always found it deeply moving.

Uncle Vanya is a masterpiece which I can never see without crying. Gorki says: "I have recently seen *Uncle Vanya* and I blubbered like a green girl." Why? Because it is the story of the failure and the sacrifice of fine and splendid people (Uncle Vanya himself, Sonia who deserved to be loved, but is passed by because she is plain, and, above all, Astrov, the country doctor, who dreams of a noble future but is condemned to live an obscure and hopeless life.) And here the further question arises: why should such things be? Why should only people like the celebrated and intolerable Professor Serebrakov and his young wife, the very—the too—beautiful Elena Andreevna, be capable of shining and of breaking away from the mediocrity of a country existence. Apparently Tchekov was unable to imagine more than three types of womanhood: the young, pure and idealistic girl; the radiant, rather silly and distinctly dangerous beauty; the ugly duckling who has every good quality and is fated to be humble and unhappy.

At the end of the play, the Proud take flight from the calamitous countryside, and the Humble are left alone. All the same, in the final passage of dialogue Tchekov leaves a great hope with them:

"VOITZKI (*stroking Sonia's hair*): Oh, my child, I am so miserable—if only you knew how miserable. . . .
SONIA: There is nothing we can do about it. We must

[248]

live our lives as they are. Yes, uncle Vanya, we shall
go on living through the long procession of days before
us, and the long evenings: we must bear patiently the
trials imposed on us by fate. We shall work for others
endlessly and without rest, both now and when we
are old. And when our last hour comes we shall meet
it humbly, and, beyond the grave, we shall say that we
have suffered and wept and known bitterness, and
God will have pity on us. Ah, then, dear, dear uncle,
we shall know a bright and beautiful life, and we shall
look back upon our sorrows here with a tender smile—
and we shall have peace. That I believe, uncle,
fervently, passionately. (*Sonia kneels at his feet and
rests her head on his hands. She speaks in a weary voice.*)
We shall rest at last. (*Telegin plays on the guitar.*)
We shall rest, and we shall hear the angels. We shall
see heaven gleaming like a jewel. We shall see all the
evil of the world and all our pain drowned in a great
compassion which will fill the whole universe. Our life
will be as tranquil, sweet and tender as a kiss. I believe
that, I believe it. (*She wipes away her tears.*) My poor,
poor uncle Vanya, you are crying! You have never
known happiness: but wait, uncle Vanya, wait, for we
shall have rest. (*She kisses him.*)
(*The watchman's rattle is heard in the garden. Telegin
plays softly. Mme Voitskaya makes a note on the margin
of her pamphlet: Marina goes on knitting her stocking.*)
We shall have rest."

Almost the same tone, the same movement, marks the
conclusion of *The Three Sisters*. The sisters have been
hoping for a long time. They have been living in the
belief that love will set them free from provincial life, and

that they will go to Moscow. But their hopes have fallen in ruins. Olga will remain an old maid: Masha has seen her lover depart with his regiment which is being posted to another garrison town: Irina's fiancé has been killed in a stupid duel. It is all over. The three sisters are in their old garden. The band of the marching regiment is heard in the distance. They stand pressed closely together:

"MASHA: Oh that band! They are leaving us: one has already left us, and for ever. We shall be all alone. We shall have to start our lives over again ... they must go on.

IRINA (*laying her head on Olga's breast*): A time will come when the purpose of all this suffering will be revealed, and there will be no more mysteries. ... Until that time comes we must go on living ... and working ... and nothing else. Tomorrow I shall go away alone ... to teach, to devote my whole life to those who perhaps can make use of it. It is autumn now: it will soon be winter. The snow will cover everything, and I shall be working, working. ...

OLGA (*embracing the other two*): The band is so gay, so lively, and one does so long to live. Oh, dear God!—the years will pass and we shall disappear for ever and be forgotten. People will forget what we looked like, the sound of our voices and even how many of us there were. We have suffered, but those who come after will rejoice: happiness and peace will reign on earth, and those who are living now will be remembered with kindly words and blessings. Our lives are not yet at an end, dear sisters. We shall live on. The band is so gay, so joyful, and we shall believe that in only a little while we shall learn why it is that we are living, why it is that we are suffering. . . . If only we could know, if only we could know!

(*The music dies away slowly into the distance. Kuligin, smiling happily, enters carrying his hat and coat: Andrey wheels on little Bobik in a go-cart.*)

CHEBUTIKIN (*singing in a low voice*): Ta-ra-ra-boom-deay. . . . What does anything matter! (*He reads the paper.*)

OLGA: If only we could know! If only we could know!"

In what way do Tchekov's plays differ from those of all other dramatists? In the first place, like the stories, they are simple. The characters speak naturally. Plot matters scarcely at all. The spectator is witnessing a situation, and he witnesses it in time, which is what makes the plays so like the stories. The two techniques closely resemble one another.

Dialogue, with Tchekov, is important less because of what is said than because of what is left unsaid. Beneath the spoken words there is a wordless and, somehow, distressing exchange. Occasionally, but very rarely, when the suffering of a character is too great for him to bear, he cries out in pain or anger (for example, Uncle Vanya's explosive outburst against the bogus great man), but the part played by the silences is of capital importance. Now and again a character launches out into a long monologue, and somebody replies with another monologue which has no bearing on the first. In the give and take of dialogue, too, Tchekov uses the same method, and this is true to life because people do have a way of following their own thoughts and not listening to their interlocutor.

On one occasion when he was abroad, so Stanislavski

tells us, he sent a telegram demanding the deletion of a brilliant piece of monologue in which Andrey, in *The Three Sisters*, describes what his wife means to a ruined provincial. "He issued the most stringent orders that the whole tirade should be suppressed, and replaced by just five words: 'A wife is a wife.' That short phrase set up the necessary overtones which expressed everything that needed to be expressed." "I don't know how it is," he once wrote, "but the extremes of happiness and misery are, more often than not, better conveyed by silence than by speech. Lovers understand one another better when they say nothing."

In this he was following the example of the great composers who, by means of a brief interval, can create or sustain an emotion, or provide the period of rest which is so necessary when it is a question of stressing or isolating a theme, or of passing from one theme to another. He even inserts scraps of music into his silences. A guitar or a balalaika picks out a few poignant notes. A character whistles or hums. The sound of a military band dies away in the distance. *The Seagull* is punctuated with fragments of sentimental tunes. In *The Cherry Orchard* we hear the melancholy twitter of birds, a guitar and "a distant sound which seems to come from the sky and resembles the vibration of a string too tightly stretched". It heralds unhappiness, an unhappiness which becomes specific in the muted sound of an axe cutting down the cherry trees.

One day he said to a friend: "I've just finished a new play." ... "What is it called? What is it about?" ... "You'll see soon enough when it is produced." Then, with a smile, he added: "Stanislavski hasn't read it yet: but *he* doesn't want to know what it's about. All he's interested in is what sound-effects will be needed in it. You see, he guessed. In one scene there is a rather complicated sound which comes from the wings. I can't describe it, but it must be *exactly* as I intend: and Stanislavski has found the very thing. . . . He takes the play on trust," he said with another smile. "Is this sound so important, then?" asked his friend. Anton Pavlovitch looked at him sternly, and replied with a brief "Yes".

A play by Tchekov is, in fact, a musical composition. He loved *The Moonlight Sonata* and Chopin's *Nocturnes*. One has a feeling that in his work for the theatre he was trying to transpose something of those masterpieces, the impression they convey of sweetness and airy lightness, of a melancholy and fragile beauty. In this he succeeded, and as we look and listen it is borne in upon us that if life is indeed sad, it is also marvellous and can provide us with moments of pure joy. His stage directions resembled Japanese poems. "The stage is empty. We hear the doors being locked. The sound of carriages driving away. There is complete silence. It is broken by the dull thud of an axe striking on wood. Sad, isolated blows." . . . "It is evening. The room is lit by a single shaded lamp. There is a sound of rustling trees and the wind whistling down the chimney. The night watchman taps on his drum."

A lot has been said about his realism. It is poetic realism, transposed realism. The instructions he gave to the actors had something unreal about them. It was almost as though he were speaking in a dream. Katchalov, a member of the Art Theatre Company, tells the following story:

"I was rehearsing the part of Trigorin in *The Seagull*. All of a sudden Tchekov asked me to talk about it to him. I went over to where he was sitting, secretly feeling rather frightened.

'You know,' he said, 'those fishing lines ought to be of unequal length, hand-made things. He has cut them himself, with a penknife. . . . His cigar is good . . . or, perhaps it's not really very good, but it looks fine in its silver-paper wrapping.'

He stopped, thought for a moment, then went on:

'But don't forget those fishing lines.'

Then he relapsed into silence. I waited. I wanted to know how I ought to handle one or two pieces of business. He cleared his throat several times, then said:

'I really can't tell you . . . as they ought to be. . . .'

But I stuck to my guns.

Seeing how determined I was, he said: '. . . that bit where Trigorin is drinking vodka with Masha . . . I shouldn't have failed to do like this.'

He got up, pulled down his waistcoat and breathed once or twice rather heavily.

'Like that—that's what I should have done. When one's been sitting still for too long, one always wants to do like that.' "

When he went, for the second time (11th September, 1898) to watch *The Seagull* being rehearsed at the Moscow Art Theatre, one of the actors told him that there were going to be sounds back-stage of frogs croaking, grasshoppers scraping and dogs barking.

"What's the point of all that?" asked Tchekov with considerable displeasure.

"It's realistic," replied the actor. "Realistic, eh?" Anton Pavlovitch smiled. Then, after a short pause, he said:

[254]

"The theatre is an art. Kramskoi[1] paints admirably rendered faces. Now see what happens if you remove one of those painted noses and replace it with a real nose. The nose will be 'realistic' but the picture will be ruined."

Another actor explained with pride that at the end of the third act the producer was going to bring on to the stage all the domestic servants and a woman with a crying child in her arms.

Anton Pavlovitch said: "Well then, he mustn't. It would have about the same effect as banging down the lid of a grand piano during a *pianissimo* passage."

"But it does quite often happen that a *forte* does intrude on a *pianissimo* in real life," objected one of the company.

"Perfectly true," replied Anton Pavlovitch, "but the stage must, to some extent, be ruled by conventions. We don't, for instance, have a fourth wall. Besides, the art of the theatre reflects the quintessence of life, and nothing superfluous must be introduced."

He hated the sort of "business" which is introduced solely for the purpose of giving an illusion of "real life". When, in the second act of *The Cherry Orchard*, he saw the actors busily killing mosquitoes, he said: "In my next play I shall make one of the characters exclaim: "What an extraordinary place this is—not a single mosquito!" Once, when he was watching *Uncle Vanya*, when Sonia, in the third act, said: "Papa, we must be charitable," she knelt down and kissed his hand.

"But she mustn't do that!" said Anton Pavlovitch. "This isn't a melodrama. The tragedy is all *interior*. There had been tragedy in Sonia's life before this par-

[1] A famous Russian painter. (Translator.)

ticular moment, and there will be more tragedy later on. The pistol shot isn't tragedy: it is an incident."

Gorki wrote to him on one occasion:

"It is being said that *Uncle Vanya* and *The Seagull* are examples of a new form of dramatic art in which realism has been raised to the level of spiritual symbolism. . . . I find that very true. As I listened to your play, I found my mind dwelling on the thought of life sacrificed to an idol, of beauty intruding into the wretched lives of human beings, and on many other essential and important matters. Other plays have not got that power to lead audiences on from realities to philosophical generalizations—yours have."

That is the real point. With Tchekov a simple concrete case always opens immense perspectives on to human nature and the world of ideas. In all his plays there are certain intelligent and meditative characters who, from time to time, rise above their personal destiny, and see the world as it is and as it will be.

"MASHA: . . . People will forget us.
VERSHININ: Yes, people will forget us. Life is like that, and there is nothing we can do about it. A time will come when what today seems to us to be important, serious and heavy with consequences will be forgotten, or regarded as trivial. (*Pause.*) And the curious thing is that we have no way of finding out what will seem great and important, and what feeble and silly. Didn't the discoveries of Copernicus, say, of Columbus, seem pointless and ludicrous at first, while any sort of rubbish written by a fool was looked upon as holding the key to all truth? Just in the same way

it may well happen that our present way of living, which gives us so much satisfaction, will, one day, come to appear strange, uncomfortable, stupid, unclean and even sinful. . . .

TUZENBACH: Who knows? It is no less possible that it will seem to have been not altogether lacking in nobility. People may even honour its memory. We have done away with torture and capital punishment, we're free from invasions but, at the same time, how much suffering there still is.

SOLENI (*in a feeble voice*): There, there . . . the Baron is perfectly prepared to go without his dinner if only you'll let him talk philosophy.

TUZENBACH: Vassili Vassilievitch, kindly leave me out of this (*changing his chair*), it gets on a fellow's nerves, you know."

Or, again, in the same play (*The Three Sisters*):

"TUZENBACH: . . . Laugh if you like (*to Vershinin*) but that doesn't alter the fact that in two or three centuries' time, in a million years, life will be still the same. Life doesn't change, it just goes on and on, for ever following its own laws, which don't concern us, or which, at least, we shall never discover. Migrant birds, cranes, for instance, fly and fly, and whatever thoughts there may be in their heads, great or small, they will still fly, not knowing why nor how. No matter what philosophers may be born among them, they will go on flying. They may philosophize to their hearts' content, but they'll never stop flying. . . .

MASHA: But there must be some meaning in it all.

TUZENBACH: Meaning? Look, it's snowing. What meaning has that?"

And that leads us on to wonder what Tchekov's philosophy was. It is a rash question to ask, for he would have denied that he had any. Well, then, let us not say philosophy, but *Weltanschauung*—view of the world. Every intelligent man has one. Tchekov's was courageous and original.

But before starting on that, let me sum up what I have been saying about his work in the theatre. Today it is universally admired, and justly so. But not because of its dramatic construction. He cared very little about that. All his subjects can be epitomized in three sentences: a group of characters are unhappy. There is no solution for them. They cling desperately to their hope in an unknown future. The originality of Tchekov's plays lies in their musical quality. He was the Chopin of the stage. His silences, his pauses, his "repeats" and, on the visual level, his half-tones, his "soft water-colour effects"—all combine to make something unique in the history of the theatre: something washed clean of all vulgarity in feeling and expression.

4

If we are to hope to understand Tchekov's ideas, we must first of all remember (*a*) that his outlook changed as he grew older. At first he had a weakness for moralizing, like a young Polonius, as his early letters to his brothers show. Later, he refused to judge. (*b*) That, for all his poetry, his mind was essentially scientific, that he looked at people and things with the eyes of a doctor.

"An ordinary, simple-minded man gazes at the moon and is emotionally stirred, as though by something mysterious and incomprehensible. . . . But an astronomer can have no fond illusions about it. I, too, because I am a doctor, have very few illusions . . . and that is a pity because they keep one from becoming dessicated."

His rules of behaviour during the first period are expressed in the now famous letter which he wrote, when he was twenty-six, to his brother Nicolas. That was the period at which he had brought the basic formation of his own character to completion, and was anxious that his brother, who was talented, but aimless, should take his place among those whom Tchekov called "culti-vated", but I should call "civilized" people.

"In my opinion," he wrote, "no one can be con-sidered cultivated who does not fulfil the following conditions.

(I) He must have a proper respect for human per-sonality: consequently, he must be good-hearted, gentle, polite, and ready to give way to others. He must not make scenes over such things as a mislaid hammer or a piece of indiarubber. If he lives with someone else he must not take the view that he is conferring a favour, and, when the arrangement is terminated, must not say to his companion: 'You're an impossible person to live with.' He must be tolerant of noise, cold, tinned food, jokes and the presence of strangers in the house.

(II) His sympathy must not be confined to cats and beggars. He must have a heart which can bleed for what the eye cannot see. He must be willing to work late into the night to help a friend, to pay his brother's fees at the university, to buy clothes for his mother.

(III) He must have a proper respect for other people's property, and, consequently, must pay his debts.

(IV) He must be sincere, and dread a lie as he would dread the plague. He must never lie even in small things, for a lie is an insult to the hearer, and puts him in an inferior position to him who tells it. Cultivated people do not put on airs, but behave in the street as they do at home, and do not show off in front of their poorer friends. They are not given to idle chatter, and do not force on others confidences that are not wanted. From a feeling of respect for the ears of others, they say less than they might.

(V) A cultivated man must not run himself down in order to arouse compassion. He must not play on other people's feelings so as to get sympathy and enhance his own importance. He must not say: 'Nobody understands me' or 'I'm nothing but a second-rater', because that sort of thing is merely aimed at making an easy effect, and is vulgar, false and conventional.

(VI) He must never be fatuous and vain, nor must he flash such false diamonds as being intimate with the famous, shaking hands with a drunken poet or listening to the vapourings of a chance visitor to a picture show just because he happens to have a bar-parlour reputation."

"Is that all you mean by morality?" a saint might ask. No, most certainly it is not, but it is, a least, what Charles du Bos called that standard of decency, that minimum of consideration for others and for oneself, without which there can be no civilization. *It is because this bare, basic decency has been lost to us that human society is dying.*

To behave "in the true spirit of national socialism" as preached by Hitler is to deny all human decency. It was Tchekov's ardent desire that civilized behaviour should become a second nature in all men. "A wish to serve the general good should be felt as a simple human need, a condition of personal happiness. As soon as it comes to be regarded as no more than an intellectual theory, it ceases to be genuine." In him this wish was authentic and constant. Painful though his own life had been, for he had long been poor, and was always ailing, he was never heard to complain on his own account. When his sufferings were at their worst, none of those closest to him ever guessed what he was going through. When people commiserated with him, he would change the subject, and talk about unimportant matters with a sweet and melancholy humour.

As he grew older his general view of the world, and his personal ethical standards as a writer, became modified, though he never expressed them dogmatically. They can be read between the lines of his stories and plays. He was of the opinion that a writer's duty was to portray, not judge. "When I describe horse-thieves, there are people who maintain that I ought also to point out that stealing horses is wicked. But that is not my business but the law's."

Again:

"It is not for the writer of fiction to resolve such problems as the existence of God, the nature of pessimism, etc. What he has to do is to exhibit his characters and record the circumstances and the way in which they talk about God and pessimism." ... "You are confusing two entirely separate things: the solving of a problem and the presentation of that problem correctly. Only the second is the concern of the artist. In *Anna Karenina* or *Eugene Onegin* no problem is resolved, but those works are satisfying, all the same, because the problems are correctly presented."

It is clear, from this, that Tchekov did not hold the view that a writer should be "committed", partly because to be so runs counter to the very principle of art, which is contemplation, and, more especially, because no one should talk of what he does not know. The artist knows that such and such a landowner, such and such a capitalist is ridiculous, but he does not know what is the best form of economy to impose upon a nation. One day, when several people were discussing, in front of him, certain rumours to the effect that he had no religion and no philosophy, he frowned.

"People say a great many things about me, but it is all a lot of nonsense. I am just a man like other men. I love nature and books: I hate routine and despotism."

"Political despotism?"

"Despotism in any form, no matter where, nor in what form it operates."

He describes moujiks and landowners without taking sides. When he published *The Peasants*, the critics were in a quandary. Should he be praised or blamed? He showed certain peasants in a distinctly unfavourable light, whereas the fashion of the moment was to champion them. Tolstoy had said much the same thing in *The Power of Darkness*, but had later regretted it. Tchekov, however, said quite simply, "that's how things are". This caused a deal of heartburning, and the members of the *intelligentsia* were touched on the raw. Obviously one could not love what one didn't find sympathetic, and now . . .

"The *moujiks* don't ask for love," replied Tchekov, "what they want is bread: work, bread and land."

Hard words, but it was no use deceiving oneself. Similarly with religion. Tchekov was a non-believer, and said so. Nevertheless, he was still attached to the faith of his childhood, to icons and church bells. Some of his stories are impregnated with religious emotion. But the scientist in him could not affirm what he did not know. "When one is thirsty, one feels that one could gulp down a whole sea: that is faith. But when one begins to drink, one swallows only a small part of the sea: that is science." He also said: "One must respect even one's own indifference, and not change it for something else, because, if a man is worth anything, his very indifference can be a religion." He has left with us the words of the prayer he would have offered up had he been in the habit of praying: "Oh, God, let me not judge anybody nor speak of what I do not know or understand. . . . The important thing is to be intellectually honest, morally pure and physically clean."

Three months before his death, he wrote to his wife: "You ask me what life is. . . . That is just about as sensible as asking me what a carrot is. . . . A carrot is a carrot, and that's all you can say about it."

But it must never be forgotten that, though he refused to judge, that did not mean that he was not ready to help all who were suffering. We have seen how devoted and courageous he was during the cholera epidemic, and how he gave medical help and moral support to the peasants at Melikhovo. He held, also, to the opinion that "it is the duty of the writer neither to accuse nor to persecute, but to defend even the guilty once they have been sentenced and are undergoing punishment. At the time of the Dreyfus Affair he publicly approved of Zola's attitude, and almost quarrelled with Suvorin, who was an anti-dreyfusard. "Whatever the verdict, Zola will feel a lively satisfaction when the trial is over. His old age will be happy, and he will die with an easy conscience."

Tchekov had no old age, but we know that he died with a clear conscience. He says somewhere that a great writer should point his readers the way to a great end. What was the end he had in view? "Liberation from brute force and lies, no matter what form they take—that would be my programme, were I a great artist." And it was, with the addition of an active compassion. Beyond his scepticism and agnosticism there is faith, a belief that deep down in the human heart there exist true feelings of love. This is most easily seen in the man-woman relationship. But "what we feel when we are in love is, perhaps, a normal state. Love shows man what he ought to be."

What he ought to be, that is to say, good, disinterested, and with a deep regard for others. That is the better life to which Tchekov points the way in his stories and his plays. Not that he says it in so many words, but only with an infinite shyness, a timid tenderness. But we know that we are better for seeing a performance of *Uncle Vanya* or *The Cherry Orchard*, and, for the artist, the knowledge that he has brought that about is the only glory worth having.

CHAPTER XII

NICOLAS GOGOL

IT IS CUSTOMARY for critics, personal preferences apart, to rank as equal those four giants of Russian literature, Pushkin, Gogol, Tolstoy and Dostoievski. To this list I, personally, should add Turgenev and Tchekov: but there can be no doubt that Russia's national literature began with Pushkin and Gogol. It would be difficult to imagine two more different writers. Pushkin, warm-hearted and generous, had come to terms with life. Gogol, a strange and sombre figure, never freed himself from his own inner drama. His life was the tragedy of a man at grips with his genius, which revealed to him an essential truth. He was irresistibly driven to express this truth, but there was a streak of weakness in him which made it impossible for him to carry on his shoulders so great a burden. One part of him was a being of flesh and blood whom the other, the spiritual part, held in detestation. This divided personality produced a painful lack of balance. "Whether there was ever anybody who actually loved Gogol the man I do not know," said Aksakov, "but I should say that to do so was impossible." It is sad not to be loved, and sadder still not to love oneself. Yet, such was the fate of this solitary bird with the hard and watchful eyes, of this spirit, seemingly so dead, who produced that masterpiece which goes by the name of *Dead Souls*.

[265]

I

Yet in childhood his life had promised happiness. He was born in the Ukraine, a land of fabulous harvests, where the black soil needs no artificial fertilizers, where a plough left abandoned in a field is covered, in the space of a few days, with thick vegetation, and where rivers of honey flow quite literally, so numerous are the bees. Its great plains ripple with golden corn. The days there are aflame with sun and flowers, the nights mild under a wonderful sky which seems to be the very granary of light. "You don't know our Ukraine nights? Then I will bring them before your eyes. From the middle of the sky the moon looks down. Divine nights! spellbinding nights! On a sudden everything comes alive—the forests, the lakes, the steppes. The trill of the lordly nightingale trembles upon the air, and the moon seems to stand still and listen."

That might have been written by Chateaubriand dreaming beside the lake at Combourg. As Chateaubriand looked for his Sylph, so did Gogol, child of a land where magic was in the very air, lie in wait for the nymphs whose home was in the running streams. All his life long the white translucence of the female body filled him with desire and terror. Undine's body, diaphanous and fragile. The people of Little Russia had a great love of legends. Wandering minstrels, with baggy trousers tucked into high leather boots, and sheepskin caps on their heads, sang them to him. Ballads, too, he learned, full of heroic deeds. The Ukraine, or Little Russia, was a frontier province which had seen much fighting against the Moslem Tartars and the Poles. A nomad race of Zaporogue Cossacks had carried out counter-offensives in defence of the country. These warrior horsemen, led by their *ataman*, had been the Knights-Templar of the Dnieper.

Gogol was descended from these Zaporogues. In his family there had been soldiers and priests. His parents, Vassili Aphanassievitch Gogol and Marie Ivanovna Kossiarovsky, belonged to the class of those small landowners who, at that time, were plentiful in Russia, never very rich, robbed by their peasants, but in easy circumstances thanks to the inexhaustible abundance of the soil. His father was a mild and unassuming man who had been educated in a seminary. He knew Latin and wrote comedies. His mother, who was pious, simple-minded and affectionate, had been married at fourteen. They were a model couple, almost ridiculously fond, and, one suspects, rather like that *Family of Other Days* described by their son. Not very lordly lords they were, in a land of plenty over which there hung one dark shadow—serfdom. The peasants in those days were slaves whom their masters could buy or sell at will. It was said of so-and-so, "He owns a hundred—or a thousand—souls." Gogol's parents, never having known any other system, thought it perfectly natural, and there was no evil in them. But nobody has the right to own souls with impunity. The phrase was as ugly as the thing. The devil was prowling in this paradise.

Nicolas Vassilievitch Gogol was born in 1809. He was a delicate child, but quick-witted and something of a little oddity, a diminutive Cossack who danced the *trepak*. He had a face that was out of the ordinary, with a long, pointed nose like a bird's beak, and ferrety eyes under a crop of pale fair hair. At the Niejin secondary school, where he got his education, the other boys were frightened of him, and called him the "mysterious dwarf". He had a gift for mimicry and a sharp tongue, and took off his friends' tricks of behaviour, and even their ways of thinking. In adolescence he developed a passion for the theatre and a taste for writing. But his dream was of "some great destiny". He was fond of preaching, and made a great show of wanting to "serve", to make himself useful, and to lead Russia along a high and noble road. Now, in those days, a "great destiny" could mean only one thing, State employment, and that involved entering the *tchin*, the administrative hierarchy with its fourteen different grades, where the tyro began as an "assistant" and rose by degrees to the post of Councillor of State, or even higher.

Gogol longed passionately to be one of this mandarin caste. Being by nature something of a sentimental exhibitionist, he missed no opportunity of "spouting" about all the good he was going to do. His talk was always curiously exaggerated, as were his letters. If he spoke to his mother about his health, it was always in a highly dramatic manner. To judge by what he said he must be at death's door, but he didn't believe a word of it. When his father died in 1825, Nicolas, aged sixteen, declared that he would put an end to his life, and did nothing. To his mother he sent a series of homilies: "In this time of grief, turn to the Almighty." His religion was nothing but words, but he was afraid of death. Certain sermons on the subject of Hell had a frightening effect on him. As long as he lived he was obsessed by a terror of the Last Judgment. As a youth his worst torment was the thought that he might pass through the world without leaving a trace. Ambition, but also nobility of heart. Desire for some great sacrifice. And always, that trick of over-emphasis: "With the aid of my iron will I hope to establish the unshakeable foundations of the tremendous edifice I mean to raise." What that edifice was to be, nobody knew, not even he.

When he was nineteen, he set out for Saint Petersburg to begin his great climb to glory. The journey in a *kibitka*, the discovery of the world of Russia, went to his head, but the capital was a sad disappointment. He was poor, solitary and unknown. He shared an attic with some other young men from Little Russia, and dreamed of the radiant skies of the Ukraine. Seen from a distance, the country life from which he had so longed to escape, had all the charm of an idyll. He wrote home asking his mother and his sisters to send him precise information about the legends of his homeland, because lack of money had turned his mind to the possibility of becoming a writer. His first book, published under a pseudonym, was an idyll in verse, *Hans Küchelgarten*. It was a complete failure, and Gogol, deeply chagrined, burned it.

He did not, as a matter of fact, think that he was cut out to be a writer, but a great Civil Servant. What a strange fellow he was. Women scared him, and he peopled his imagination with haughty beauties dying for love of him, divinities set by God upon his way, to save him from Saint Petersburg. To his poor, adoring mother he described a *femme fatale* from whom he must escape at all costs. There was no such person, and the whole letter was a lie. The future creator of myths began with mystification. Eager to leave the capital after the failure of his book, he invented a rich friend who was going to take him to Lübeck. The finger of God, he said, was sending him away. God did not mean him to be a Civil Servant. The friend was no more real than the woman, and the money for his journey had been sent him by his mother for the purpose of paying the interest on a mortgage with which the family property was encumbered. But this new myth enabled him to get to Germany, there to discover a whole new universe: the West.

The value of travel is that it helps us, by providing contrast, to see the normal setting of our lives in perspective. On his return to Saint Petersburg, where he had found a minor post in the Department of Crown Lands, Gogol studied the *tchinoviks* with a sharp eye. He was poor and contemptuous. Since he had only a summer overcoat "lined with wind", the northern winter was a severe trial. He suffered not only in his body but in his pride, because his cravat and his jacket were not in the mode. Balzac, and even Stendhal, had similar weaknesses. Those who would describe strong feelings must feel strongly. The year 1831 looked like giving a new and happier direction to his destiny. He made the acquaintance of Alexandra Ossipovna Rosset, a brilliant and cultivated young woman of twenty-one, the darling of the Imperial Family, who opened the door of Pushkin's enchanted circle to this strange *khokol*, as she called the Little Russian.

If we are to have any idea of the position occupied by Pushkin in the Russia of those days, we must think of Byron in England, or of Victor Hugo in the France of the early 'thirties. He was deeply cultured and had read not only Byron but Chénier and the German romantics. With *Boris Godunov* he had introduced into Russia a taste for historical drama, as, later, Dumas, Hugo and Vigny were to do into France. He treated with genius the romantic themes of Melancholy and Fate. But like all really great romantics, he gave a classic perfection of form to his writing. In all countries the excesses of romanticism were bound, sooner or later, to provoke a realistic reaction. Balzac, Dickens and Gogol all responded to the same need, but in Pushkin the two principles had achieved a remarkable state of equilibrium. The Czarist despotism shocked him, and, in 1825, he had been involved in the Decembrist Plot. Nevertheless, the personal charm of Nicolas I was not without its effect upon the poet, who had a temperamental liking for elegance in all its forms. Nicolas, for his part, admired Pushkin, welcomed him at Court, but had him closely watched, and would not let him travel abroad. The Czar had a certain generosity of mind, but—"all power corrupts, and absolute power corrupts absolutely." There was something tyrannical even in his generosity.

A curious contrast, this of Gogol and Pushkin: an embittered ambition in the presence of a radiant glory of achieved triumph. Pushkin gave a friendly welcome to the awkward, shy, depressed beginner. "How good Pushkin is!" said Alexandra Rosset. "He has at once accepted the refractory *khokol*." When Gogol published a collection of Ukrainian tales, called *Village Nights*, Pushkin was enthusiastic. "Here is true gaiety, sincere, spontaneous, and without any pulling of faces ... and now and again, what poetry! what sensibility!" The book was indeed charming. On the bored readers of the capital it had much the same effect as Alphonse Daudet's Provençal stories had upon the Parisians of his day. In it Gogol had taken refuge in his childhood from the nastiness of an odious present. His rustic idylls had the same sort of grace as those of George Sand later in the century. Sand told hers through the mouth of an old hemp grower: Gogol cast an old bee-keeper for a similar part. Everyone fell in love with these tales, from the printers who set them up in type to the Empress. Gogol became famous overnight: "Behold me now," he said, "a free Cossack."

2

But success did not bring him peace of mind. In spite of it he continued to observe humanity with a hard and jaundiced eye. He had written some delicious idylls, but he did not believe in them, since he was conscious only of an underlying hollowness. He was very proud, and spread his net for nobler game. He wanted to "help his fellow men", to free them from the eternal flatness of their lives which, with a merciless lucidity, he saw on every side. He became the victim of an obsession. He must conquer the Devil and so write that, after reading his books, people might be able to laugh at the Devil and all his works. For him, the Devil was a real person in whom was concentrated the negation of God; the embodiment of the uncompleted, giving himself out to be infinite, the incarnate denial of all height and all depth, God's ape. The worst of all evils in Gogol's eyes lay not in grave infractions of the moral law, but in the complete absence of the tragic sense. "The Devil does not sport magnificent Byronic clothes. He goes about, I know, in a ready-made suit from a slop-shop."

But that suit was his own, and he found the Devil within himself. Was not he, more than anyone else, the uncompleted giving himself out to be infinite?—a man who hungered after greatness but thought about his cravats? a man with a commonplace face and pointed nose who dreamed of exalted loves? And so it was that in the next two volumes, *Mirgorod* and *Arabesques*, the tone hardened. Instead of the poetry of childhood's fairyland he depicted the misery of the world as seen by a clear-sighted observer. *A Family of Other Days*, the story of an old countryman and his wife, could have been an idyll, but the eye with which he sees it is severe, and the old man's greediness, the unhappiness of the widower, prompted not by true sorrow but by resentment at having to break the habits of a lifetime, seem, not so much pitiful, as ridiculous. *The Overcoat*, a wonderful story, "the mould from which we all came", said Turgenev, contains discords which anticipate Flaubert's *Bouvard et Pecuchet*, and a degree of pity which is reminiscent of Tolstoy's *Death of Ivan Ilitch*. It is the story of a poor clerk in one of the Ministries, Akaky Akakievitch, who has dreamed for years of some day having a new overcoat. He spends all his life's savings on buying one, only to have it stolen that very same evening.

Here Gogol shows himself to be very much in accord with Flaubert's aesthetic theory: "the more ordinary the poet's subject, the higher should he fly." But Gogol wanted art to be a reconciliation with life.

"Every true work of art has in it something to soothe and comfort. . . . While we read, we cease to feel the need of anything, to be envious of anything: we are conscious of no indignation at the expense of neighbour or brother: we are filled with a sense of love and pardon. . . . Art brings to us order and harmony, not trouble and disorder."

And again: "Art should show us all the good qualities and virtues of people, as well as their weaknesses and vices." In short, beauty is to be found in *total* truth (as it was found, later, by Tolstoy). But here, again, the horror of Gogol's spiritual adventure lay in the fact that the Devil, with unholy joy, allowed him to see *only* the weaknesses and vices of men. He loved Homer and Pushkin, and poetry that was noble and spacious, but the Devil compelled him to write stories with an ugly grin in them: *The Nose* and *The Diary of a Madman*.

One of his more fantastic tales, in the manner of Hoffman, a *genre* in which he excelled, is very revealing. It is about a picture which is acquired, turn and turn about, by several collectors, and brings unhappiness, death and ruin wherever it is hung. Why does it carry this curse? Because it has been painted with the collaboration of the Devil, and has in it *an element of reality in the raw*. The eyes of the portrait are not the effect of art: they are *alive*, and this is what they should not be. If a work of art is to produce a sense of purification, it must transpose. It is remarkable that this story, written when he was a young man, precisely exemplifies Gogol's later attitude to all his work. He disliked what he had done because it contained reality in the raw. He had, according to himself (but not according to us) worked in the service of the Demon.

About the same time, he did, however, make an effort to depict noble feelings. He once again had recourse to the memories of his childhood, and in *Tarass Boulba* wrote the epic of the Zaparogue Cossacks as it had been told him by his grandfather, who had played a part in that *Iliad*. The book was yet another proof of his great talent, and contains many fine scenes. There are battles between Cossacks and Poles: there is the hero's secret journey to Warsaw in order to be present at his son's execution: there is the scene of Tarass Boulba's death by burning, and a description of a mass plunge of Cossacks into the river. In the spacious quality of the writing this prose-poem bears a certain resemblance to Chateaubriand's *Les Martyrs*. But the shadow of Gogol's disenchantment dims the bright light of this epic tale. In particular, a love story which runs through the drama completely misfires. What did Gogol know of love?

His austere temperament was better suited to comedy than to epic. "What a deal of laughter and of bile!" For some time he played with the idea of writing a satirical play about Saint Petersburg officialdom. But the censor would never have allowed its production on the stage. Gogol, discouraged and in despair, turned to Pushkin who had always been so kind to him. "Give me a subject," he begged, "and I guarantee that I will sit down straight away and write a devilishly funny comedy. In heaven's name, help me! Both my head and my heart are starving." Pushkin had no lack of subjects, and no lack of affection. He there and then presented Gogol with the plot of *Revizor* (*The Government Inspector*). It runs as follows. The officials in a small provincial town are, one and all, thoroughly dishonest. They are told that a Government Inspector will soon be coming incognito for the purpose of showing them up. It so happens that a stranger has just arrived at the inn. Terror reigns. The guilty men do everything in their power to thwart the Inspector. Money, women, all the classic tools of bribery are employed. The young traveller, at first surprised by so much generosity, joins in the fun. He accepts the bribes, and makes love to wives and daughters. Everything is discovered when the real Inspector turns up, but by that time the impostor has vanished.

Out of this comic subject given him by Pushkin, Gogol made a terrible satire on the baseness, the venality and the laziness of the *tchinoviks*. But, more especially, he painted in the central character, Khlestakov, a cruel portrait of himself. The man is not a deliberate impostor. He is shrewd, but "gentlemanly". He has a worldly standard of morality, and delivers himself of pious, soothing discourses which have a close resemblance to the homilies to which Gogol used to treat his mother. Like his creator, like all artists, Khlestakov has a guileless genius for lying. He is incapable of pursuing any feeling through to the end. There is something sickening in his levity, and even Christianity seems flat and uninteresting when he talks about it. He is not Gogol as he was, but only as he saw himself in his worst moments, a man with a touch of the satanic. The final scene is, in the words of Dmitri Merejkowski, a "Last Judgment". The real Inspector appears like the angel at the end of a medieval mystery play, and the Spirit of Evil, in the person of Khlestakov, is carried off by his *troika* into the void. But the mystical symbolism is kept well hidden, and the play is irresistibly funny. "The firmer the grip of old torments on our heart," Gogol had written, "the noisier should be our gaiety."

How came it that the Czarist censorship allowed this vitriolic comedy to be seen upon the stage? For two reasons. In the first place, since the scene was laid in the provinces, the officials in Saint Petersburg could be justified in supposing that it was not they who were aimed at. In the second, the Emperor had read the piece in manuscript, and had been much amused. "Nobody escapes a trouncing, not even I," said Nicolas, and gave orders that the play should be performed. It opened in Saint Petersburg in 1836 and made a great sensation. The literary world, solidly hostile to a corrupt administration, was delighted. The *tchinoviks* were furious. They attacked Gogol, and got others to follow suit. This came as a painful surprise to the author. He had hoped that his play would cure them of their vices. Besides, had he not made fun of himself? Very soon he felt that he was being buried under an avalanche of hatred. "Everyone is against me: officials, the police, merchants and writers, every man jack of them is busy tearing my play to pieces. I've got a real horror of it." The wretched victim preferred flight to fighting. How wonderful never to be more than two days in the same place! "I'd like to be a despatch rider, a courier, a post office messenger. . . . I am going abroad. A comic writer should always live away from his own country."

3

Before leaving, he once again asked Pushkin for a subject, so that he might be able to work on a book while he was away. The inexhaustible Pushkin made him a present of one which was both strange and beautiful. In Gogol's hands it was destined to become for Russia what *Don Quixote* is for Spain. The idea was based on a fraudulent custom which in fact existed at that time. Once every few years every Russian landowner had to make a "return" of his "souls", in other words, his serfs, and to pay a tax on the figure declared. If any of his serfs had happened to die in the interval between two of these returns, the tax was still levied on them. Now, a sort of central "bank" had come into existence which was prepared to lend money to the owners, reckoned at so much per "soul", in fact a sort of mortgage on souls. It was this that had suggested the possibility of working a colossal fraud. Why not buy up the dead souls which their owners would sell for next to nothing so as not to have to pay the tax? The purchaser would then be in a position to draw a considerable amount from the central bank, after which he could quietly disappear. The perfect swindle!

Gogol was enchanted. He saw in the theme not only a theme for a picaresque novel, a chance to set his hero moving among many different Russian types, but also a piece of symbolism, for are we not, almost all of us, dead souls? He completed the first chapters before leaving Saint Petersburg, and read them to Pushkin. "He, who took such delight in laughter," said Gogol, "grew gloomier and gloomier as I read, and when I had finished, remarked in a voice of despair: 'Dear God, what a sad place this Russia of ours is!' " Gogol was amazed. He had painted the picture black because he saw it black. Taking the precious idea with him, he started off. He visited Switzerland, Paris—which dazzled, though it did not captivate, him—and Rome, to which he became deeply attached, by reason both of its strength and its simplicity. The humble people of the city, so gay, so spontaneous, so unworried, had a calming effect upon his own tormented spirit. In these new surroundings he worked away at *Dead Souls*. It was while he was living in Rome that he learned of Pushkin's death in a duel. "No news could have been worse, for with him has gone the supreme happiness of my life." But he no longer needed Pushkin now that he had given him the essential matter for a masterpiece. For two years he stayed on in Rome writing, correcting and as much at peace as a man of his temperament could be. He had very little money, but appealed for help to the Emperor Nicolas, who had a hundred thousand roubles sent to him. Russia, seen from a distance, awoke in him a tender love for his country, and he took a lively pleasure in describing it. He believed that, in spite of all her faults, she was destined to revive the civilization of the West. "Italy and Russia," he said, "are, neither of them, materialist." He himself was becoming more and more drawn to religion: "It is only in Rome that people pray." He remained loyal to the Orthodox Church, but saw little difference between the formularies of the Russian faith and those of Roman Catholicism.

His work was progressing. The hero of the book, Tchitchikov, the buyer of dead souls, was, once again, a caricature of the author, a sententious Gil Blas, correct and negative, not fundamentally bad, but corrupted by society, a very ordinary sort of man, wholly absorbed in his pet scheme, and driving about the country with his coachman, Selifane, and his three horses, a grotesque group which was to become as celebrated as Don Quixote, Sancho Panza and Rossinante. Pushkin had advised him to call the book a *poem* rather than a *novel*, and it is, indeed, the *Odyssey* of Tchitchikov, who goes from landowner to landowner, buying souls and coming in contact with strange human types—the miser who drives a hard bargain for his dead souls, and ends by getting two roubles apiece: the superstitious woman who is terrified at the idea of selling the dead, and offers, instead, her honey and her wheat. As in *The Government*

Inspector he shows all the officials of a small town cringing to Tchitchikov, because they think that a man who can buy so many peasants must be very rich.

The esoteric significance of the book is gloomy in the extreme. Stupid, greedy, hypocritical humanity is shown as damned beyond any possible hope of remission. Not that Tchitchikov and those who sell to him are conscious criminals. But they are dead to all finer feelings. Tchitchikov is the property-owner, or, as Gogol called him, the purchaser, who buys non-existent things in the hope of drawing material profit from them. Comfort and easy living is all he thinks about. "His kingdom is of this world ... and you must realize that Tchitchikov was the most respectable fellow to be found anywhere." That is what is so frightening. Humanity cannot repudiate Tchitchikov, because it *is* Tchitchikov.... What does humanity do if not accumulate dead souls? The book is admirable, monstrous and deeply troubling. Gogol's humour reminds us most, not of Lesage, not of Sterne, not even of Cervantes, but of Swift. The two of them share the same contempt of their fellow-men, the same cruelty in their painting of them, the same disgust with humanity, the same stark precision of their prose, and, what should cause no surprise, the same erotic deficiency. Continence engenders not only lucidity but fanaticism.

Rome had been for Gogol a place of refuge. Deep down in his Ukrainian nature there was a pagan joy of living, a longing to make contact once again with the basic, primitive folk-elements in human nature. In Rome he found the possibility of doing so, but, all the same, he was homesick for Russia. In 1841 he was back again in Moscow, submitting *Dead Souls* to the censor's department. Its Director was shocked. "The soul", he argued, "is immortal: consequently there can be no such thing as a dead soul. . . . Besides, the very idea of selling souls at two and a half roubles each! . . . so low a price is an insult to human dignity!" A permit was refused in Moscow, but in Saint Petersburg Prince Wiazemsky intervened with the Emperor, and the book duly appeared.

Once again, Gogol found himself faced with universal disapproval. Pro-Westerners and Slavophils combined to loose a flood of abuse against him. Every reader was appalled by the vision of his own utter emptiness. Pushkin had once told Gogol that, more than anyone else, he had the supreme gift of expressing the flatness of existence. That was true, and who can *love* the master painter of flatness? In vain did Gogol say to his enemies: "The book is the story of my own soul. . . . In me are united all the possible forms of beastliness, but in small doses." To a friend, he wrote: "In addition to my own defects, my characters have certain features borrowed from my friends, you included."

Men are afraid of the comic when it contains an element of bitterness, and it is true that all writers of comedy make us see what it is that is dead in human souls, or, as Bergson was to say later: "*a veneer of the mechanical applied to the living person*"—which amounts to the same thing. Both Tartuffe and Harpagon are dead souls, but Molière contrasts with them his *soubrettes*, his argumentative characters and his lovers, thereby doing something to rehabilitate the white races. But in Gogol's world there are *only* dead souls. His people are either commonplace malefactors, or else they skate on the surface of lunatic hallucinations, or live their lives in a state of somnolence like the protagonists of *A Family of*

Other Days. "And those dead souls are you and me," he says. These caricatures are, at one and the same time, the author's private diary in which he exposes his true self, and portraits of his readers. Such a lesson is too hard to be endured. The passage of time was necessary before the genius of this Daumier could be appreciated at its proper value. Gogol in his life-time paid a high price for his clear-sightedness. He had seen "the corpse he carried about within himself, and, as an artist, he had found freedom from the terrible burden". But, as a man, he still had a hard battle to fight.

4

The last part of Gogol's life was a long search for salvation, at first moral, then religious. Gogol's most severe critic was Gogol. On re-reading *Dead Souls,* he said: "If anyone could have seen the monsters who, much to my surprise, broke free from my pen, he would have trembled." Already, in his novel, he had excused himself to the reader for having chosen so negative a character as Tchitchikov to be his hero:

"Alas, the author knows all that only too well, yet it was impossible for him to choose a virtuous man as hero. But . . . it may be that in this book of mine strings, till now unsuspected, may be heard to vibrate, that there may be conjured up before the reader's eyes the power and the might of the spirit of Russia which nowhere has its equal in the world, a spirit radiant with divine beauty, filled with noble aspirations and burning with a desire to dedicate itself. By comparison, the virtuous of other nations seem dead, as a book is dead when set against the living word. The moral treasure of the Russian nature will manifest itself, and then it will be apparent to all how deeply embedded in the Slav soul is what merely moves on the surface of the souls of other peoples."

At the end of the volume he had inserted a lyrical invocation to the swift-moving *troika*:

"Oh! troïka, bird of the steppe, who first invented thee? Thou couldst have come to birth only among a daring people, in a land which never does things by halves, but spreads like a patch of oil over one half of the world, covering so many versts that the eye grows weary in the measuring of them! . . . Dost thou not, Russia, fly like the ardent troïka which cannot be out-paced? Speeding past in a cloud of dust, leaving all else behind? The watcher, dumbfounded by the divine prodigy, stops dead in his tracks. This must surely be a thunderbolt shot from the skies! What means this wild and onward dash the sight of which fills all hearts with terror! What unknown power lies deep concealed within these horses? Oh! coursers of sublimity, what whirlwinds lift your manes! It is as though your quivering bodies were all ear. When they catch above their heads the old familiar song they expand their breasts of bronze in unison, and, scarcely touching the earth with their hooves, make but a stretched and single line, cleaving the air. Just so does Russia pursue her onward flight, inspired by Heaven. . . . Whither dost thou fly? Answer me that, but no answer comes. The bells tinkle melodiously: the tormented air gathers to a wind, and all upon the earth is left far behind. Then, with eyes of envy, the other nations stand aside to give it passage!"

When a satirist turns lyrical it is because he has caught sight of something on the further side of satire. Having written a masterpiece about dead souls, Gogol, the moralist and preacher, longed to set out in search of living souls. Between 1842 and 1848, leading a wandering existence in many parts of Europe, he tried to continue the adventures of Tchitchikov, this time introducing into the narrative some noble characters; a certain Mourasov who reminds us, as has been justly said, of M. Madeleine in *Les Misérables*, and a prince-governor who, like the King in Molière's comedies, is an enemy to all dishonesty. At the same time he was writing numerous letters to his Russian friends, in defence of himself: "The essential feature of my talent is to cast a revealing light upon vulgarity."

"If *Dead Souls* has been received in Russia with such a show of consternation, the reason is not that the book uncovers so many sores and reveals so much of inner sickness: nor that it offers a sensational spectacle of vice triumphant and innocence oppressed. No, no, my heroes are not criminals. I had but to add a single sympathetic feature to any one of them, and the reader would readily have accepted all the rest. What has repelled him is the vulgarity of the whole. My heroes pass before his eyes, one more vulgar than the other, and, his patience exhausted, he seeks some consoling episode, some spot where he may halt awhile and draw breath. When he shuts the volume, he feels that he has come from an airless cavern into the light of day. I should have been forgiven for portraying picturesque ruffians: what I cannot be forgiven are my flat-footed vulgarians."

But Gogol asserts that he has been fully aware of this danger, has realized that the absence of light in the book is distressing in the extreme. He is going, he says, to supply it in the second volume.

> "I love the good and ensue it. It fills me with enthusiasm. Far from taking pleasure, like my heroes, in my turpitudes, I detest them. I abhor the baseness that estranges me from the good. I fight against it, and, with God's help, shall overcome it. . . . I have already freed myself from much of my meanness by passing it on to my heroes, thereby delivering them over to my own mockery as well as to the sarcasm of others. By stripping the picturesque rags from vileness, and pulling from its face the mask of chivalrous knighthood which is presented to us, I have begun to liberate myself. When I confess my misdeeds to Him who put me into this world and willed me to correct my defects, I am still conscious of my many vices. But they are no longer those of the years gone by. From those a divine power has helped me to break free."

But to paint living souls one must be one of them. They cannot be invented. To bring light into a book, one must strike light into oneself: one must become better. What Gogol was saying now was, in other words, that one must turn back to Christ. During these years of penitence, he did much reading in the Fathers of the Church. He studied *Les Elévations sur les Mystères* and *Le Traité de la Concupiscence* of Bossuet. He dreamed of going to the Holy Land, to Jerusalem. In Russia, his friends who received these emotional letters were terrified.

"Be careful," Aksakov wrote to him, "you are walking on a knife-edge and are well on the way to falling into mysticism." The critics warned him that he would kill his art stone dead if he turned into a layman playing at being a Father of the Church: "And what sort of a layman? a satirist!" He, on the contrary, believed that he was working in the interest of his art by making it worthy to give birth to nobler characters: "I have no love for my horrors: I fight against them and with God's help, shall drive them out."

He returned to the dream of his youth, to be of service. He wanted to do good in the sphere of action. "I have always thought that I could play an important part in working for the common weal, that I could make myself indispensable." The position he was now taking up was the very reverse of that adopted by Pushkin, who used to say that he was "born for sweet sounds". Gogol could not understand contemplation without action. It was a courageous attitude, but ambivalent, and, therefore, dangerous for the artist, and, perhaps, for the saint. There is a deal of pride in this wish to act on the hearts of men. May not to *serve* mean to *command*? Was not the Devil, in a new disguise, again taking possession of Gogol? Whether or no, the writer no longer doubted where his mission lay, and thought that he would begin it by publishing *Select Extracts from Letters* which should reveal a new Gogol.

The effect was a staggering blow to him. He had thought that he would find forgiveness for *Dead Souls*. What happened was that the critics attacked him more violently than ever. From Herzen to Bielinsky, the liberals, all of them more or less atheists, who had believed that he was one of them, were irritated at seeing him falling into bigotry. "He will be buried as a mystic, but he was no such thing." The public was exasperated. He was accused of parading an arrogant humility. He was called *Tartuffe Vassilievitch*. Nevertheless, he was sincere, or as sincere as he could be. He genuinely believed that, by his books, he was going to create in himself, and in others, an interior Kingdom of Heaven, that society would be better because men would be better, that his country would become an Earthly Paradise administered by virtuous officials. But, in the eyes of his readers, all this preachifying was bringing him into disrepute. It was all so very much like the homilies of Khlestakov and Tchitchinov. "He fought the Demon like one possessed of the Demon." This he soon saw for himself. "Once again I have been playing the Khlestakov game," he said, and wrote to his mother: "Pray that the merciful God may drive out of me the spirit of self-confidence, blindness and pride." Many of his colleagues said that he was mad. He recognized, with humility, that his true strength lay in creating "living images", in works of the imagination. "I feel that I am a great deal stronger as a writer than as a reasoner . . . if all this had been put into my novel, the critics would have found nothing to object to."

So, to the making of images he returned; in other words, to the second part of *Dead Souls*. It was there that he proposed to sublimate the real. From then on he refused to make use of his formidable gift for the comic. In spite of himself, however, it still crackles and glows in such few fragments of the book as were rescued from the flames to which he consigned it. But speaking generally, it is safe to say that, whereas his dead souls had been very much alive, his living souls were undoubtedly dead. Unlike Tolstoy and Dostoievsky, who made living persons of Levine and Pierre Bezoukhov, of Muichkin and Alexis Karamazov, Gogol could give true animation only to his more monstrous puppets. His genius was for comedy, and, in his heart of hearts, he knew it. On two separate occasions he burned what he had written of this second part. Why? "Because," he wrote, "if a man is to rise again, he must first die." But he began again almost at once. What he now intended was that his novel, like the *Divine Comedy*, should have three sections. The first had been the *Inferno*: a world of damned spirits who did not even know that they were damned. The second was to be the *Purgatorio* in which the characters should become aware of their degradation; the third, the *Paradiso*. But why, even in Dante's hands, is the *Inferno*, as a work of art, superior to the *Paradiso*? Why does *Paradise Regained* add nothing to the reputation of Milton, whose *Paradise Lost* is almost the only one of his major poems now read?

In 1847 Gogol set off on a pilgrimage to the Holy Land, hoping that in Jerusalem, in the presence of the tomb of Christ, God would instruct him in his duty both as a writer and a man. From the very first, however, he knew that his journey would be in vain, since he was embarking upon it without faith and without love. He was painfully aware that certain things left him cold, though cold was what he least wanted to be. He was perpetually haunted by the knowledge that his soul was arid, dry, in short, dead. To his religious friends, Alexandra Rosset, now Mme Smirnov, and Count Alexis Tolstoy, he confessed that before the Holy

Sepulchre, he had felt as though his heart were made of ice. Count Tolstoy had recommended him to consult his own Spiritual Director, Father Matvei. The choice was not a good one. Father Matvei was a narrow-minded sectarian, who held the stage and all literature in abhorrence, both *The Government Inspector* and *Dead Souls*. He saw salvation for Gogol only in fasting and mortification.

Gogol thought that by returning to the Ukraine, to his mother and his sisters, he might find the refreshment of which he stood in need. But the love of his native land had also dried up. He found the pettiness of provincial life more shocking, more intolerable than ever. Gloomy and preoccupied, he did nothing and found gaiety in nothing. At forty-two he looked like an old man. Was he sick? He thought so, but the doctors could find nothing organically wrong with him. Many of them believed that he was shamming, whereas the truth was that all his life had been nothing but a prolonged process of dying. At Moscow, in 1850, he announced that *Dead Souls* had, at last, been completed. This was just another lie. Turgenev, who was one of his admirers, saw him at this time, and was struck by the signs of secret disquiet which showed in the shrewd, observant eyes. "The long pointed nose gave to his face a crafty look which made one think of a fox." While listening to him, he thought: "What a strange, diseased creature he is." Gogol had taken pains to be pleasant to Turgenev, who was a young writer much in favour at that period. With other visitors he remained silent, and yawned. Many said that he was well on the way to going mad: others, that his seeming madness was merely another deliberate mystification.

Father Matvei urged him to abandon writing for good

THE ART OF WRITING

and all. This priest was a peasant in his sixties who had
lived an ascetic life. "In my view," said Gogol, "he is the
most intelligent man I have ever come across." He ended
a letter to the Father with these words: "Yours eternally
grateful both on this side of the grave and beyond it."
But, all the same, he put up a stubborn fight in defence
of his work. "Not to write at all would be for me the
same thing as not to go on living." Then, towards
the end of 1851, the death of a woman friend had an
overwhelming effect on him. He put his manuscript
aside.

> "This is not the moment for me to be concerned
> with all that sort of thing. . . . Life would lose its
> beauty if there were no death. . . . The time has gone
> by for joking and philosophizing. . . . The earth is
> already burning with an incomprehensible anguish.
> . . . All is silence . . . all is but a grave. Oh God!—how
> empty and terrifying has Thy world become."

He made his confession and took Communion. He
thought that he had heard a voice in a dream speaking to
him of his approaching death. He had a stormy interview
with Father Matvei, in the course of which the priest
threatened him with eternal damnation. "Enough!" cried
Gogol. "Let me be! . . . I can bear no more. . . . It is too
frightful!" He shut his door against all visitors, told his
servant to light the stove, and threw the manuscript of
Dead Souls into the blaze. The lad had an obscure feeling
that some terrible crime was being committed before his
eyes. "Why are you doing that?" he asked. "Be silent!"
said Gogol, "it is none of your business." Then he burst
into tears as he looked at the ashes. To Count Tolstoy
he said:

[290]

"See what I have done. . . . What power the Devil has . . . this is what he has driven me to!"

"Nonsense!" said the Count, "it is a good sign: it means that you will live to do better."

These encouraging words put new life into Gogol:

"Yes," he answered, "it is all here, in my head."

But he never again left his sofa. He lay there motionless, with his eyes shut, and refusing all food. "Don't touch me, I beg you," he murmured. He received extreme unction. "I have no pain," he declared, "all I want is to be left in peace." One cannot help thinking of the death of Marcel Proust, who worked until the very end, and clung to life so that, before he died, he could write "Finis". Gogol, on the other hand, destroyed his work and died with it.

His last words were: "A ladder, quick! a ladder. . . ." A few lines in one of his letters explains the exclamation: "God knows, perhaps the ladder is even now ready to be thrown down to us from the sky, and the hand which will help us to climb it, is already stretched." He died on 21st February, 1852. His will contained these words: "Be living souls and not dead souls. There is no other gate than that shown us by the Lord Jesus Christ."

5

Never was there a more mysterious end to a life. The doctors all asserted that Gogol was not suffering from any mortal disease. Of what then did he die?—of the desire for death. The life of the body, the harmonious life of a Pushkin had been denied him. Having imprisoned himself within a false and terrible dilemma—

either Art or God—he had felt himself compelled to make the choice of death. Why, knowing that he was lost, did he burn his manuscript? That he might stand naked before God? But was it not the Devil who, once again, had tempted him and driven him to make a sacrifice, not of love but of overweening pride. "It is useless," said Boris de Schloezer, "to try to make out that his life ended on a concord of sweet sounds." "Art," Gogol had once declared, "should bring a reconciliation with life." Is it possible for any biographer to see such a reconciliation in his end?

For my part, I think that can be said. The reading of Gogol's books, and the close study of his life, does not leave me with any feeling of despair. He was a writer of genius who had something to say, and said it. To his literary heirs, to Turgenev, to Tolstoy, to Dostoievsky he bequeathed some admirable examples. When Turgenev said: "He is the mould from which we have all come", he was speaking the truth. His misfortune was that he never knew how well he had carried out the task for which he had been made. He believed that he owed to his country a second part of *Dead Souls*, whereas it was the first part of which Russia stood in need, the masterpiece which is still of universal application. He thought of himself as a dead soul, "but a dead soul could never have been capable of so heroic a feat of extravagance". Proust wrote: "One had knocked on all the doors, only to find that they opened on to nothing, until, suddenly, one came by chance upon the only one through which it was possible to pass."

Gogol, too, by accident had come upon the only "door" which led into his secret nature, namely, a gift of dark and gloomy humour shot through, at rare moments of slackened tension, with deeply moving lyric flights. And, at last, that door had swung open to give egress to masterpieces. All his life long he had had a feeling that he owed some great duty to Russia, and had concluded wrongly, that it could be performed by his becoming either a great administrator or a saint. His only real duty was that of the artist, that is, to paint with absolute truth and unwavering courage what he saw, and this he did. He gave to his country, and to the world, something more precious than dead souls—legendary figures over-flowing with more intensity of life than the living, and that phantom troïka the bells of which sound down the centuries like the "jerky and metallic tinkle" at a garden gate in Combray. Had he but been aware of this success, this passport into immortality, with what peace of mind and heart would he have come into the presence of the greatest of all Government Inspectors. At the end of the sublime and painful symphony which is what the life of almost every true artist is, the closing chord sounds, not the harmonious and impossible resolution of a man's life and work, but the reconciliation of that work with Time.

The sad renunciation which, a hundred years ago, marked the end of that tormented life, could not be, and was not, the last movement of his symphony. Far from perishing with its creator, the work broke free from him. Gogol dying had turned away from it, but now it makes of Gogol a living being. The readers of his day saw in it the Russia of their time, a posting house upon the road along which the troïka was sweeping onward into the future. "Tell me, whither dost thou hasten?" The bells sound melodiously, and hard on the heels of a funeral march comes an *allegro furioso*. The unhappy and divided man, Nicolas Vassilievitch Gogol, has been dead for a century, but the artist now set free continues still, throughout the world, to liberate his readers.

CHAPTER XIII : THE ART OF
TURGENEV

LITERARY QUARRELS are one of those violent and futile games without which, it seems, men find their brief existence too long to be endured. There is no good reason why two different writers should be thought to compete for the favours of the reader, nor why their books should be regarded as waging an internecine war. But, just as in the seventeenth century the admirers of Racine behaved like jealous lovers intent on purging their mistresses' minds of every trace or hint of Corneille, so, too, in our own age has Russian literature aroused in Western Europe strange and guileless passions. Those who give to Dostoievsky a fanatical devotion (very natural and very proper) seem to think that they must, therefore, turn their backs on Tolstoy, and, more particularly, on Turgenev. Robert Lynd has said in one of his essays that those who are loud in praise of this or that Russian writer proclaim their devotion by denigrating others. They are, he says, monotheistic in their worship of literature, and cannot bear to see altars raised in honour of rival divinities.

As almost always in human affairs there is a substratum of truth beneath this apparent absurdity. What we champion with such fervour in our chosen God is not so much his work as our own taste. Our literary choices, our preferences, are dictated by our emotional and intellectual needs. Having found in a novel the precise expression of our own restlessness or our own serenity, we look upon the hostile critic as a personal enemy. The modern disciples of Dostoievsky feel for Turgenev very much what Dostoievsky himself felt. In the world of readers no less than in that of writers, temperaments are in violent opposition. Nothing could well be more natural, and nothing, perhaps, more healthy. But it would be a strange critical method that should seek to transform subjective reactions into absolute judgments. To blame Turgenev for not writing like Dostoievsky is about as sensible as to feel resentment because an apple tree does not produce peaches.

But surely we may be allowed to classify fruits in an order of preference? Obviously we cannot expect to find peaches on a bramble bush: but are we not entitled to say that in the general scale of fruit values, the peach is superior, in our opinion, to the blackberry? If, say the ardent followers of Dostoievsky or Tolstoy, one compares the worlds created by the three great Russian novelists, there can be no denying that Turgenev's is perfectly consistent with the man, that it is, in fact, the most Turgenevian of all possible worlds. Admittedly it has a certain charm and elegance: up to a certain point it is even true. That we must all agree. But, granted its merits, it remains a very small world. The reader can very soon make its complete circuit. After reading two of the novels he will know the typical Turgenev "setting" like the back of his hand. It is unvaryingly, or almost unvaryingly, a Russian country house belonging to aristocrats of moderate means, containing the "old familiar round-bellied chests-of-drawers with their brass fittings, the white painted chairs with their oval backs, the chandeliers with their crystal lustres"[1]—and, we might add, the narrow beds with their old-fashioned striped curtains, the bedside table with its icons, the shabby carpets spotted with wax-droppings. The landscapes also run true to form: the steppe in the administrative area of Oriol, the copses of birch and aspen, the eternal mists. One knows, too, his human types: the Russian Hamlet—Bazarov and Rudin: the old gentleman who is a relic of the eighteenth century: the young civil servant, contented and ambitious: the talkative and ineffectual revolutionary. The same is true of the women. They can be divided into two or three recognizable groups: the sweet young girl, all perfection and frequently pious: Tatiana in *Smoke*, Lisa in *A House of Gentlefolk*; the temperamental woman, dangerous and misunderstood: Irene, in *Smoke*; finally, the Marianne of *Virgin Soil*, physically strong, unmarried, with grey eyes, a straight nose and thin lips which seem to express a deep-seated need for struggle and devotion. These garrulous men, infirm of purpose, these passionate and generous-hearted women make up a tiny, shut-in universe. How far removed, we tell ourselves, from those serried ranks of human beings to whom Dostoievsky and Tolstoy could give life and movement.

True, no doubt. But I cannot, for the life of me, see why an artist's world should be found lacking on the mere score of its being small. The quality of a work of art is not to be measured in terms of size, any more than it is to be judged by the importance of the object represented. We might just as well complain of the triviality of a piece of still-life. We might just as well say that Vermeer was not a great painter because he painted

[1] Haumant.

only small interiors, or that Chardin is a lesser artist than Cormon because he drew his models from one social level only (the hard-working lower middle class of Paris). The truth seems to lie all in the other direction, that it is often an excellent thing for the artist to work within a strictly limited field. It is impossible to know everything well, and a small picture painted with close attention to detail may teach us more about human beings than a "vast and sprawling fresco". A novelist can tell us the truth about three Germans or ten Germans, but he may not be able to give us much information about Germany; or, rather, he can tell us about Germany only in so far as he can describe, to the extent that his temperament permits, the Germans he has known. It matters little to me that in *A Sportsman's Sketches*, Turgenev gives us nothing but the portraits of a few peasants living round Spasskoïe. In doing so he tells me more about the Russia of 1830 than I could learn from any number of long books about Russian history.

Besides, though the types with which Turgenev works belong to a fairly small social species, within that species there are numerous and well-defined variants. In every Turgenev novel, so it is said, you will find the temperamental woman and the Russian Hamlet. Perhaps, but these different Hamlets are none of them really alike. Bazarov is not the same man as Rudin. Bazarov is as silent as Rudin is talkative. He is misanthropic, desperate and moody. He is capable of love, whereas the other is not. Lavretzky, in *A House of Gentlefolk*, is another Hamlet type, but less complex, more simple-minded. Nejdanov, in *Virgin Soil*, is a Hamlet with something in him of Julien Sorel, but an aristocratic Julien, which

makes of him quite a different character. The same can
be said of the peasants in *A Sportsman's Sketches*. They
have certain features in common, as is only natural, but
they are thoroughly individualized. One might, perhaps,
with more reason complain of the monotony of Turgenev's women, but the same defect is to be found in
other great novelists. Most men are obsessed by a certain
type of woman, and find it difficult not to run after her.
Not seldom they write for the sole purpose of painting
her portrait. When we say that this or that woman
"might have stepped out of a Racine play", we evoke a
type sufficiently generalized to contain women as different
as Roxane, Esther and Phèdre, yet, at the same time,
clearly defined in terms of type. Is Racine to be blamed
for that? Like all artists of the front rank, Racine and
Turgenev chose, from among the immense variety of
human beings, those whom their art could best assimi-
late. That is a perfectly natural and a perfectly legitimate
process.

Another complaint is that Turgenev was deficient in
creative genius.

We must be quite clear about the meaning of that
word, creative. Is a novelist to produce his characters
from some unimaginable void, or should he, more simply,
try to paint nature as he has seen it? I hope to show,
later on, that the question seems to me to be badly
framed. But we do know what Turgenev's own answer
would be. "I have never", he said, "been able to create
anything simply from my imagination. All my characters
have to be modelled on real people."

Thanks to the labours of M. Mazon, who has published
a remarkable analysis of the papers, drafts and plans for
future work, left by Turgenev in Paris, we are now in a

position to study the methods he employed in absorbing and utilizing living persons in his stories. These papers show him to us at his desk. When he started on a novel, he first drew up a list of characters. Quite often the real name of the model is indicated side by side with that of his hero. Thus, in the draft of *First Love*, we read:

> Myself, a little boy of thirteen.
> My father, thirty-eight.
> My mother, thirty-six.

Then, later, he made a correction—Myself, a little boy of fifteen—having, no doubt, decided that his own emotional precocity might seem improbable. In the "cast" of *On the Eve*, Karataïev, a *real* person round whom the book is constructed, is called by his own name, as is, also, the Bulgarian, Katranov.

Turgenev filled out these lists with biographical notes on the characters. These tell us about their physical attributes and their antecedents. For example: "epilepsy in the family: one of the mother's cousins was mad". Then follow moral judgments: "Sensual, though rather shy. . . . Naturally good and honest—doesn't cost him any effort. . . . Has a tendency to religious mysticism." Sometimes these notations of character and temperament are suggested by real persons whose names are given: "The expression of his face is that of the late Savin and of the lunatic, Verokin"—Golouchkin wants to be taken for a progressive—"same sort of type as the soldier, Tankov."

All those who have made a study of the way in which novelists work will realize that in this respect Turgenev resembled some of the greatest. Balzac made no bones about talking of the "fish-pond" from which he, also, drew nutriment for his works. We know the identities of several of Tolstoy's models. Perhaps a day will come when Dr Robert Proust will publish Marcel's notebooks, and we shall be able to see how, with the aid of jottings, he built up the characters of his book, and read, as in Turgenev's memoranda, the actual names of those who contributed to their realization. Artistic creation is not creation *ex nihilo*. It is a re-grouping of elements taken from the real world. It would be easy enough to show that even the strangest tales, those which seem to us to be furthest from actual observation, such as *Gulliver's Travels*, Poe's *Tales*, the *Divine Comedy* and Jarry's *Ubu-roi*, owed much to memories, just as Leonardo's monsters and the devils carved on the capitals of cathedral pillars were constructed with the help of the features of human beings and of animals, or as a mechanical invention is not a creation of matter, but a new assemblage of parts already known. "The artist", says Valéry, "accumulates and composes, *through the medium of matter*, a quantity of desires, intentions and conditions which have come from all the points of the human spirit." It should also be pointed out that such a piece of mechanism, once set up, becomes a generator of life by its own movement. Thus Proust, having created Charlus by making use of Montesquiou, was very soon able to "talk Charlus" without further reference to his model. This power which fictional characters have of developing a life of their own, is seen to a remarkable extent in Balzac, especially towards the end of his life.

But though creation *ex nihilo* is impossible, it remains true that the novelist may keep, more or less, close to nature. "I am a realist," said Turgenev, and maintained that the sole duty of the artist is to paint honestly what he sees. But the problem is more complex than that.

It is easy enough to say: "Paint what you see, reproduce nature." But how is to to be done? Nature is inexhaustible: it is multiple both in space and in time. Enough images and ideas pass through a man's mind in one hour to fill a book of four hundred pages. If, in such a book, the author wishes to create a sense of life, not only in one man but in a group of men and women, it becomes obvious that the realistic method will have to make concessions, will have to suppress, cut, choose. Delacroix inveighed against realism in painting. "If you want to paint 'real' pictures," he said, "then all you have to do is to carve statues in the shapes of men, give them the actual colours of living people, and impart movement to them with the aid of a concealed spring. You will have been 'real' sure enough, you will have kept close to life, but will you have produced a work of art? You will not. You will, in point of fact, have done the exact opposite."

Art is not nature. It is an essentially human activity. The need men feel for art is the need to make nature (which is confused) intelligible to the human mind by imposing upon it constructions which, in nature itself, are not visible. Turgenev knew this very well. He liked quoting what Bacon said, that "Art is man added to nature", and Goethe's remark to the effect that "we must raise the real to the level of poetry".

If we are to judge works of art it is essential for us to understand that the two ideas of realism and poetry are not contradictory (and that is all that Turgenev's doctrine amounted to). A novel does not resemble life—common sense tells us that. It is limited in scope, it is organized, it is composed. But the ordered whole must be made up of details which are true to life, and it must, in itself, be convincing. A Shakespearean tragedy is not a "slice of life", though the characters in it are living beings. Polonius is a genuine courtier, Hamlet a real young man. A novelist must no more attempt to paint without a model than a dramatist. In the novels of Turgenev you will never find a character who gives the impression that he is playing a part in a melodrama. The sportsmen are "real" sportsmen who see things with the eye of a sportsman. The peasants talk like peasants and do not react to nature as a painter would. The women are feminine. I said, a while back, that Turgenev's world is small. But, precisely because he had the courage to limit his universe to what he could himself observe, he is one of those rare novelists who almost never lie.

But if Turgenev is a realist because his details are true to life, it is by the choice he makes of them that he proves himself to be an artist. M. Paul Bourget once heard M. Taine give a summary of the Russian novelist's theories about description. "According to him, the descriptive talent is all a matter of choosing evocative details. He took the view that description should always be indirect and *suggestive* rather than *laboured*. Those were the very words he used, and he quoted with admiration a passage from Tolstoy in which the silence of a lovely night on a river bank is made almost perceptible merely by the mention of one simple feature of the scene: a bat in flight. One could, he maintained, actually *hear* the sound of the wing-tips touching. . . ." It was always by the evocation of such details that Turgenev handled his descriptions. Here are two examples, taken at random. The first is from *A Lear of the Steppes*:

"So profound was the silence that one could hear at a distance of more than a hundred paces, a squirrel skipping across the dead leaves which already lay thick on the ground, or the faint crack of a dead branch breaking off from the top of a tree and rebounding from other branches in its fall until it reached the ground, where it lay in the withered grass, never to move again."

And this, from *A House of Gentlefolk*:

"Peace had descended on the salon, where nothing was to be heard but the faint spitting of the wax candles, the sound of a hand striking the card table, an exclamation, a voice adding up the score.

Through the windows came great waves of the cool night air, bringing with them the challenging song of the nightingale, clear-toned and ardent."

These examples, which it would be very interesting to compare with similar passages in Flaubert, are sufficient to give us an understanding of Turgenev's habitual method of procedure. He lets the vision buried within him rise again into consciousness, and notes which detail it is that first solicits his awareness. He then makes of that the key element of the required scene, round which the others gather like a retinue.

To hold tight to the essential detail, to suggest rather than demonstrate, those are the rules and methods of a certain form of art which combines delicacy with strength. Turgenev's art has frequently been compared to Greek art, and the comparison is accurate, because in both a complex whole is evoked by means of a few perfectly chosen details.

No novelist has ever employed so great an economy of means. It comes as something of a surprise to those of us who are, to some extent, familiar with the technique of novel-writing, that Turgenev should have been able, in books so short, to give an impression of solidity and abundance. An analysis of the method shows a skill in construction which is carried to perfection but is never obtrusive. A Meredith, a George Eliot delight in following their heroes from childhood to maturity. Tolstoy takes his point of departure somewhere well removed from the central episode of his story. Turgenev, on the other hand, almost always plunges straight into the main action. *Fathers and Children* covers only a few weeks, as, also, does *First Love*. *A House of Gentlefolk* opens with the return of Lavretzky, *Smoke* at the moment of the meeting with Irene. It is only later, when the reader's emotions have already been engaged, that the author turns back into the few paths which he considers it necessary to explore. When reading Turgenev one is almost inevitably reminded of that unity of time which is so marked a feature in the classic French tragedies. He is, indeed, a great classic. He even shares with the great classical writers their contempt for "plot". Like Molière, who made use of the most hackneyed subjects and the most familiar *dénouements* for his plays, Turgenev was primarily concerned to portray certain characters and to bring into a clear focus certain emotional shades. In the case of *Virgin Soil* we now know, from M. Mazon's documentation, that he finally found his subject after working and meditating on his central character for eighteen months. Like Molière, too, he was satisfied with an almost archaic symmetry. With the *femme fatale* (Varvara, Irene) he contrasts the pure woman (Lisa,

Tatiana): the artist with the practical man: children with their fathers. His construction is a great deal more ingenuous and primitive than that of either Tolstoy or Dostoievsky.

There is a similar economy of means in the portraying of character. As in his descriptive passages, a few well-chosen details are given the task of suggesting the rest. For instance, in *A House of Gentlefolk*, Lavretzky has left a flirtatious wife who has been false to him. He thinks that she is dead. She suddenly turns up again in his own house, and not unnaturally he receives her with some degree of severity. She shows him his little daughter in an attempt to work on his feelings:

" 'Look, Ada, your father,' said Varvara Pavlovna, pushing back the curls which hung low over the child's eyes and passionately embracing her, 'join your prayers with mine!'

'That is papa,' lisped the child.

'Yes, darling, and you love him, do you not?'

Lavretzky could stand no more:

'From what particular melodrama did you borrow this scene?'

And he left the room.

For a moment, Varvara Pavlovna did not move, then, with a faint shrug, she led the little girl into another room, where she undressed her and put her to bed. She, herself, took up a book and sat down under the lamp. She waited for about an hour, after which she decided to go to bed.

'Well, madame?' said the French maid whom Madame Lavretzky had brought with her from Paris. as she helped her mistress to undress:

'He looks much older, Justine, but he is still (I think) at heart as good as ever. Bring me my night-gloves, lay out my high-necked grey dress for tomorrow, and don't, whatever you do, forget the mutton cutlets for Ada. . . . You may find it difficult to get any here, but you must try.'

'We must do with what there is,' replied Justine, and blew out the candle."

There is an unforgettable note of callousness about the scene. Varvara Pavlovna's lack of heart, the egotism of a pretty woman who is completely sure of herself, her husband's weakness—all this we see in a single short page, as we should do in life were we in the presence of those particular characters. Yet nothing has been said by the author. We have been given no elaborate analysis of the workings of Varvara Pavlovna's mind. But, after the painful scene with her husband, the only thing she bothers about is the beauty of her hands. She asks for the gloves she wears in bed. That is enough. We know her through and through.

But as I have already pointed out, it is not enough in describing Turgenev's art to use the word "realist". It is essential to add that his realism is "poetic". What, exactly, does that mean? Poetry is one of the worst defined words in the language. We should never lose sight of the fact that, in the etymological sense, the poet is "he who makes". Poetry is the art of remaking, of re-creating the world for man, of imposing upon it a form and, above all, a rhythm. To reconstruct this mysterious unity, to establish a relationship between Nature and the human emotions, to set the individual adventure within the vast rhythmic movement of clouds and sunlight, spring and winter, youth and age, that is what being a poet and, at the same time, a novelist means.

It is impossible to think of Turgenev's books without being conscious of those great phenomena of nature which, in some way, associate it with human passions. In *Smoke* we watch the white clouds slowly drifting over the countryside. The garden in *First Love* is unforgettable, the night in *Bèjine's Meadow*, the lake beside which Dmitri Rudin has his last meeting with the girl he is about to desert.

A poetic realist knows that men's lives are not filled only with humdrum details, but that they also have their great moments, their periods of restlessness, mystery and noble illusions. To dream is a part of reality. If we overlook that or deliberately try to avoid it, we impoverish reality and take from it all that makes it human. That is what Turgenev meant when he wrote: "The trouble with Zola is that he has never read Shakespeare."

That statement needs annotating, for there is a great deal to be said about Zola's poetry, though it is not difficult to see why the art of Zola seemed to Turgenev to be limited. In his view, any picture of life which neglects certain tender feelings, certain movements of happiness, is incomplete and false. There is a realist pattern just as there is a romantic pattern: the tremolo is as dangerous as the roulade. "I am not a naturalist," said Turgenev, "I am a supernaturalist" — which is strictly true. What was lacking in his friends (and as markedly in Flaubert and the Goncourts as in Zola) was a genuine experience of the simplest and strongest of all human feelings. After a dinner at which Turgenev had

explained with extreme delicacy why it is that love is an
emotion with a very special colour of its own, and why
Zola was on the wrong road if he refused to recognize
that colour, Edmond de Goncourt rather artlessly noted
in his Journal: "What it all amounts to is that neither
Flaubert, in spite of all his exaggerated talk about the
subject, nor Zola, nor I have ever been seriously in
love, with the result that we are incapable of dealing
adequately with love in our writings." That they were
so lacking is perfectly true. "It is not that they are devoid
of talent," said Turgenev, "but that they are not on the
right road. They use their imagination too much. Literature, in their hands, 'stinks of literature'."

He had most certainly been in love, or at least, halfway to being in love. He had known romantic passion.
In his attitude to Pauline Viardot there had been a touch
of the chivalrous. But whether what he felt had been
friendship or love, there can be no doubt that he had
experienced at first hand those warm and durable feelings
which free from all meanness of mind and heart those
whom they have touched, and impart to their spirit the
distinctive "colouring" which we recognize at once,
whether in a statesman or a businessman, by reason of
a sort of noble serenity, so that we feel convinced that
they have known true love. Much of the quality of
Turgenev's books comes from that.

No doubt, purely animal sensuality is also true, and
it is necessary. It will, however, be generally admitted
that it can very soon become monotonous and tedious.
There can be no question but that all novelists who have
written well about passionate love—and I am thinking
as much of Stendhal as of Turgenev—have been chaste
novelists. Even Proust, who cast such a revealing light

on the part played by the physiological mechanism in all emotional experience, does so, almost always, with a remarkable measure of restraint, and, when he oversteps the limits, comes a cropper. I point this out, not because I am at all preoccupied with morality, for morals and art have nothing in common, but because it seems to me to reveal the existence of an important aesthetic law.

The characteristics in Turgenev to which I have drawn attention (the desire to paint only what he knew well from his own experience, the prevalence in his work of those great emotions which he himself had felt) might lead us to expect a highly subjective art. He maintained, on the contrary, that a novelist must be *objective*, and "disappear from view behind the people in his books". "The umbilical cord which ties a writer to his characters must be cut," he said to M. Taine. To a young man who wanted to make writing his profession, and had asked him for advice, he wrote:

> "If the study of human beings, of other people's lives, interests you more than the expressing of your own feelings and your own ideas; if you find more pleasure in painting truly and accurately the exterior, not only of a man but of any quite ordinary object, than in writing with elegance and warmth about what *you* feel about those men or those objects—then you are an objective writer and fitted to undertake a story or a novel."

This attitude, which was that as much of Flaubert as of Turgenev, would seem to be at odds with the methods of our present-day practitioners of fiction. Most of us prefer the subjective approach, and try to re-create in

the reader the emotion provoked in us by some important
event, rather by analysing the emotion in question than
by recording the facts which gave rise to it. It seems to
me that both manners are equally acceptable, and that
nothing could be more erroneous than to condemn
Proust in the name of Turgenev. Why must we take
sides in the quarrel between the objective writer and the
subjective? There is more than one way of suggesting
the world. The truth is, I think, that no writer, however
objective he may want to be, can ever wholly prevent
his personality from showing in his work. A man is
marked by a certain number of preoccupations, and they
will come to light whether he likes it or not. It is impossible to read Meredith without concluding that, in
middle age, he fell in love with a young girl—which is
strictly true. In all his young women there is a grace, a
perfection which is obviously linked with some deep
feeling in himself. Similarly, in Turgenev's novels we
get a very clear impression of what he was like—languid,
sentimental, honest and for ever searching in vain for
some strong woman who might arouse his passion. It is
this, what we might call congenital, monotony that gives
life to a writer's work. A novelist can cut the umbilical
cord which binds his characters to the imagination which
gave them birth: what he cannot do is to keep them
from having a recognizable resemblance to their creator,
and to one another.

Besides, Turgenev was very far from refusing to
indulge in introspection. He thought that an artist should
be willing to accept everything and everybody, including
himself, as a possible object of observation. "A writer,"
he said, "should never let himself be crushed by suffering. He should make use of everything that comes his

way. He is, by definition, highly strung. He feels more intensely than other people. That is precisely why he should exercise self-control. He should always and exhaustively contemplate himself and others. If unhappiness comes to you, sit down and write: 'This, that or the other has happened: this, that or the other is what I feel.' The pain will pass, an excellent piece of writing will remain. It may, perhaps, become the vital centre of a piece of work which will be truly a work of art, because it will be genuine, and painted from life." And, elsewhere: "If all unhappy artists blew out their brains, there would be no artists left, for they are all more or less unhappy. There is no such thing as a happy artist. Happiness bring tranquility, and tranquility never created anything."

It seems clear, then, that he was both subjective and objective. As a matter of fact, he had little liking for systems and classifications. He held that liberty is necessary for the artist. "You feel swept upwards on a surge of joyous, childlike faith, do you? You want to let yourself go in a great lyrical outpouring? Well, let yourself go. Perhaps, on the other hand, you feel like blowing all your emotions sky-high, to see everything with an inquisitorial eye, analyse until the objects of your analysis crack like nuts. Well, get on with it!" An artist should be loyal only to himself, not to a system.

About one thing only was he intransigent. He believed that no novelist should ever consciously set out to prove a thesis. The artist and the moralist are two essentially different persons. Art is a way of escape, not a demonstration. A novelist can be as much interested in ideas as anybody else. The expression of ideas, like the expression of feelings, is part and parcel of that human life which he is trying to paint, but ideas should figure in his work as belonging to his characters. They should spring from, not mould, them. They should provide moments of dramatic tension, and leave us free to choose between them. Turgenev made no effort to "understand life". He had no system of morality to preach, no metaphysics, no philosophy. That was not his job. He confined himself to telling a story, to introducing his readers to human beings. For some time now there has been a great deal of talk in France about pure poetry. Turgenev provides us with one of the best examples of the pure novel.

It was from this point of view that he had so great an influence on his French friends. The young Maupassant owed much to him, and from him, even more than from Flaubert, got his taste for story-telling. "In spite of his age," wrote Maupassant, "Turgenev was always expressing the most modern, the most advanced ideas, rejecting the old theories of the manipulated novel, of the contrived drama, and basing his work directly on life, without plots, without crude adventure themes." Turgenev, for his part, thought highly of Maupassant. Tolstoy tells how, one day, when Turgenev was staying at Yasnaïa Polyana, he took from his bag a small French book which he handed to his host. "Read that when you have a moment to spare," he said; "it's by a young French writer, and it's not at all bad." The book was *La Maison Tellier*.

In matters of style and composition Turgenev was the master of the French writers between 1860 and 1880. We should derive a good deal of benefit from re-reading him now, at a time when, as André Gide said, a writer can no longer speak of an object without comparing it with ten others. Turgenev, like Stendhal and Merimée, Tchekov and Tolstoy, knew that the power of words is all that matters. A perfectly ordinary word, even used in isolation, has the power to suggest the object to which it refers. If it can't, what is the use of language? But, if the word is enough, why adorn it with a lot of ugly and merely ornamental rock-work? I know that the facets and the prickles will always attract the *blasé* reader. I know that one can say: "It is easy enough to paint with a subdued palette when one feels nothing strongly." But that was not the case with Merimée, Stendhal or Turgenev. All three had a keen and quivering sensibility. But they thought, and I agree with them, that true emotion can be recognized precisely because it refuses to make use of deliberately excessive methods of expression. Melodrama is not the same thing as drama. Byron, towards the end of his life, by which time he had had experience of real drama, developed a violent distaste for the melodramatic poems which he had written as a young man. Had Turgenev, during the two years of his last illness, tried to judge the value of his work, he would have thought of it with pleasure and, if he attached any importance to posthumous fame, with confidence. Truth does not grow old, and the children of to-day are still remarkably like the son of Hector and Andromache. "It is possible", he said, "to be original without being eccentric." I would go further, because I believe that no one can be profoundly original who does not avoid eccentricity.

Pushkin, Turgenev's master, wrote:

"Poet, set no store by popular applause. The moment of extravagant praise will pass, and you will hear about you the judgments of fools and the laughter of the cold multitude. But do you stand firm, calm and undaunted.

You are a king and, as such, must live in loneliness. Tread freely where the spirit of freedom leads, endlessly perfecting the fruit of your chosen thoughts, and seeking no rewards for noble deeds.

Your work is its own reward: you are the supreme judge of what you have accomplished. With greater severity than anybody else you can determine its value.

Are you content? If so, you can afford to ignore the condemnation of the crowd."

All through his life Turgenev had been his own exacting critic and supreme judge. Now, after fifty years, we can ratify the silent verdict which he gave in favour of his creatures.[1]

---

[1] In the aphorisms by Paul Valéry published in 1952, just before his death, I have been delighted to find two passages which provide a perfect comment on Turgenev's statement that "it is possible to be original without being eccentric". Here they are:

"That first look reminded me of something I once heard Degas say: *it is as uneventful as all really good painting.*

"Difficult to expand. Its meaning clear when one looks at a fine portrait by Raphael: no tricks, no impasto, no trimmings, no flashy lighting, no violent contrasts. I reflect that perfection can be achieved only by rejecting all those means by which one deliberately tries to enhance the value of a piece of work."

"Novelty; the striving after novelty. Novelty is one of those toxic stimulants which, in the long run, become more necessary even than food. Once they have enslaved us, we have to go on increasing the dose to a point at which it becomes destructive of life.

"It is strange, indeed, to become so dependent on precisely what is most perishable in things—their quality of newness.

"People don't seem able to understand that no matter how new an idea may be, it has to be dressed up in such a way as to make it appear to have a noble lineage, to be, not an upstart but the matured product of age, not strange, but the child of many centuries, not newly minted or contrived this morning, but merely found again after having been forgotten . . ."

INDEX OF PROPER NAMES

[317]